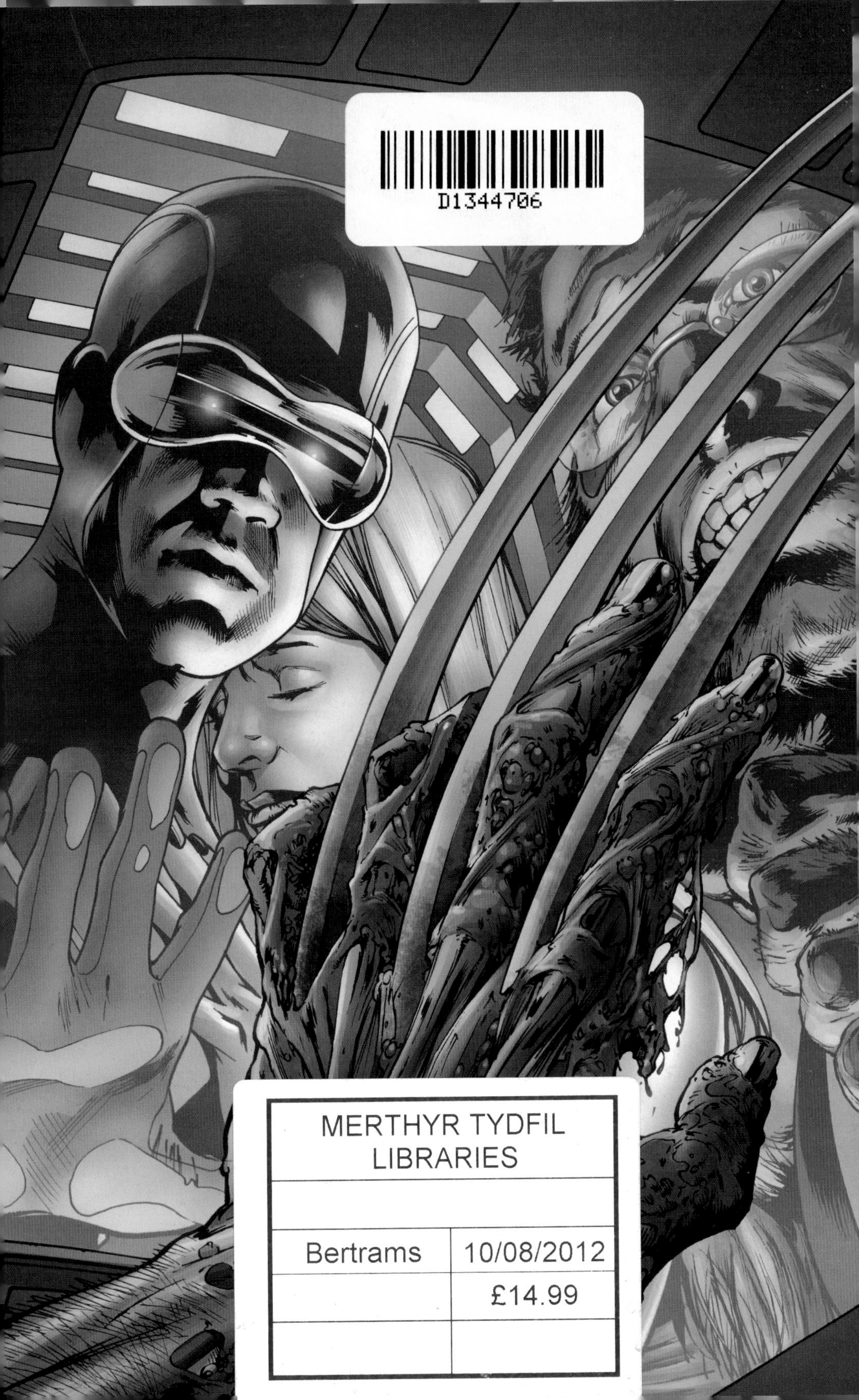

Many years ago a secret government organization abducted a man named Logan, a mutant possessing razor-sharp claws and the ability to heal from any wound. In their attempt to create the perfect living weapon, the organization bonded the unbreakable metal Adamantium to his skeleton. The process was excruciating and by the end there was left of the man known as Logan. He had become...

WOLVERINE
THE BEST THERE IS

Wolverine's mutant power, the ability to heal from any wound or sickness, put him square in sights of a man named Winsor, who captured Logan for a specific purpose.

Winsors' own body was capable of producing and incubating virulent diseases and terrible Bioweapons. Winsor infected Logan with every virus, bacteria and illness known to man, as as inflicting horrible physical wounds on his body, in an attempt to test the extreme limits Wolverine's healing factor.

Logan managed to escape and kill his captor, but with Winsor died the secret of what he w trying to achieve with his mad experiments.

Wolverine's healing factor has been pushed to its absolute limits. He barely manages to mal back to X-Men headquarters.

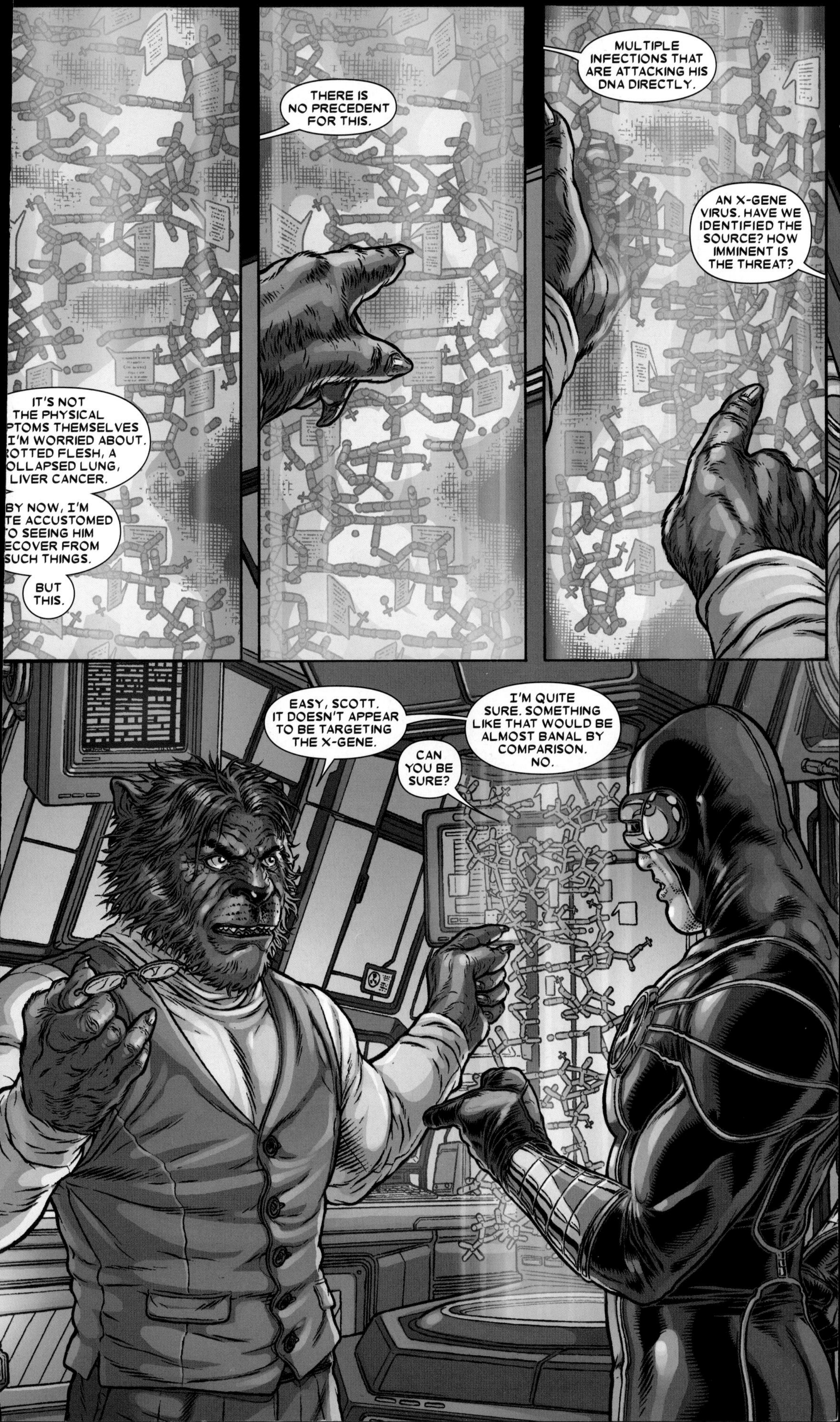
IT'S NOT THE PHYSICAL PTOMS THEMSELVES I'M WORRIED ABOUT. ROTTED FLESH, A OLLAPSED LUNG, LIVER CANCER.
BY NOW, I'M TE ACCUSTOMED TO SEEING HIM ECOVER FROM SUCH THINGS.
BUT THIS.
THERE IS NO PRECEDENT FOR THIS.
MULTIPLE INFECTIONS THAT ARE ATTACKING HIS DNA DIRECTLY.
AN X-GENE VIRUS. HAVE WE IDENTIFIED THE SOURCE? HOW IMMINENT IS THE THREAT?
EASY, SCOTT. IT DOESN'T APPEAR TO BE TARGETING THE X-GENE.
CAN YOU BE SURE?
I'M QUITE SURE. SOMETHING LIKE THAT WOULD BE ALMOST BANAL BY COMPARISON. NO.

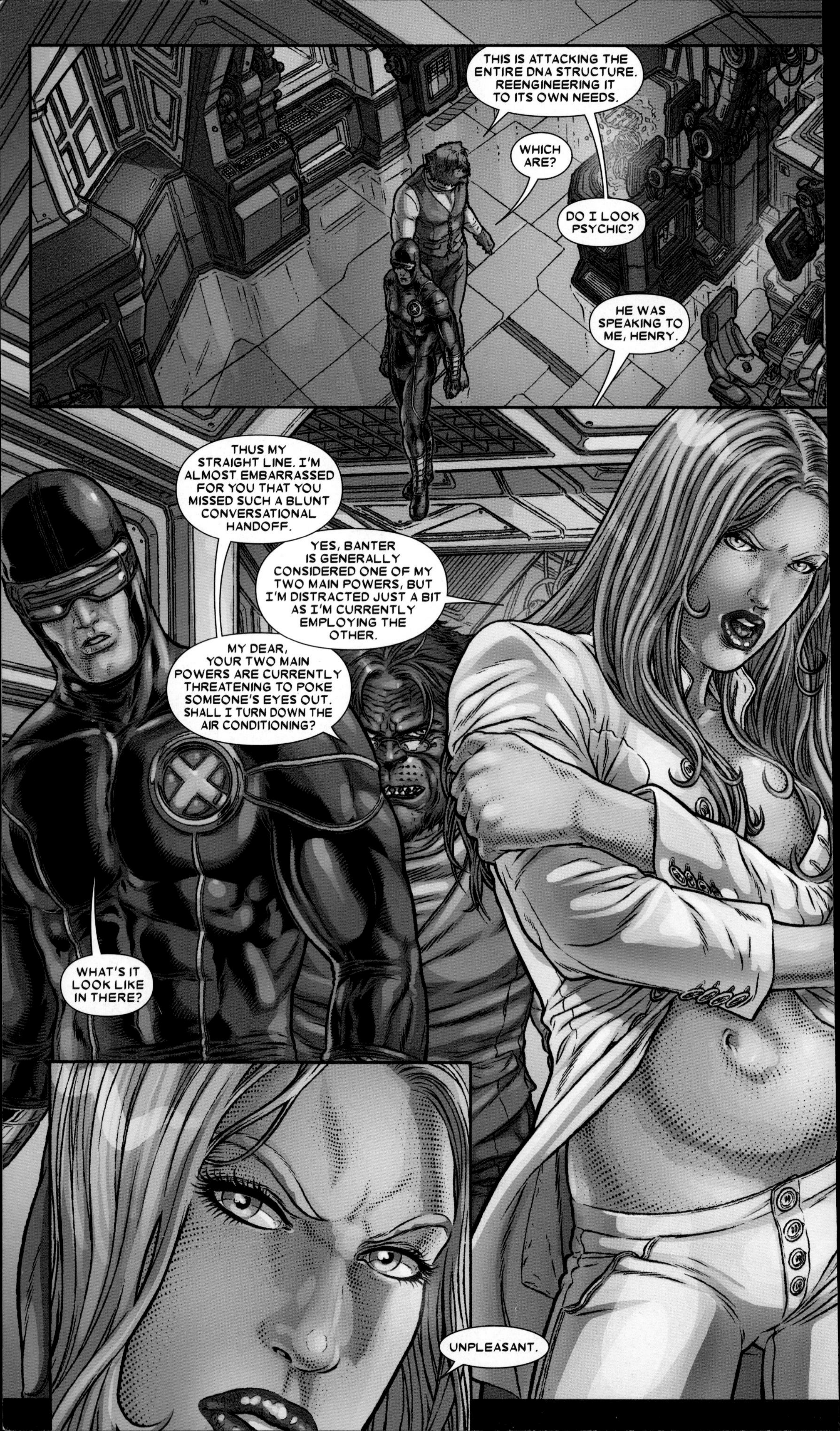
THIS IS ATTACKING THE ENTIRE DNA STRUCTURE. REENGINEERING IT TO ITS OWN NEEDS.
WHICH ARE?
DO I LOOK PSYCHIC?
HE WAS SPEAKING TO ME, HENRY.
THUS MY STRAIGHT LINE. I'M ALMOST EMBARRASSED FOR YOU THAT YOU MISSED SUCH A BLUNT CONVERSATIONAL HANDOFF.
YES, BANTER IS GENERALLY CONSIDERED ONE OF MY TWO MAIN POWERS, BUT I'M DISTRACTED JUST A BIT AS I'M CURRENTLY EMPLOYING THE OTHER.
MY DEAR, YOUR TWO MAIN POWERS ARE CURRENTLY THREATENING TO POKE SOMEONE'S EYES OUT. SHALL I TURN DOWN THE AIR CONDITIONING?
WHAT'S IT LOOK LIKE IN THERE?
UNPLEASANT.

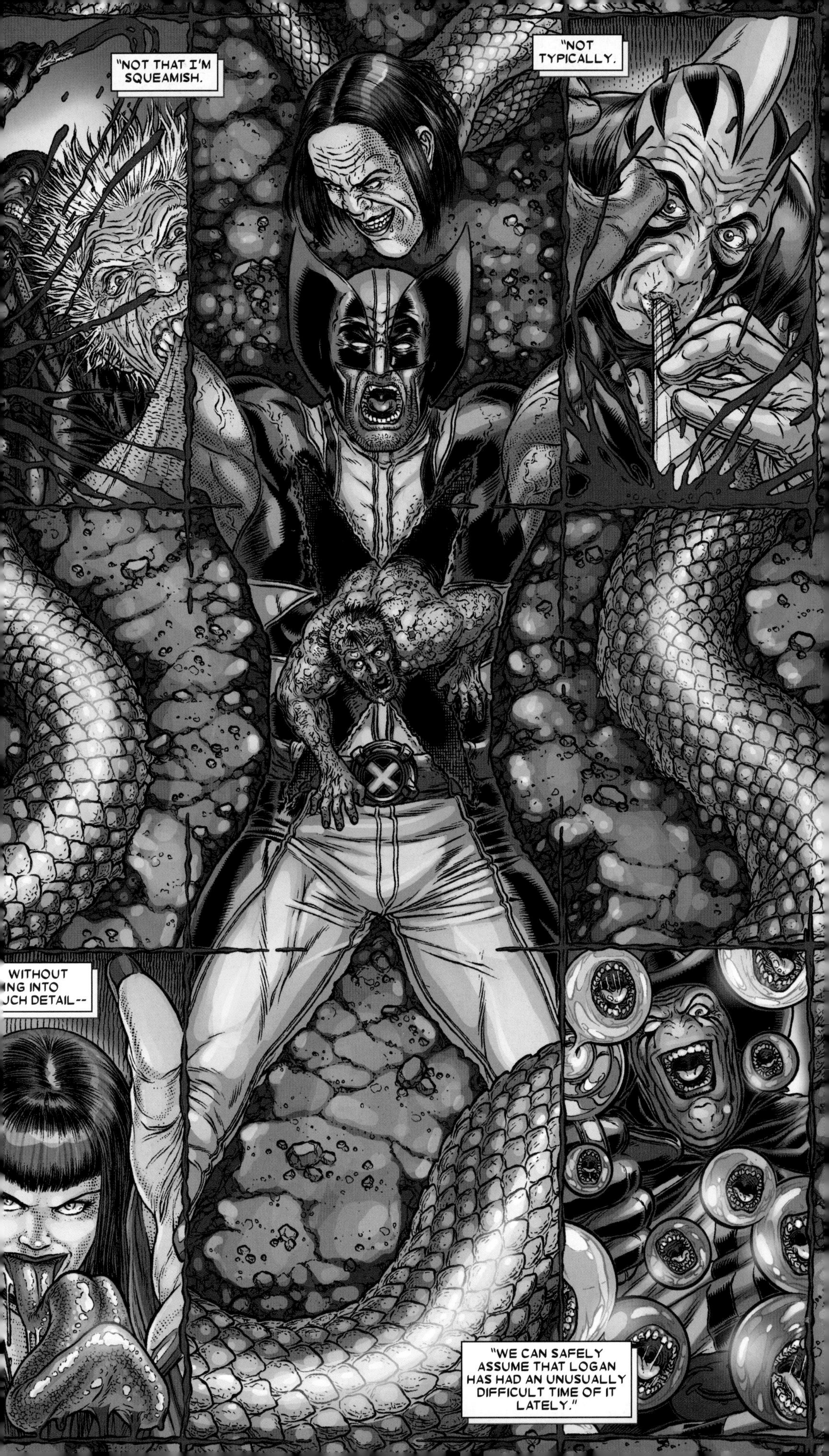
"NOT THAT I'M SQUEAMISH.
"NOT TYPICALLY.
WITHOUT NG INTO CH DETAIL--
"WE CAN SAFELY ASSUME THAT LOGAN HAS HAD AN UNUSUALLY DIFFICULT TIME OF IT LATELY."

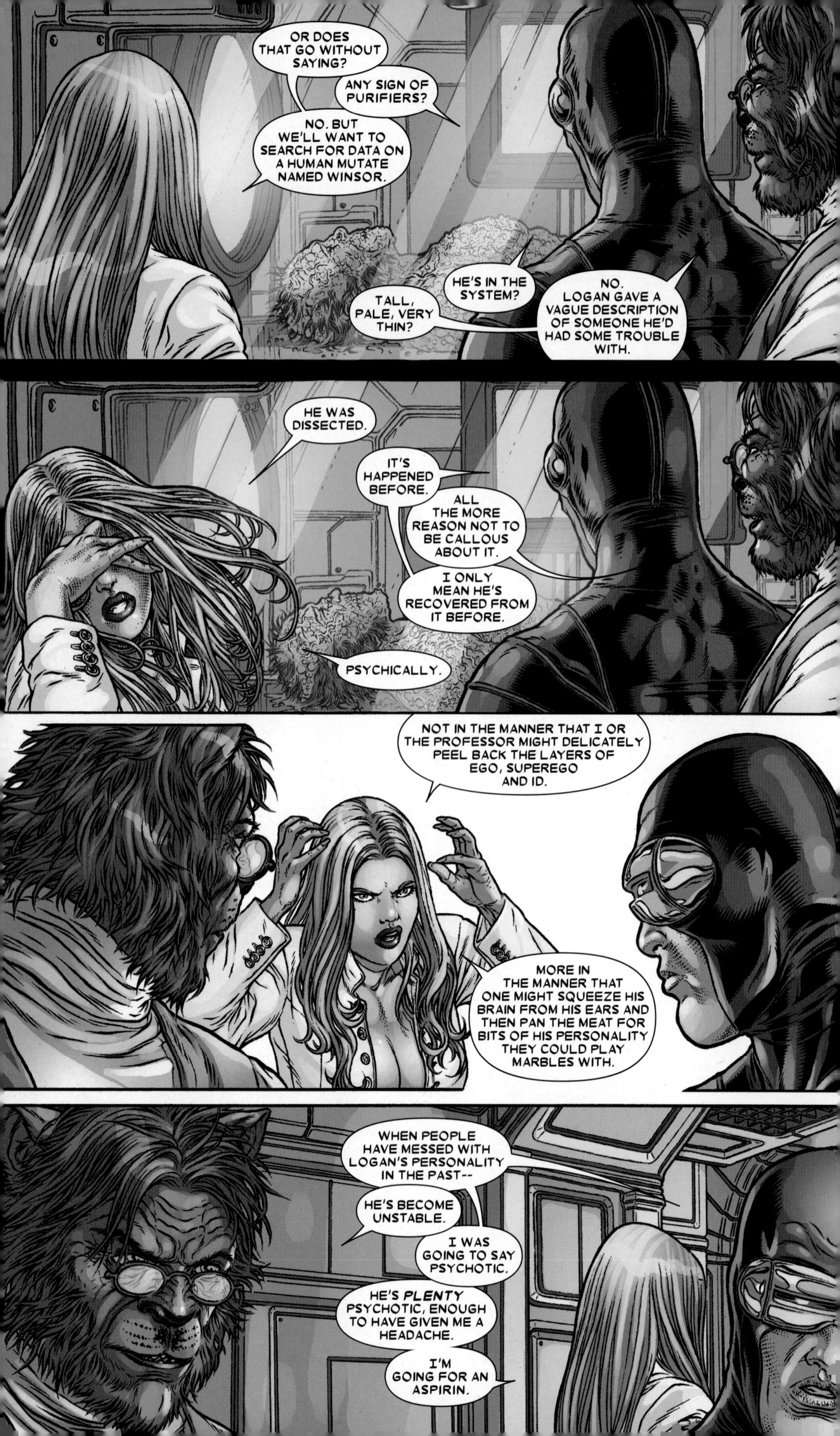
OR DOES THAT GO WITHOUT SAYING?
ANY SIGN OF PURIFIERS?
NO. BUT WE'LL WANT TO SEARCH FOR DATA ON A HUMAN MUTATE NAMED WINSOR.
HE'S IN THE SYSTEM?
NO. LOGAN GAVE A VAGUE DESCRIPTION OF SOMEONE HE'D HAD SOME TROUBLE WITH.
TALL, PALE, VERY THIN?
HE WAS DISSECTED.
IT'S HAPPENED BEFORE.
ALL THE MORE REASON NOT TO BE CALLOUS ABOUT IT.
I ONLY MEAN HE'S RECOVERED FROM IT BEFORE.
PSYCHICALLY.
NOT IN THE MANNER THAT I OR THE PROFESSOR MIGHT DELICATELY PEEL BACK THE LAYERS OF EGO, SUPEREGO AND ID.
MORE IN THE MANNER THAT ONE MIGHT SQUEEZE HIS BRAIN FROM HIS EARS AND THEN PAN THE MEAT FOR BITS OF HIS PERSONALITY THEY COULD PLAY MARBLES WITH.
WHEN PEOPLE HAVE MESSED WITH LOGAN'S PERSONALITY IN THE PAST--
HE'S BECOME UNSTABLE.
I WAS GOING TO SAY PSYCHOTIC.
HE'S *PLENTY* PSYCHOTIC, ENOUGH TO HAVE GIVEN ME A HEADACHE.
I'M GOING FOR AN ASPIRIN.

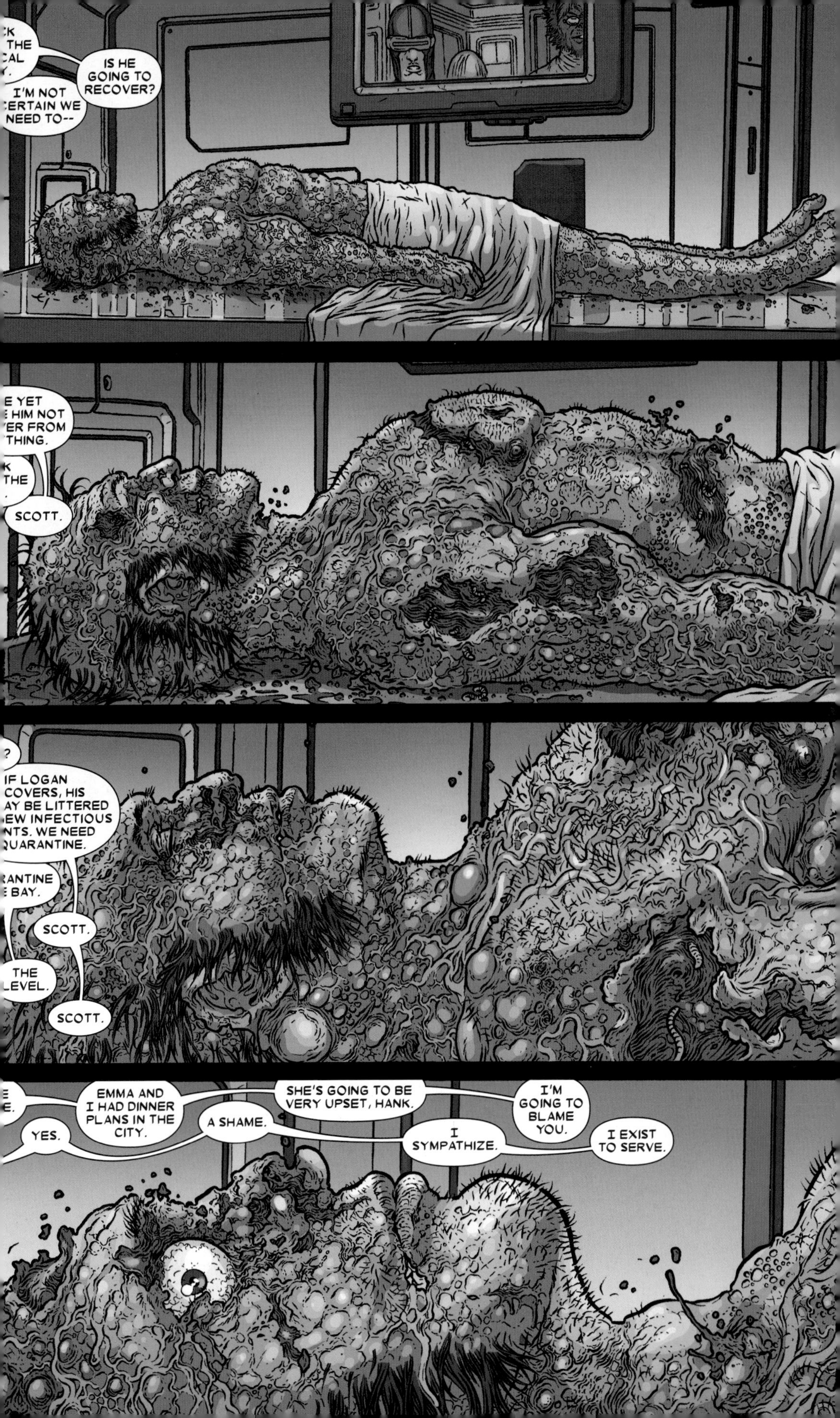

IS HE GOING TO RECOVER?
I'M NOT CERTAIN WE NEED TO--
HIM NOT ER FROM THING.
SCOTT.
IF LOGAN COVERS, HIS AY BE LITTERED EW INFECTIOUS NTS. WE NEED QUARANTINE.
RANTINE BAY.
SCOTT.
THE LEVEL.
SCOTT.
YES.
EMMA AND I HAD DINNER PLANS IN THE CITY.
A SHAME.
SHE'S GOING TO BE VERY UPSET, HANK.
I SYMPATHIZE.
I'M GOING TO BLAME YOU.
I EXIST TO SERVE.

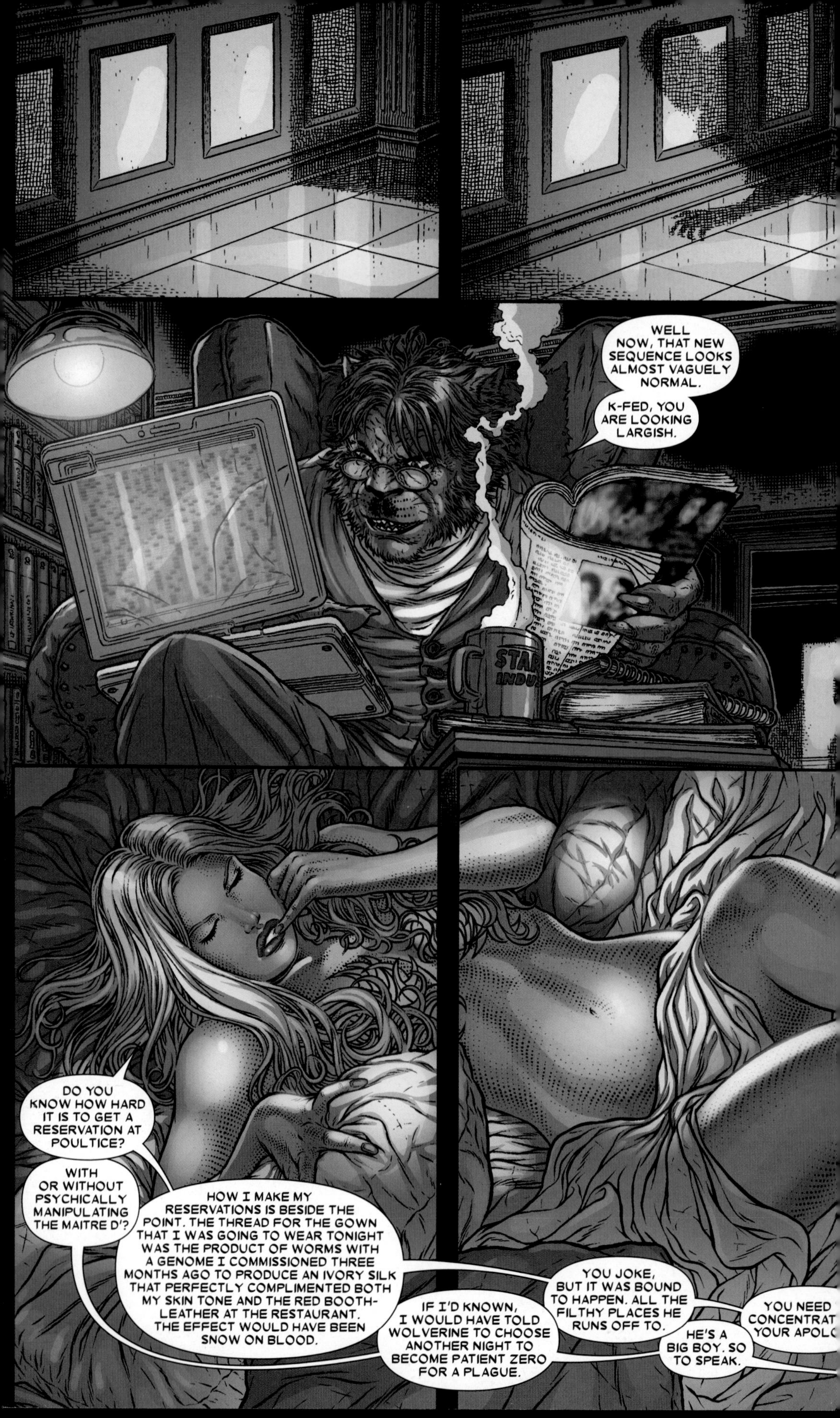
WELL NOW, THAT NEW SEQUENCE LOOKS ALMOST VAGUELY NORMAL.
K-FED, YOU ARE LOOKING LARGISH.
DO YOU KNOW HOW HARD IT IS TO GET A RESERVATION AT POULTICE?
WITH OR WITHOUT PSYCHICALLY MANIPULATING THE MAITRE D'?
HOW I MAKE MY RESERVATIONS IS BESIDE THE POINT. THE THREAD FOR THE GOWN THAT I WAS GOING TO WEAR TONIGHT WAS THE PRODUCT OF WORMS WITH A GENOME I COMMISSIONED THREE MONTHS AGO TO PRODUCE AN IVORY SILK THAT PERFECTLY COMPLIMENTED BOTH MY SKIN TONE AND THE RED BOOTH-LEATHER AT THE RESTAURANT. THE EFFECT WOULD HAVE BEEN SNOW ON BLOOD.
IF I'D KNOWN, I WOULD HAVE TOLD WOLVERINE TO CHOOSE ANOTHER NIGHT TO BECOME PATIENT ZERO FOR A PLAGUE.
YOU JOKE, BUT IT WAS BOUND TO HAPPEN. ALL THE FILTHY PLACES HE RUNS OFF TO.
HE'S A BIG BOY. SO TO SPEAK.
YOU NEED

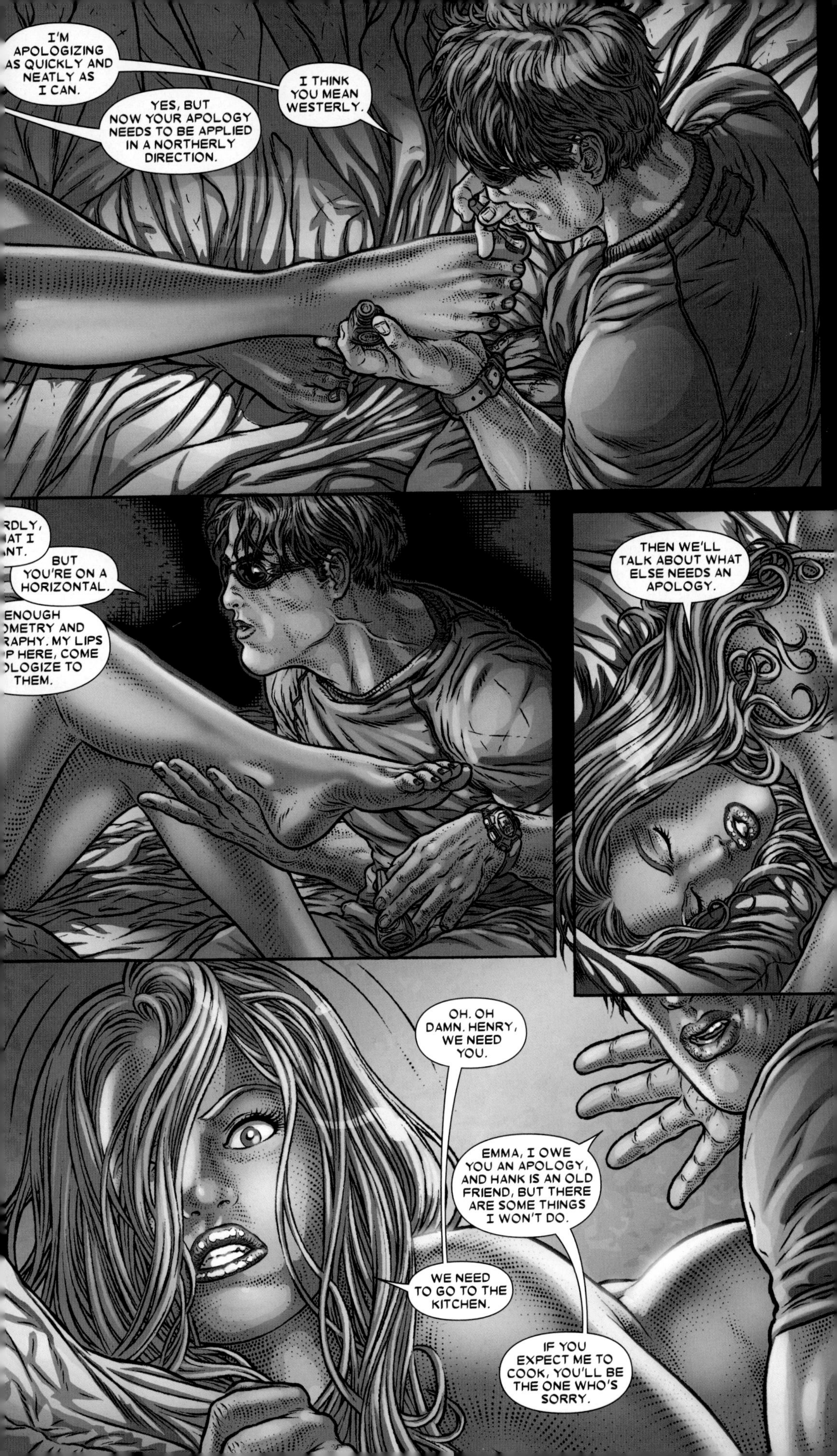
I'M APOLOGIZING AS QUICKLY AND NEATLY AS I CAN.
YES, BUT NOW YOUR APOLOGY NEEDS TO BE APPLIED IN A NORTHERLY DIRECTION.
I THINK YOU MEAN WESTERLY.
RDLY, AT I NT.
BUT YOU'RE ON A HORIZONTAL.
ENOUGH OMETRY AND RAPHY. MY LIPS P HERE, COME OLOGIZE TO THEM.
THEN WE'LL TALK ABOUT WHAT ELSE NEEDS AN APOLOGY.
OH. OH DAMN. HENRY, WE NEED YOU.
EMMA, I OWE YOU AN APOLOGY, AND HANK IS AN OLD FRIEND, BUT THERE ARE SOME THINGS I WON'T DO.
WE NEED TO GO TO THE KITCHEN.
IF YOU EXPECT ME TO COOK, YOU'LL BE THE ONE WHO'S SORRY.

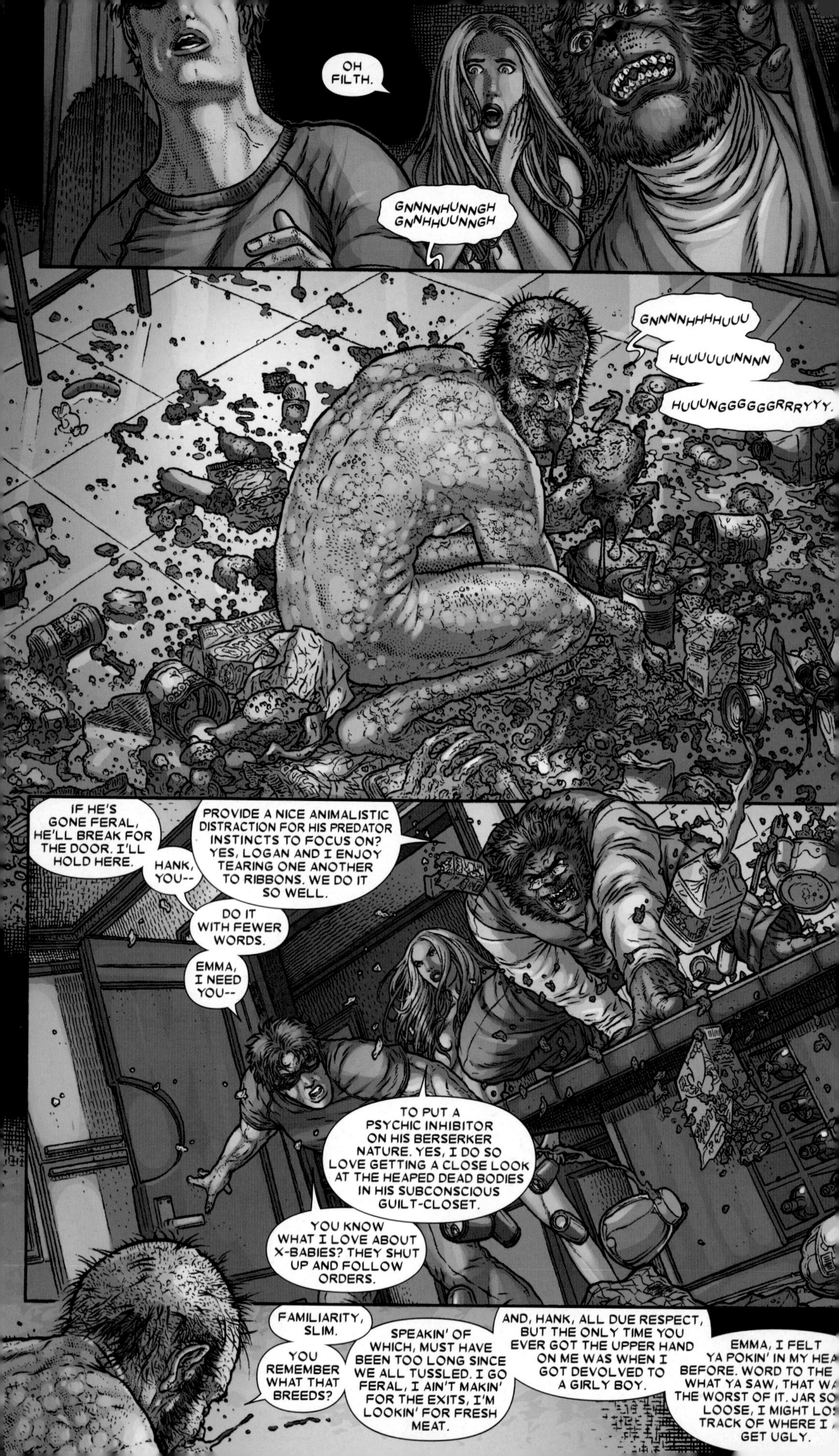

OH FILTH.
GNNNNHUNNGH GNNHHUUNNGH
GNNNNHHHHUUU
HUUUUUUNNNN
HUUUNGGGGGGRRRYYY.
IF HE'S GONE FERAL, HE'LL BREAK FOR THE DOOR. I'LL HOLD HERE.
HANK, YOU--
PROVIDE A NICE ANIMALISTIC DISTRACTION FOR HIS PREDATOR INSTINCTS TO FOCUS ON? YES, LOGAN AND I ENJOY TEARING ONE ANOTHER TO RIBBONS. WE DO IT SO WELL.
DO IT WITH FEWER WORDS.
EMMA, I NEED YOU--
TO PUT A PSYCHIC INHIBITOR ON HIS BERSERKER NATURE. YES, I DO SO LOVE GETTING A CLOSE LOOK AT THE HEAPED DEAD BODIES IN HIS SUBCONSCIOUS GUILT-CLOSET.
YOU KNOW WHAT I LOVE ABOUT X-BABIES? THEY SHUT UP AND FOLLOW ORDERS.
FAMILIARITY, SLIM.
YOU REMEMBER WHAT THAT BREEDS?
SPEAKIN' OF WHICH, MUST HAVE BEEN TOO LONG SINCE WE ALL TUSSLED. I GO FERAL, I AIN'T MAKIN' FOR THE EXITS, I'M LOOKIN' FOR FRESH MEAT.
AND, HANK, ALL DUE RESPECT, BUT THE ONLY TIME YOU EVER GOT THE UPPER HAND ON ME WAS WHEN I GOT DEVOLVED TO A GIRLY BOY.
EMMA, I FELT YA POKIN' IN MY HEA BEFORE. WORD TO THE WHAT YA SAW, THAT WA THE WORST OF IT. JAR SO LOOSE, I MIGHT LOS TRACK OF WHERE I GET UGLY.

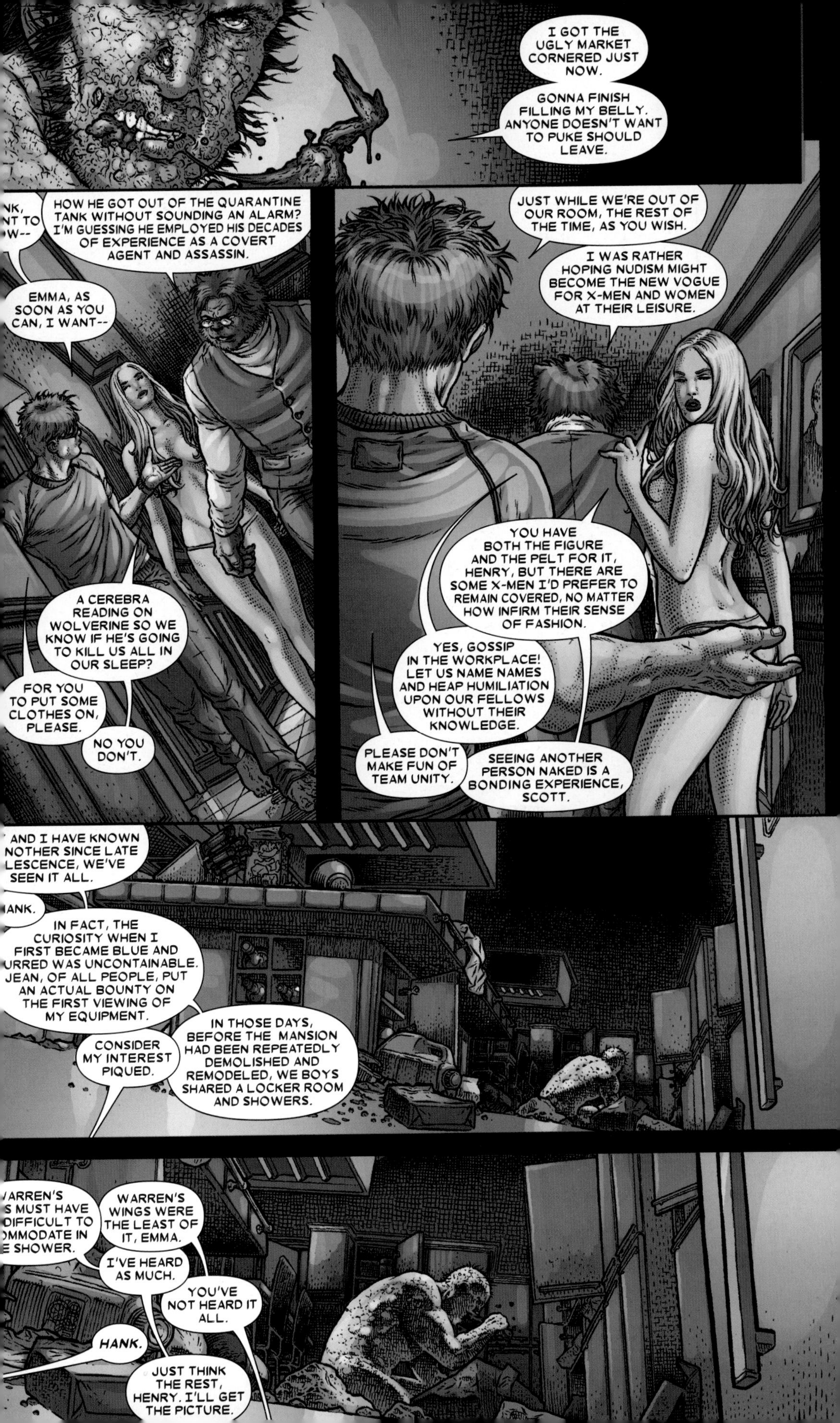
I GOT THE UGLY MARKET CORNERED JUST NOW.
GONNA FINISH FILLING MY BELLY. ANYONE DOESN'T WANT TO PUKE SHOULD LEAVE.
NK, NT TO W--
HOW HE GOT OUT OF THE QUARANTINE TANK WITHOUT SOUNDING AN ALARM? I'M GUESSING HE EMPLOYED HIS DECADES OF EXPERIENCE AS A COVERT AGENT AND ASSASSIN.
EMMA, AS SOON AS YOU CAN, I WANT--
A CEREBRA READING ON WOLVERINE SO WE KNOW IF HE'S GOING TO KILL US ALL IN OUR SLEEP?
FOR YOU TO PUT SOME CLOTHES ON, PLEASE.
NO YOU DON'T.
JUST WHILE WE'RE OUT OF OUR ROOM, THE REST OF THE TIME, AS YOU WISH.
I WAS RATHER HOPING NUDISM MIGHT BECOME THE NEW VOGUE FOR X-MEN AND WOMEN AT THEIR LEISURE.
YOU HAVE BOTH THE FIGURE AND THE PELT FOR IT, HENRY, BUT THERE ARE SOME X-MEN I'D PREFER TO REMAIN COVERED, NO MATTER HOW INFIRM THEIR SENSE OF FASHION.
YES, GOSSIP IN THE WORKPLACE! LET US NAME NAMES AND HEAP HUMILIATION UPON OUR FELLOWS WITHOUT THEIR KNOWLEDGE.
PLEASE DON'T MAKE FUN OF TEAM UNITY.
SEEING ANOTHER PERSON NAKED IS A BONDING EXPERIENCE, SCOTT.
AND I HAVE KNOWN NOTHER SINCE LATE LESCENCE, WE'VE SEEN IT ALL.
ANK.
IN FACT, THE CURIOSITY WHEN I FIRST BECAME BLUE AND URRED WAS UNCONTAINABLE. JEAN, OF ALL PEOPLE, PUT AN ACTUAL BOUNTY ON THE FIRST VIEWING OF MY EQUIPMENT.
CONSIDER MY INTEREST PIQUED.
IN THOSE DAYS, BEFORE THE MANSION HAD BEEN REPEATEDLY DEMOLISHED AND REMODELED, WE BOYS SHARED A LOCKER ROOM AND SHOWERS.
ARREN'S S MUST HAVE DIFFICULT TO MMODATE IN E SHOWER.
WARREN'S WINGS WERE THE LEAST OF IT, EMMA.
I'VE HEARD AS MUCH.
YOU'VE NOT HEARD IT ALL.
HANK.
JUST THINK THE REST, HENRY. I'LL GET THE PICTURE.

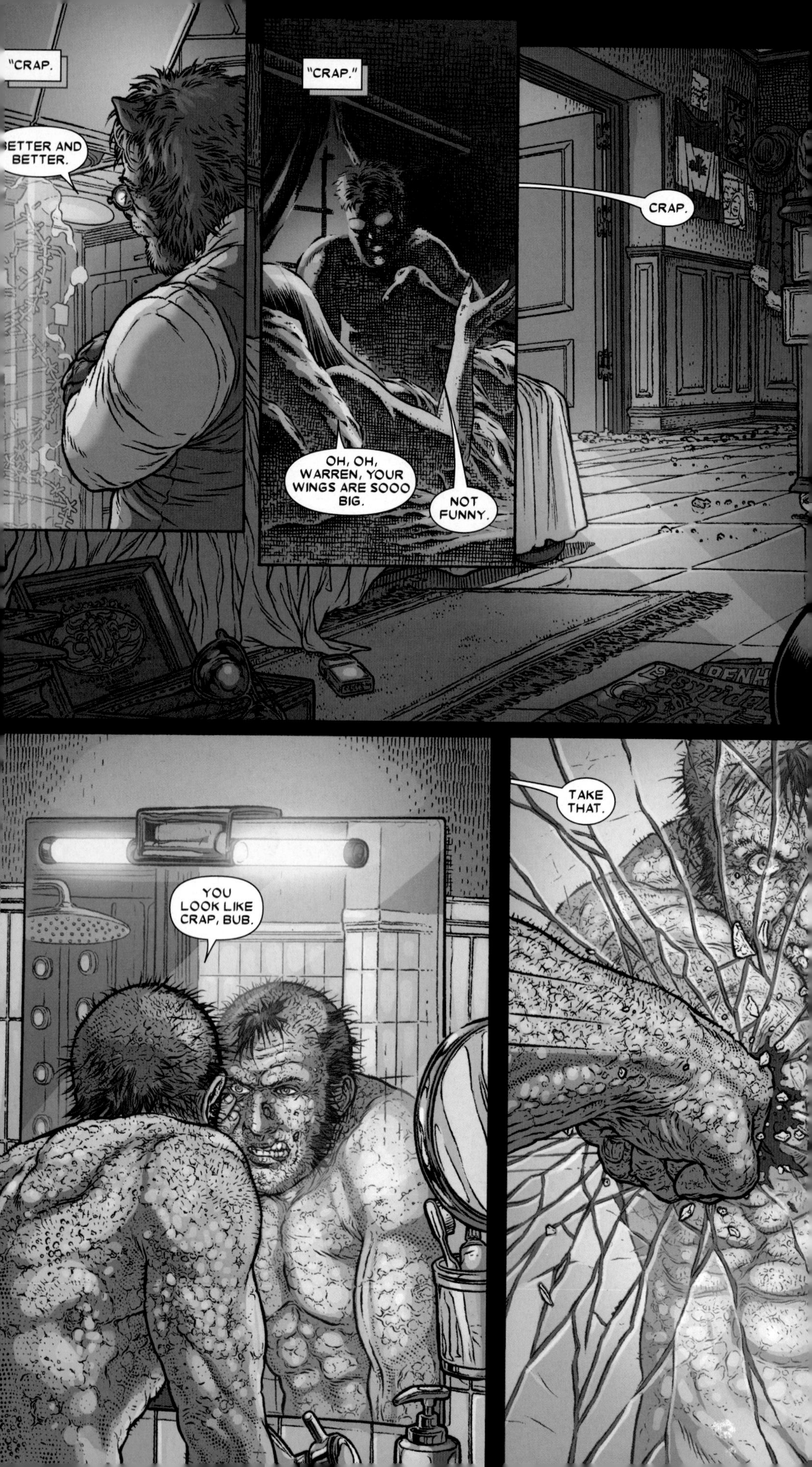
"CRAP.
BETTER AND BETTER.
"CRAP."
OH, OH, WARREN, YOUR WINGS ARE SOOO BIG.
NOT FUNNY.
CRAP.
YOU LOOK LIKE CRAP, BUB.
TAKE THAT.

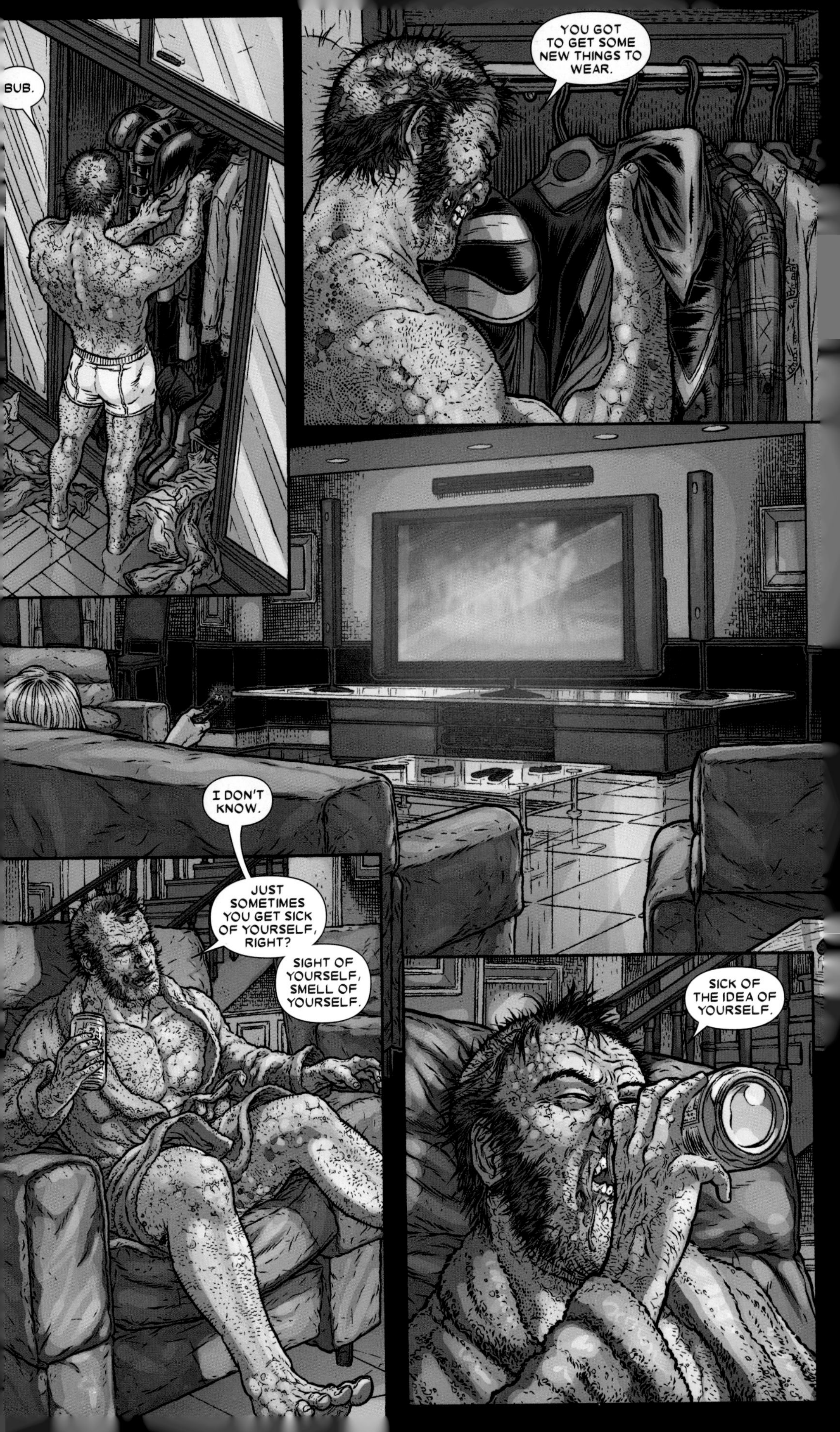
BUB.
YOU GOT TO GET SOME NEW THINGS TO WEAR.
I DON'T KNOW.
JUST SOMETIMES YOU GET SICK OF YOURSELF, RIGHT?
SIGHT OF YOURSELF, SMELL OF YOURSELF.
SICK OF THE IDEA OF YOURSELF.

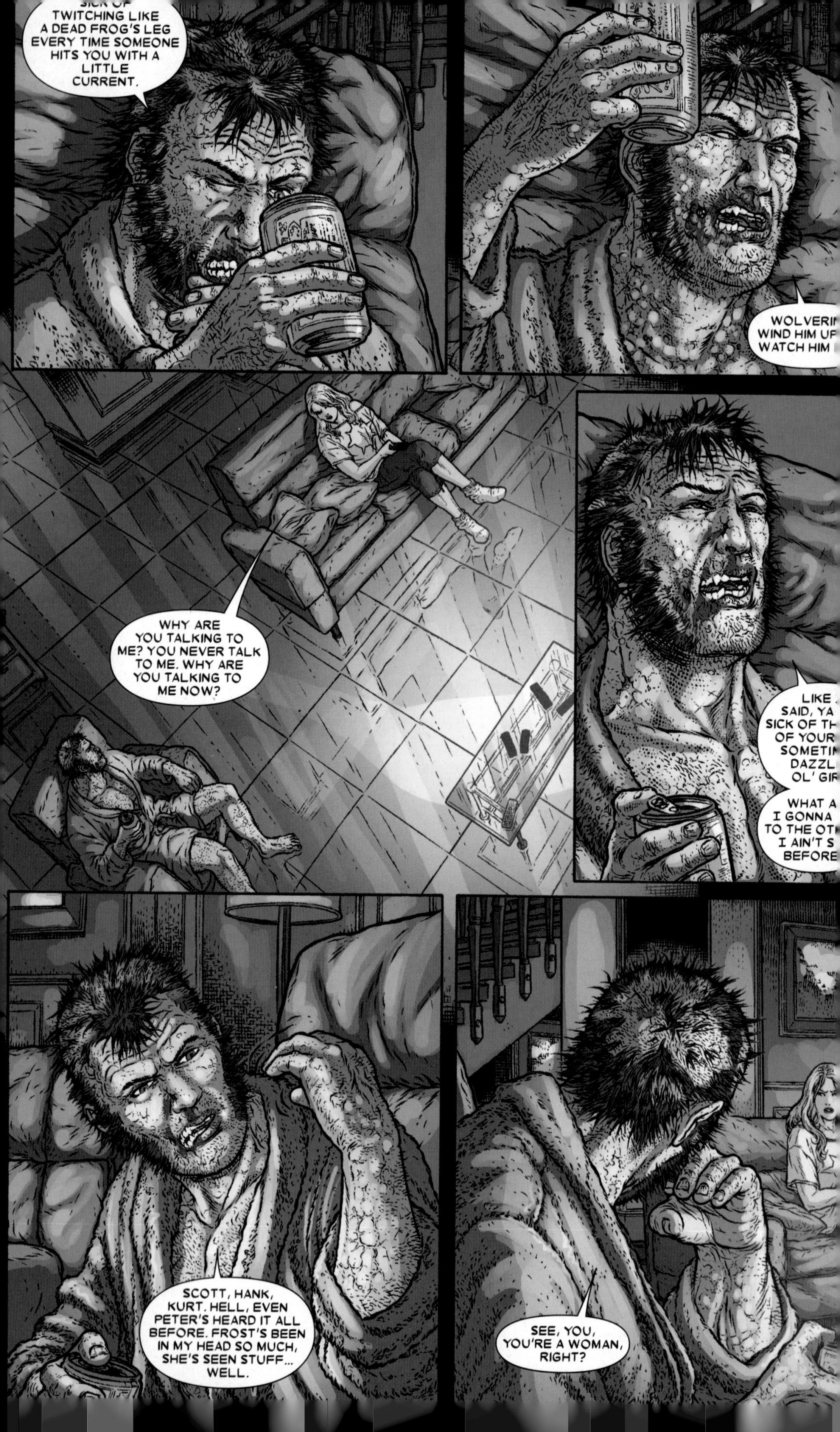
TWITCHING LIKE A DEAD FROG'S LEG EVERY TIME SOMEONE HITS YOU WITH A LITTLE CURRENT.
WOLVERI WIND HIM UP WATCH HIM
WHY ARE YOU TALKING TO ME? YOU NEVER TALK TO ME. WHY ARE YOU TALKING TO ME NOW?
LIKE SAID, YA SICK OF TH OF YOUR SOMETI DAZZL OL' GIR
WHAT A I GONNA TO THE OT I AIN'T S BEFORE
SCOTT, HANK, KURT. HELL, EVEN PETER'S HEARD IT ALL BEFORE. FROST'S BEEN IN MY HEAD SO MUCH, SHE'S SEEN STUFF... WELL.
SEE, YOU, YOU'RE A WOMAN, RIGHT?

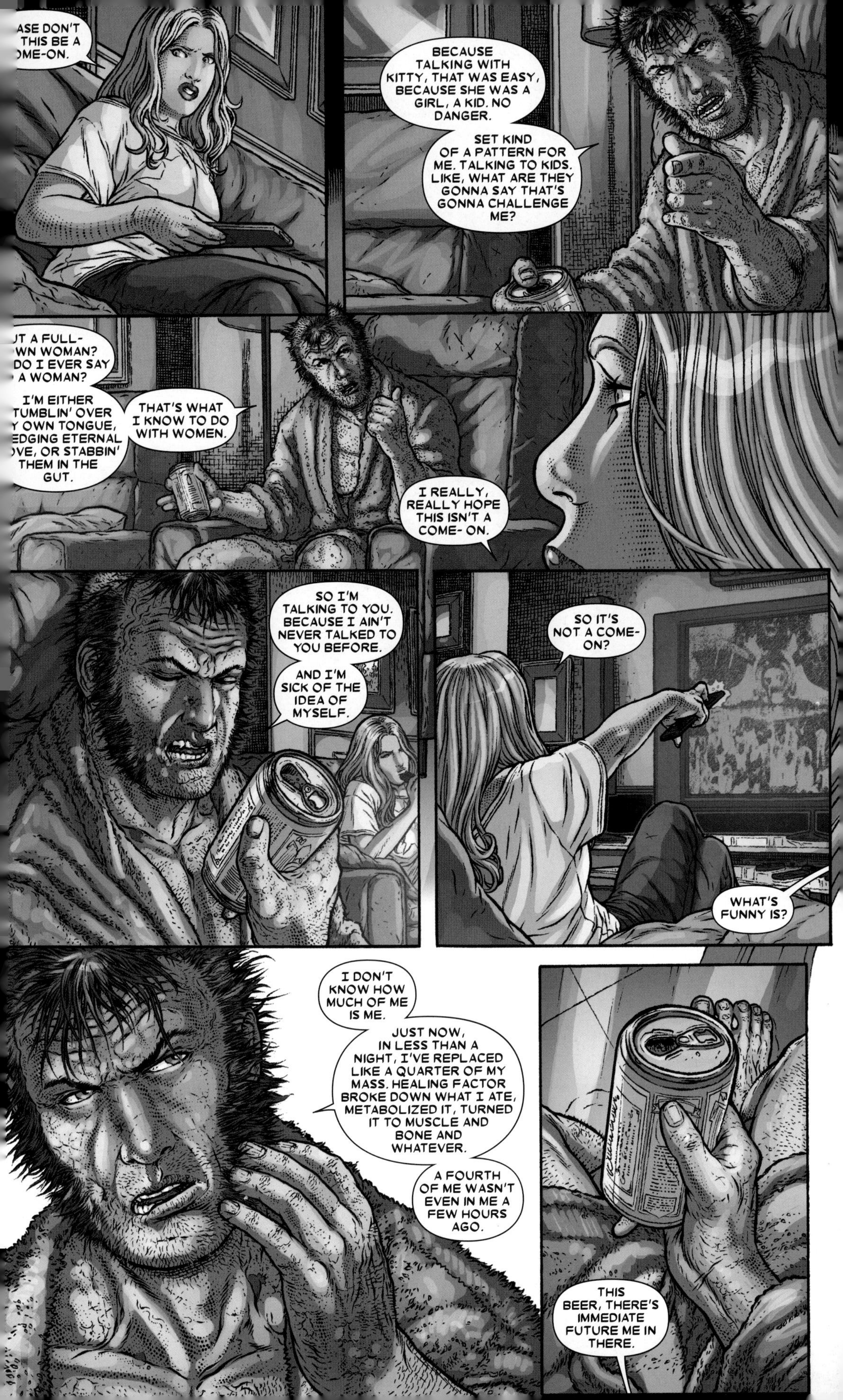

ASE DON'T THIS BE A OME-ON.
BECAUSE TALKING WITH KITTY, THAT WAS EASY, BECAUSE SHE WAS A GIRL, A KID. NO DANGER.
SET KIND OF A PATTERN FOR ME. TALKING TO KIDS. LIKE, WHAT ARE THEY GONNA SAY THAT'S GONNA CHALLENGE ME?
UT A FULL- WN WOMAN? DO I EVER SAY A WOMAN?
I'M EITHER TUMBLIN' OVER Y OWN TONGUE, EDGING ETERNAL OVE, OR STABBIN' THEM IN THE GUT.
THAT'S WHAT I KNOW TO DO WITH WOMEN.
I REALLY, REALLY HOPE THIS ISN'T A COME- ON.
SO I'M TALKING TO YOU, BECAUSE I AIN'T NEVER TALKED TO YOU BEFORE.
AND I'M SICK OF THE IDEA OF MYSELF.
SO IT'S NOT A COME- ON?
WHAT'S FUNNY IS?
I DON'T KNOW HOW MUCH OF ME IS ME.
JUST NOW, IN LESS THAN A NIGHT, I'VE REPLACED LIKE A QUARTER OF MY MASS. HEALING FACTOR BROKE DOWN WHAT I ATE, METABOLIZED IT, TURNED IT TO MUSCLE AND BONE AND WHATEVER.
A FOURTH OF ME WASN'T EVEN IN ME A FEW HOURS AGO.
THIS BEER, THERE'S IMMEDIATE FUTURE ME IN THERE.

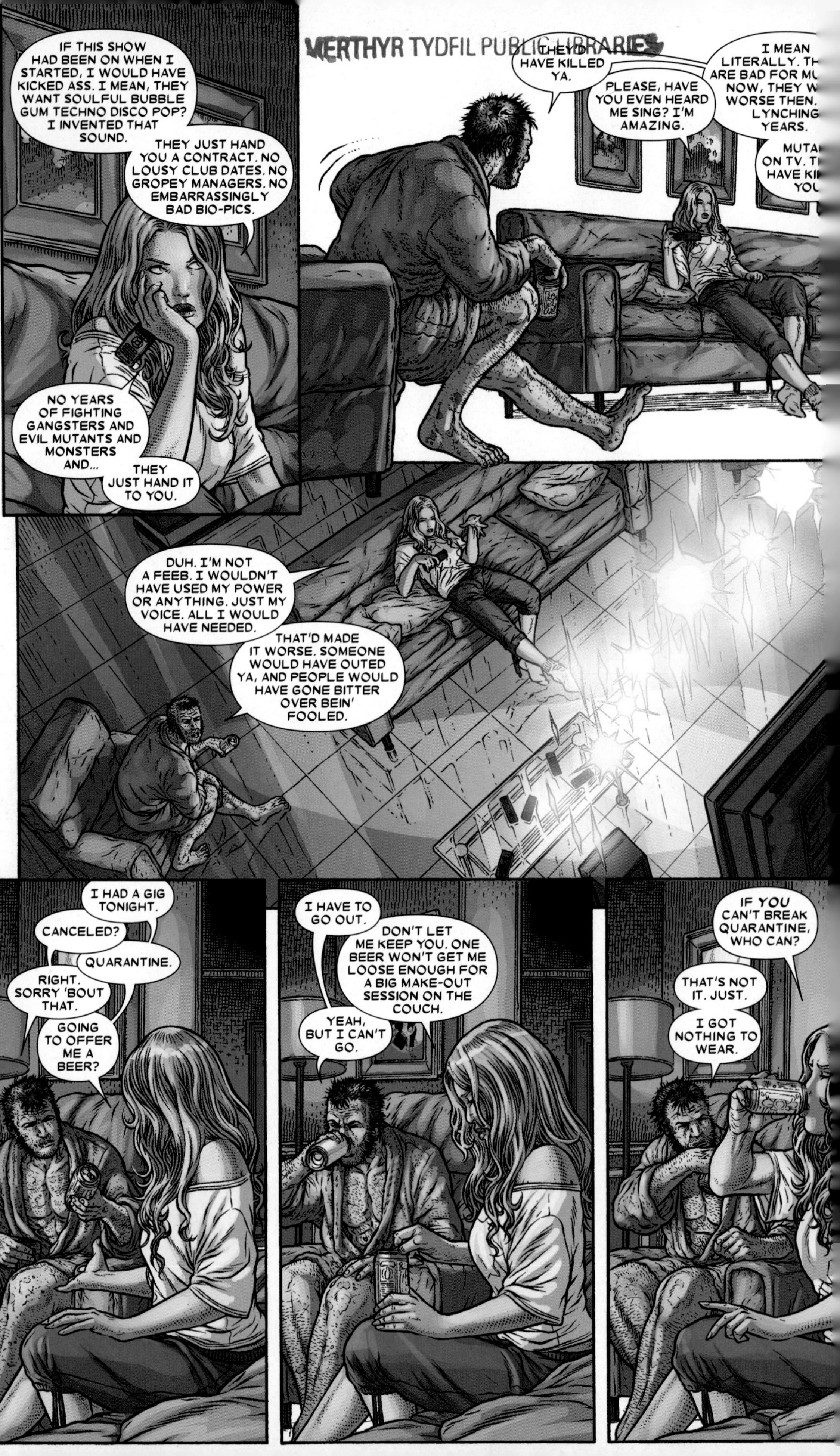
IF THIS SHOW HAD BEEN ON WHEN I STARTED, I WOULD HAVE KICKED ASS. I MEAN, THEY WANT SOULFUL BUBBLE GUM TECHNO DISCO POP? I INVENTED THAT SOUND.
THEY JUST HAND YOU A CONTRACT. NO LOUSY CLUB DATES. NO GROPEY MANAGERS. NO EMBARRASSINGLY BAD BIO-PICS.
NO YEARS OF FIGHTING GANGSTERS AND EVIL MUTANTS AND MONSTERS AND...
THEY JUST HAND IT TO YOU.
THEY'D HAVE KILLED YA.
PLEASE, HAVE YOU EVEN HEARD ME SING? I'M AMAZING.
I MEAN LITERALLY. TH ARE BAD FOR MU NOW, THEY W WORSE THEN. LYNCHING YEARS.
MUTA ON TV. T HAVE KI YOU
DUH. I'M NOT A FEEB. I WOULDN'T HAVE USED MY POWER OR ANYTHING. JUST MY VOICE. ALL I WOULD HAVE NEEDED.
THAT'D MADE IT WORSE. SOMEONE WOULD HAVE OUTED YA, AND PEOPLE WOULD HAVE GONE BITTER OVER BEIN' FOOLED.
I HAD A GIG TONIGHT.
CANCELED?
QUARANTINE.
RIGHT. SORRY 'BOUT THAT.
GOING TO OFFER ME A BEER?
I HAVE TO GO OUT.
DON'T LET ME KEEP YOU. ONE BEER WON'T GET ME LOOSE ENOUGH FOR A BIG MAKE-OUT SESSION ON THE COUCH.
YEAH, BUT I CAN'T GO.
IF *YOU* CAN'T BREAK QUARANTINE, WHO CAN?
THAT'S NOT IT. JUST.
I GOT NOTHING TO WEAR.

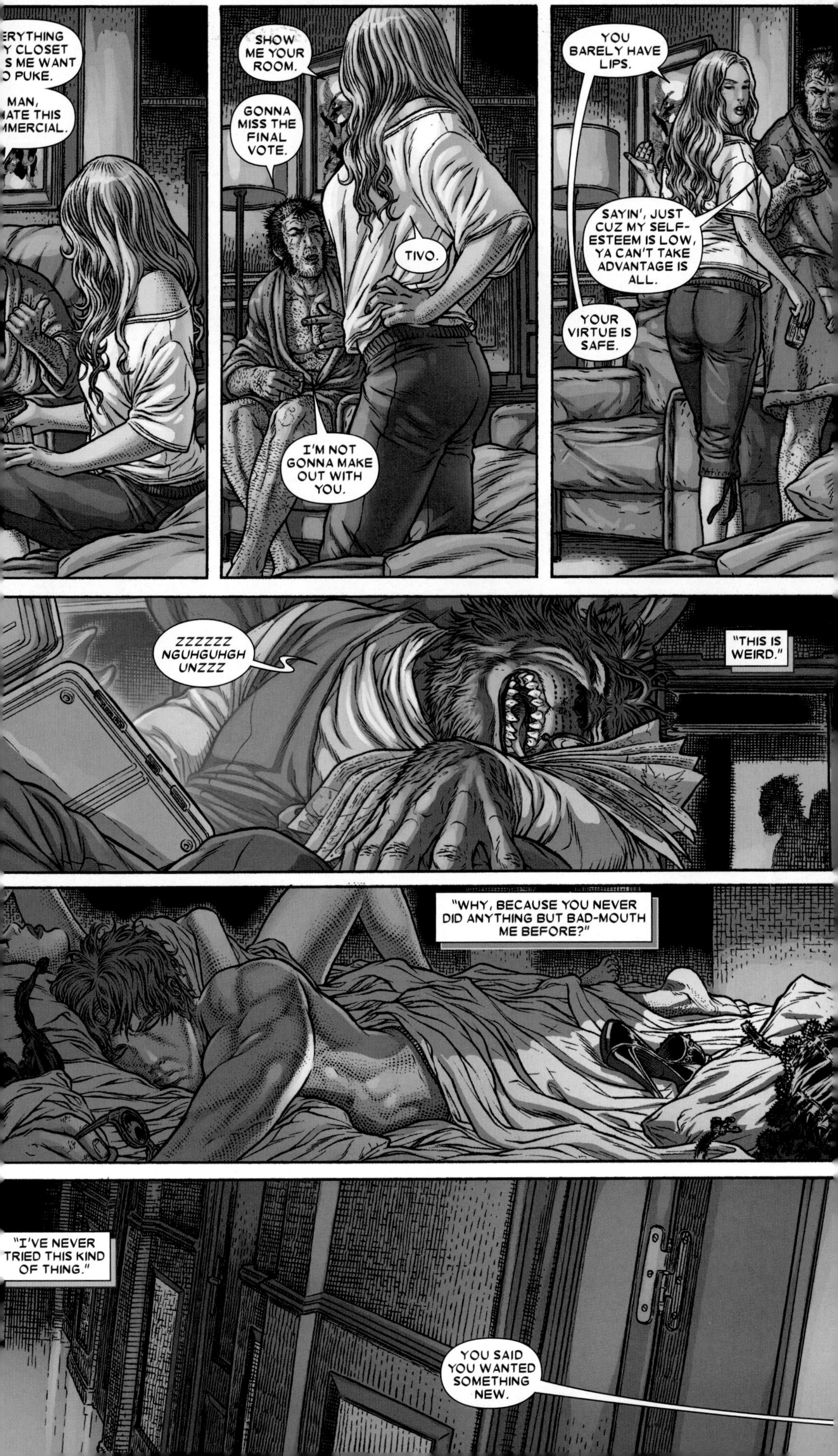

ERYTHING
Y CLOSET
S ME WANT
O PUKE.
MAN,
ATE THIS
MMERCIAL.
SHOW ME YOUR ROOM.
GONNA MISS THE FINAL VOTE.
TIVO.
I'M NOT GONNA MAKE OUT WITH YOU.
YOU BARELY HAVE LIPS.
SAYIN', JUST CUZ MY SELF-ESTEEM IS LOW, YA CAN'T TAKE ADVANTAGE IS ALL.
YOUR VIRTUE IS SAFE.
ZZZZZZ NGUHGUHGH UNZZZ
"THIS IS WEIRD."
"WHY, BECAUSE YOU NEVER DID ANYTHING BUT BAD-MOUTH ME BEFORE?"
"I'VE NEVER TRIED THIS KIND OF THING."
YOU SAID YOU WANTED SOMETHING NEW.

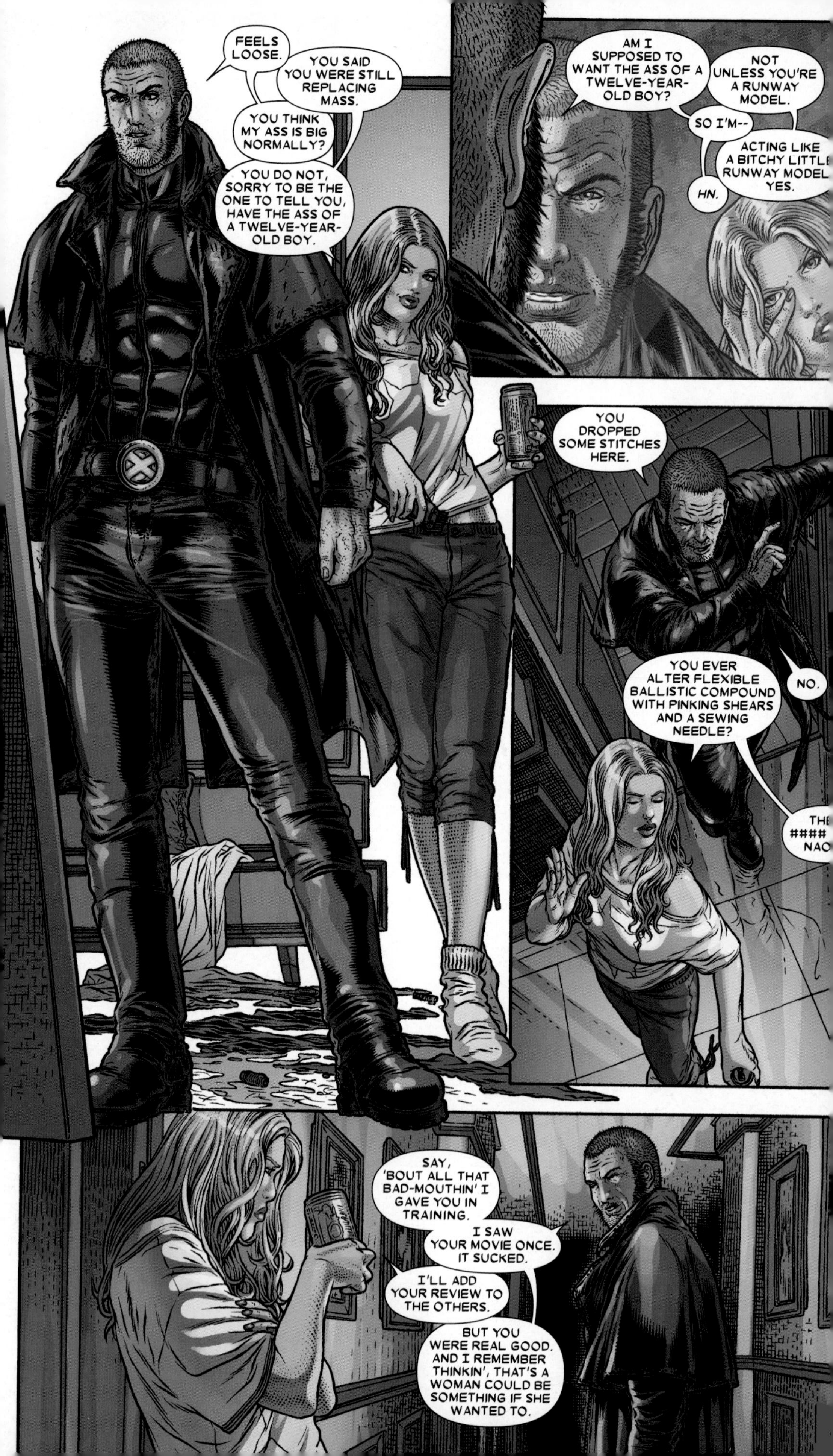
FEELS LOOSE.
YOU SAID YOU WERE STILL REPLACING MASS.
YOU THINK MY ASS IS BIG NORMALLY?
YOU DO NOT, SORRY TO BE THE ONE TO TELL YOU, HAVE THE ASS OF A TWELVE-YEAR-OLD BOY.
AM I SUPPOSED TO WANT THE ASS OF A TWELVE-YEAR-OLD BOY?
NOT UNLESS YOU'RE A RUNWAY MODEL.
SO I'M--
ACTING LIKE A BITCHY LITTLE RUNWAY MODEL. YES.
HN.
YOU DROPPED SOME STITCHES HERE.
YOU EVER ALTER FLEXIBLE BALLISTIC COMPOUND WITH PINKING SHEARS AND A SEWING NEEDLE?
NO.
SAY, 'BOUT ALL THAT BAD-MOUTHIN' I GAVE YOU IN TRAINING.
I SAW YOUR MOVIE ONCE. IT SUCKED.
I'LL ADD YOUR REVIEW TO THE OTHERS.
BUT YOU WERE REAL GOOD. AND I REMEMBER THINKIN', THAT'S A WOMAN COULD BE SOMETHING IF SHE WANTED TO.

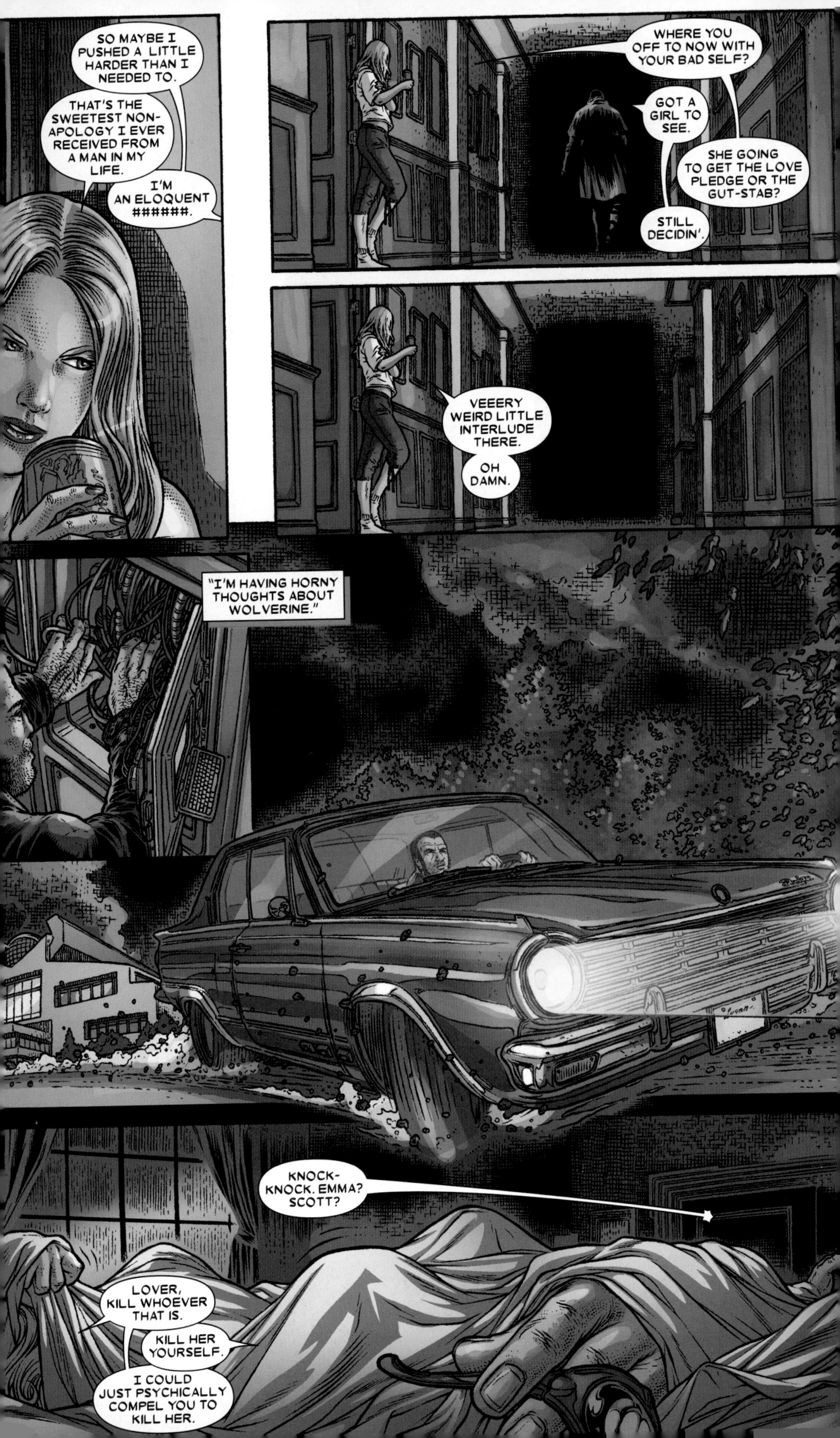
SO MAYBE I PUSHED A LITTLE HARDER THAN I NEEDED TO.
THAT'S THE SWEETEST NON-APOLOGY I EVER RECEIVED FROM A MAN IN MY LIFE.
I'M AN ELOQUENT ######.
WHERE YOU OFF TO NOW WITH YOUR BAD SELF?
GOT A GIRL TO SEE.
SHE GOING TO GET THE LOVE PLEDGE OR THE GUT-STAB?
STILL DECIDIN'.
VEEERY WEIRD LITTLE INTERLUDE THERE.
OH DAMN.
"I'M HAVING HORNY THOUGHTS ABOUT WOLVERINE."
KNOCK-KNOCK. EMMA? SCOTT?
LOVER, KILL WHOEVER THAT IS.
KILL HER YOURSELF.
I COULD JUST PSYCHICALLY COMPEL YOU TO KILL HER.

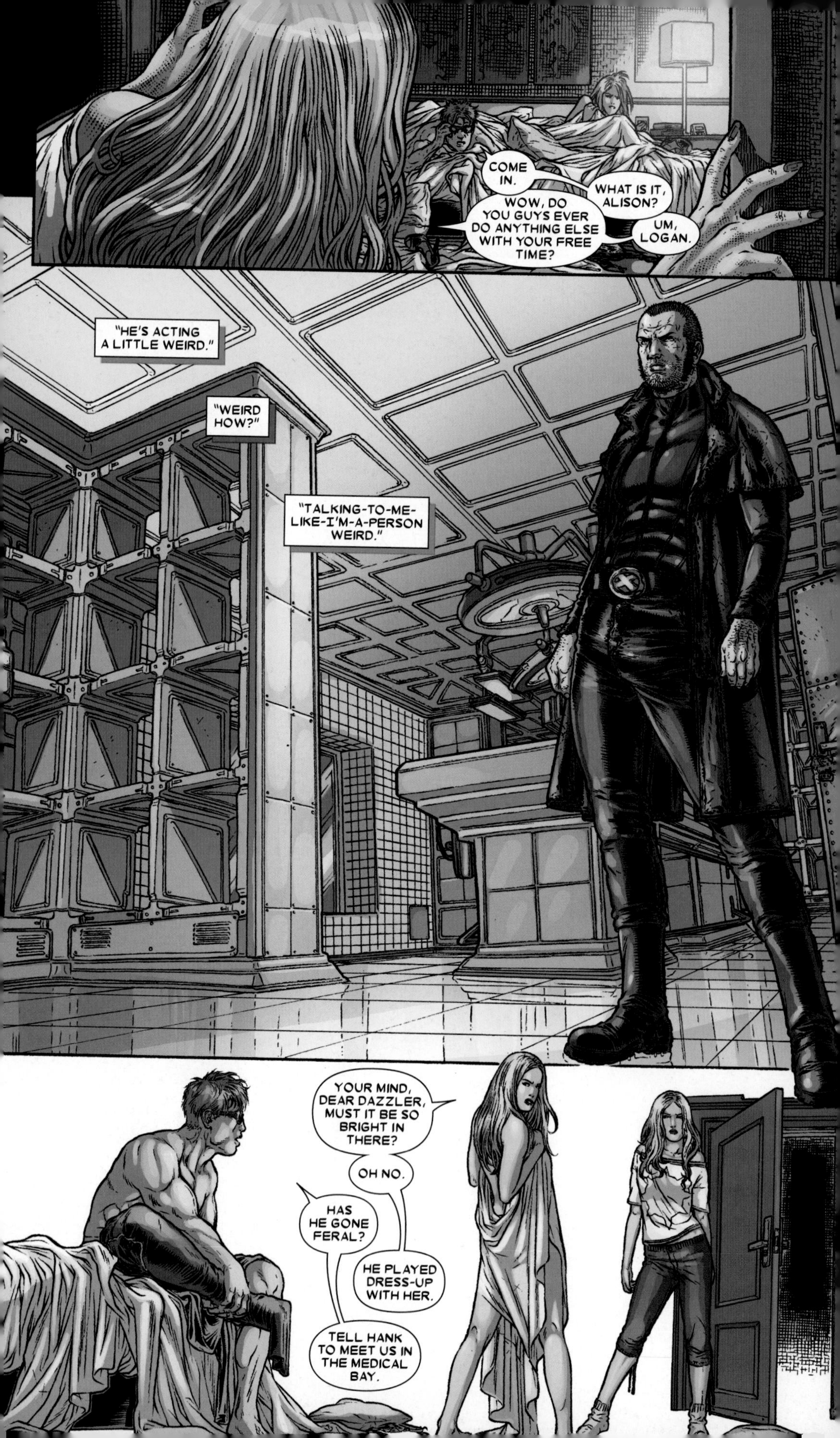
COME IN.
WHAT IS IT, ALISON?
WOW, DO YOU GUYS EVER DO ANYTHING ELSE WITH YOUR FREE TIME?
UM, LOGAN.
"HE'S ACTING A LITTLE WEIRD."
"WEIRD HOW?"
"TALKING-TO-ME-LIKE-I'M-A-PERSON WEIRD."
YOUR MIND, DEAR DAZZLER, MUST IT BE SO BRIGHT IN THERE?
OH NO.
HAS HE GONE FERAL?
HE PLAYED DRESS-UP WITH HER.
TELL HANK TO MEET US IN THE MEDICAL BAY.

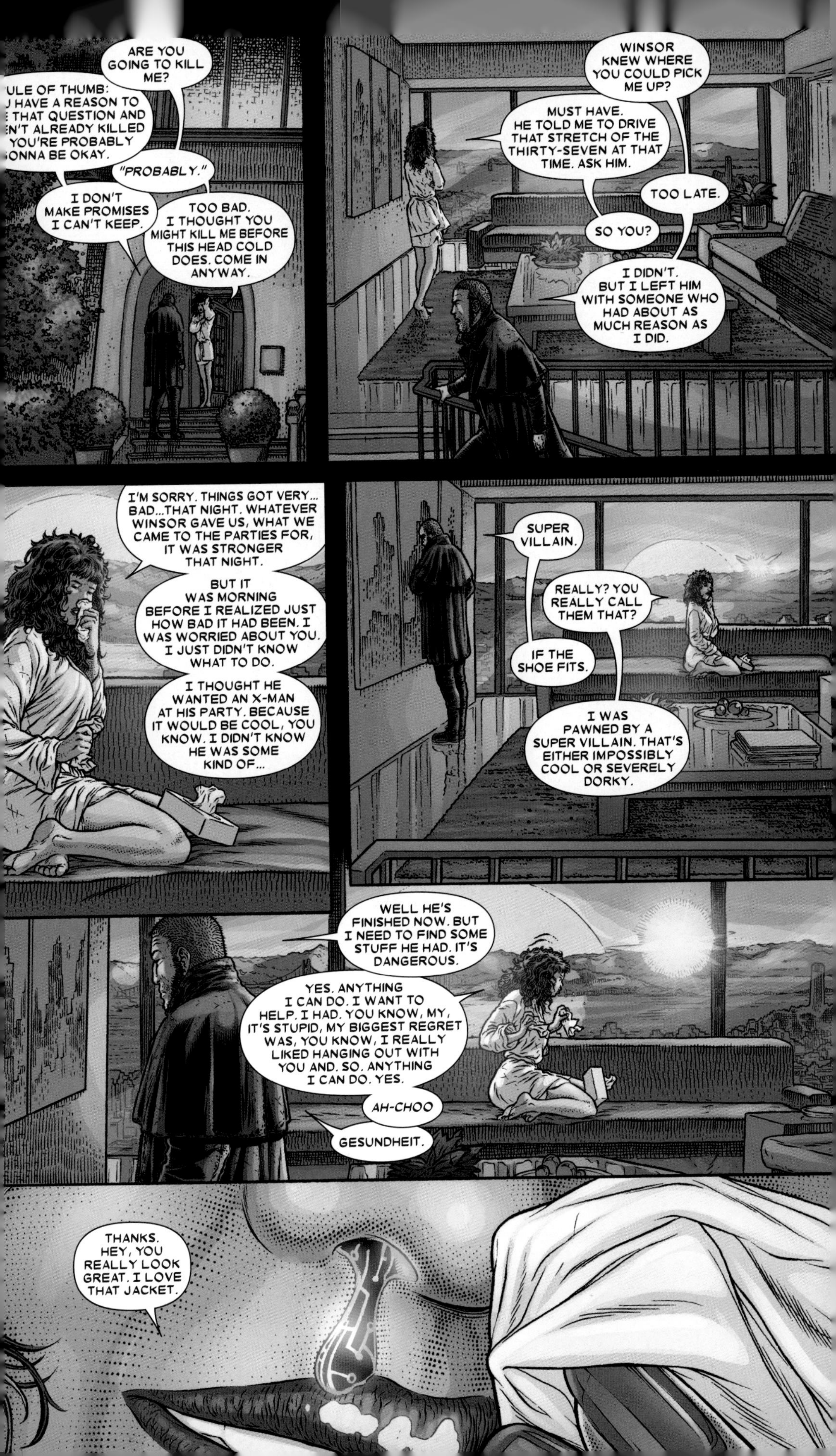

ARE YOU GOING TO KILL ME?
ULE OF THUMB: J HAVE A REASON TO E THAT QUESTION AND EN'T ALREADY KILLED YOU'RE PROBABLY ONNA BE OKAY.
"PROBABLY."
I DON'T MAKE PROMISES I CAN'T KEEP.
TOO BAD. I THOUGHT YOU MIGHT KILL ME BEFORE THIS HEAD COLD DOES. COME IN ANYWAY.
WINSOR KNEW WHERE YOU COULD PICK ME UP?
MUST HAVE. HE TOLD ME TO DRIVE THAT STRETCH OF THE THIRTY-SEVEN AT THAT TIME. ASK HIM.
TOO LATE.
SO YOU?
I DIDN'T. BUT I LEFT HIM WITH SOMEONE WHO HAD ABOUT AS MUCH REASON AS I DID.
I'M SORRY. THINGS GOT VERY... BAD...THAT NIGHT. WHATEVER WINSOR GAVE US, WHAT WE CAME TO THE PARTIES FOR, IT WAS STRONGER THAT NIGHT.
BUT IT WAS MORNING BEFORE I REALIZED JUST HOW BAD IT HAD BEEN. I WAS WORRIED ABOUT YOU. I JUST DIDN'T KNOW WHAT TO DO.
I THOUGHT HE WANTED AN X-MAN AT HIS PARTY. BECAUSE IT WOULD BE COOL, YOU KNOW. I DIDN'T KNOW HE WAS SOME KIND OF...
SUPER VILLAIN.
REALLY? YOU REALLY CALL THEM THAT?
IF THE SHOE FITS.
I WAS PAWNED BY A SUPER VILLAIN. THAT'S EITHER IMPOSSIBLY COOL OR SEVERELY DORKY.
WELL HE'S FINISHED NOW. BUT I NEED TO FIND SOME STUFF HE HAD. IT'S DANGEROUS.
YES. ANYTHING I CAN DO. I WANT TO HELP. I HAD. YOU KNOW, MY, IT'S STUPID, MY BIGGEST REGRET WAS, YOU KNOW, I REALLY LIKED HANGING OUT WITH YOU AND. SO. ANYTHING I CAN DO. YES.
AH-CHOO
GESUNDHEIT.
THANKS. HEY, YOU REALLY LOOK GREAT. I LOVE THAT JACKET.

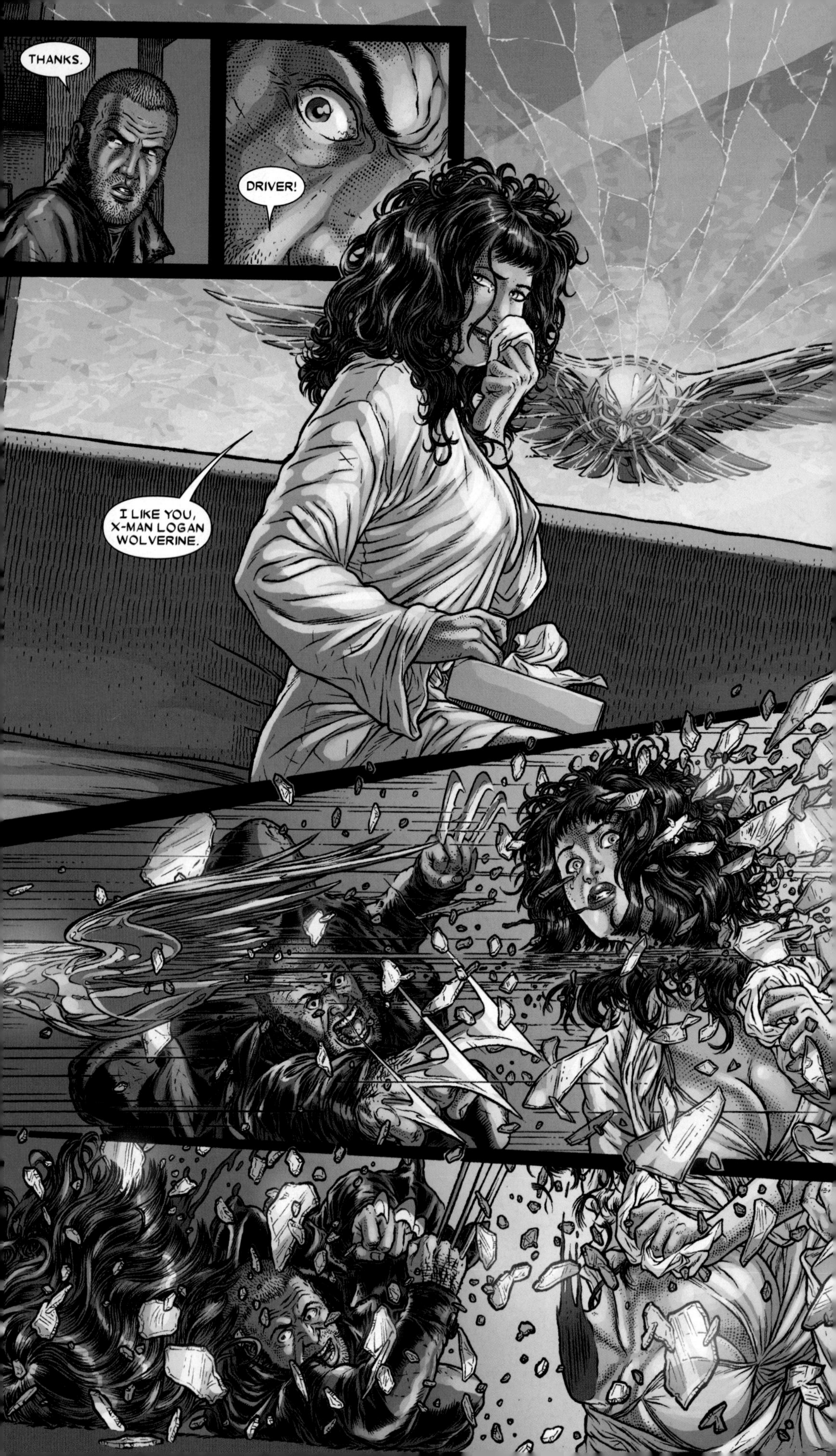

THANKS.
DRIVER!
I LIKE YOU, X-MAN LOGAN WOLVERINE.

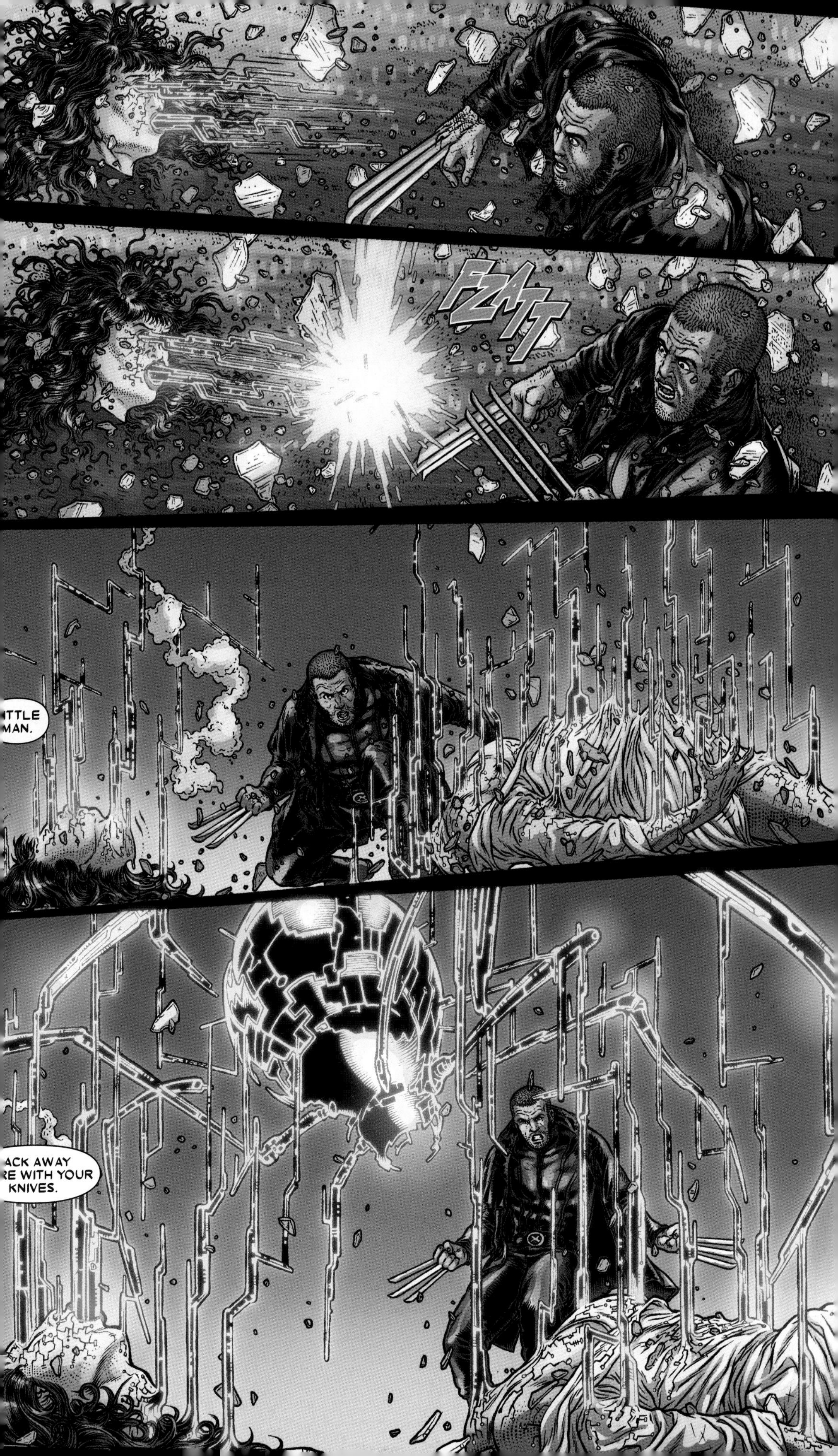
FZATT
TTLE
MAN.
ACK AWAY
RE WITH YOUR
KNIVES.

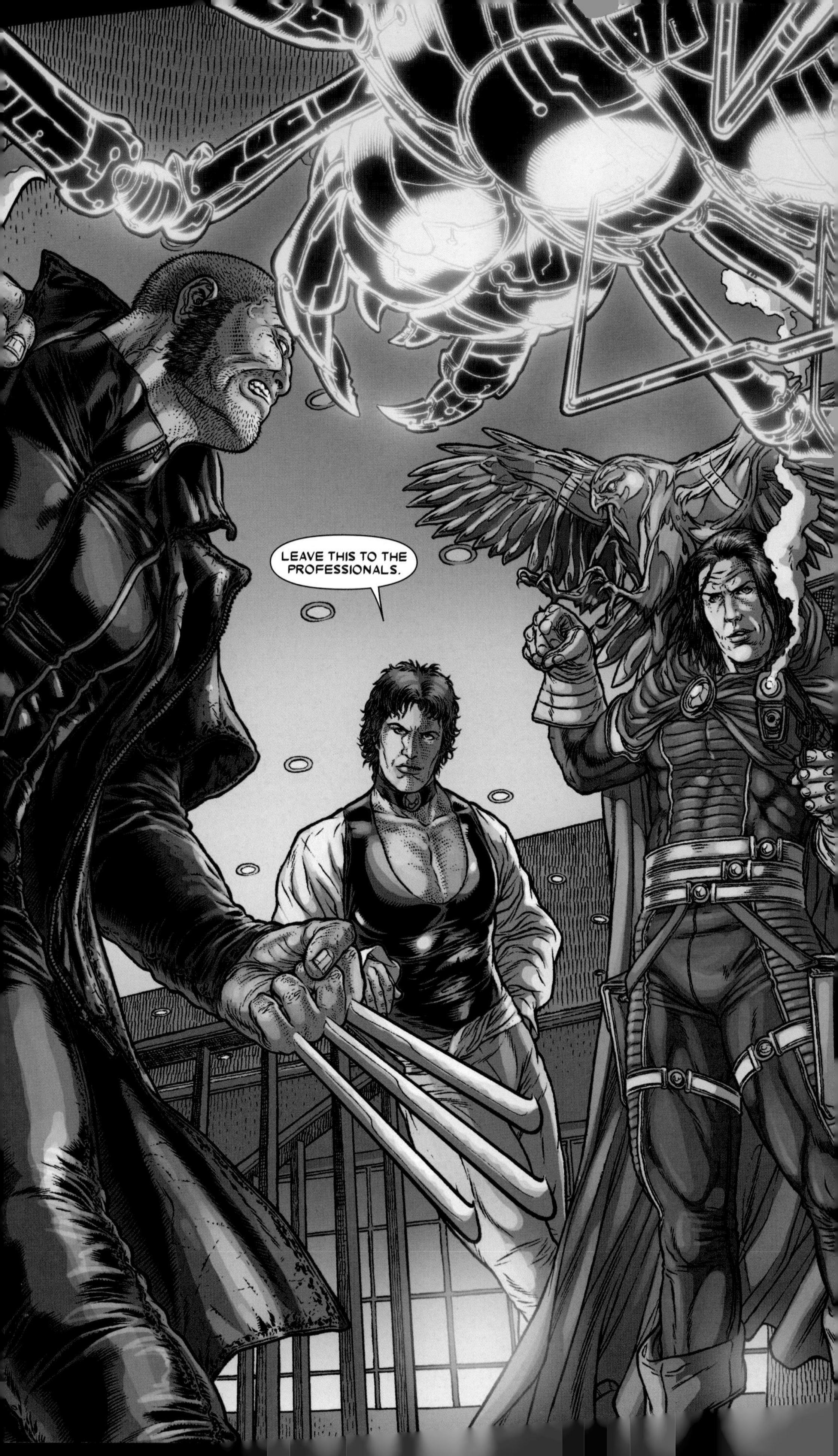
LEAVE THIS TO THE PROFESSIONALS.

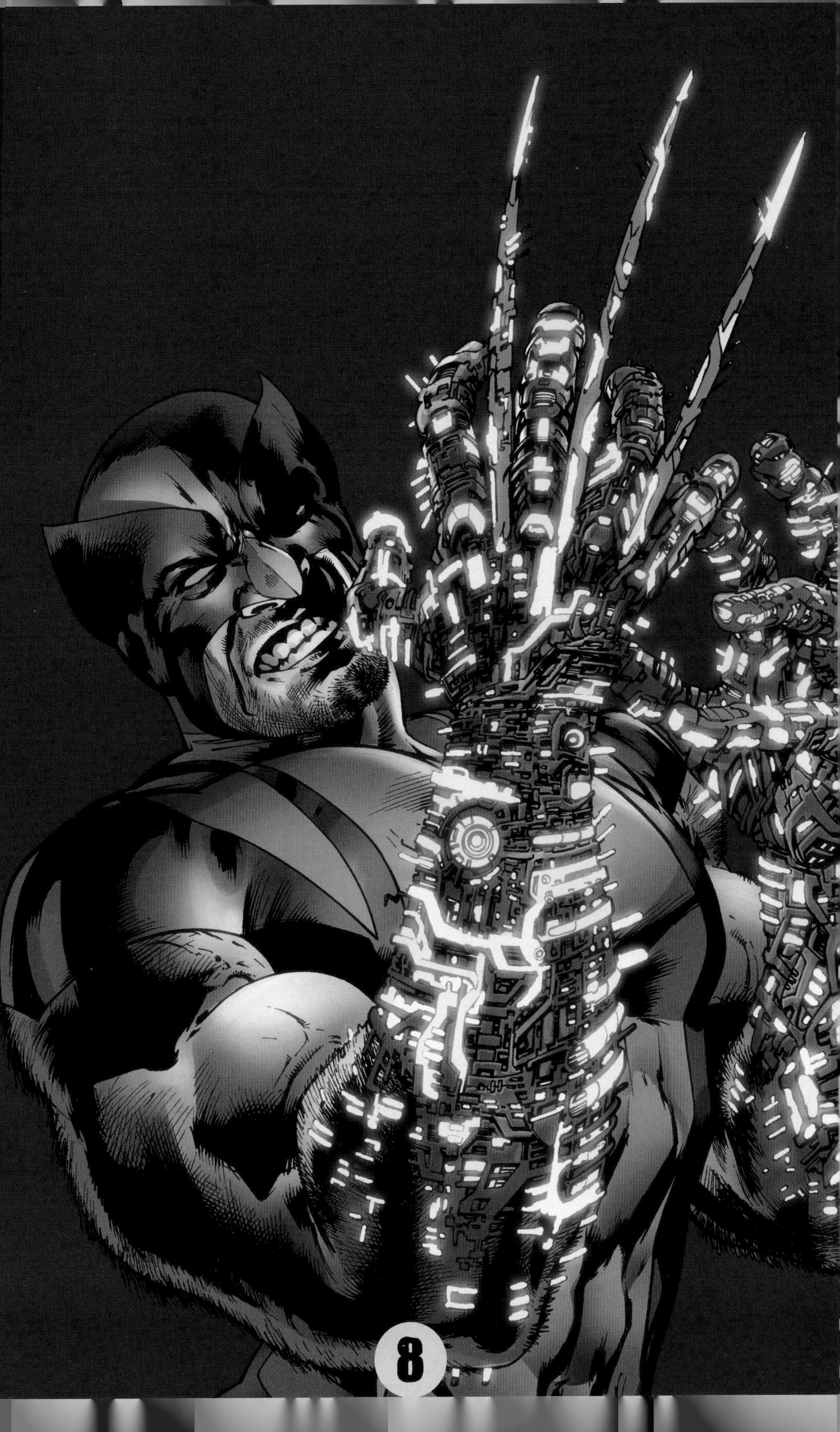
8

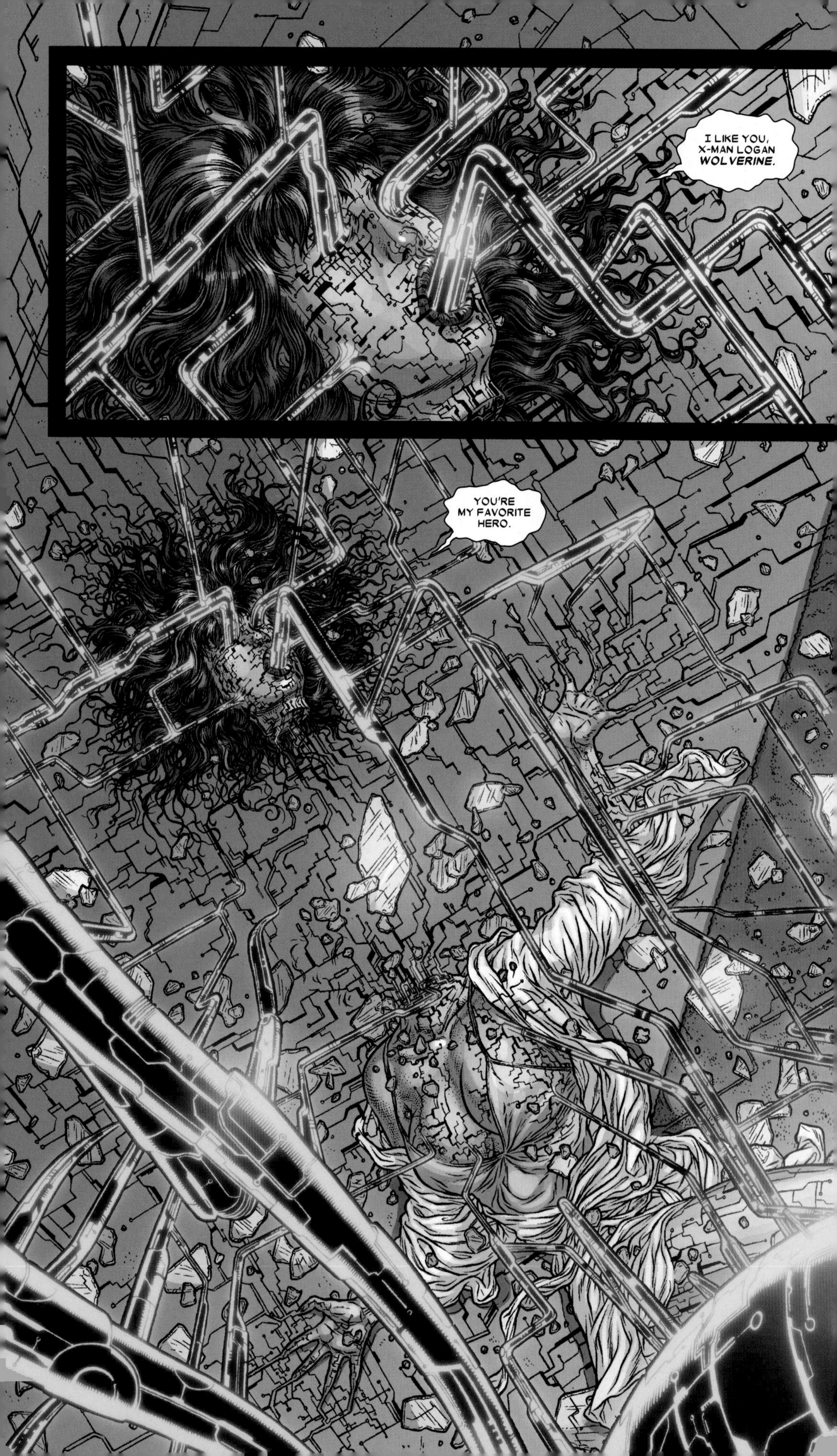
I LIKE YOU, X-MAN LOGAN WOLVERINE.
YOU'RE MY FAVORITE HERO.

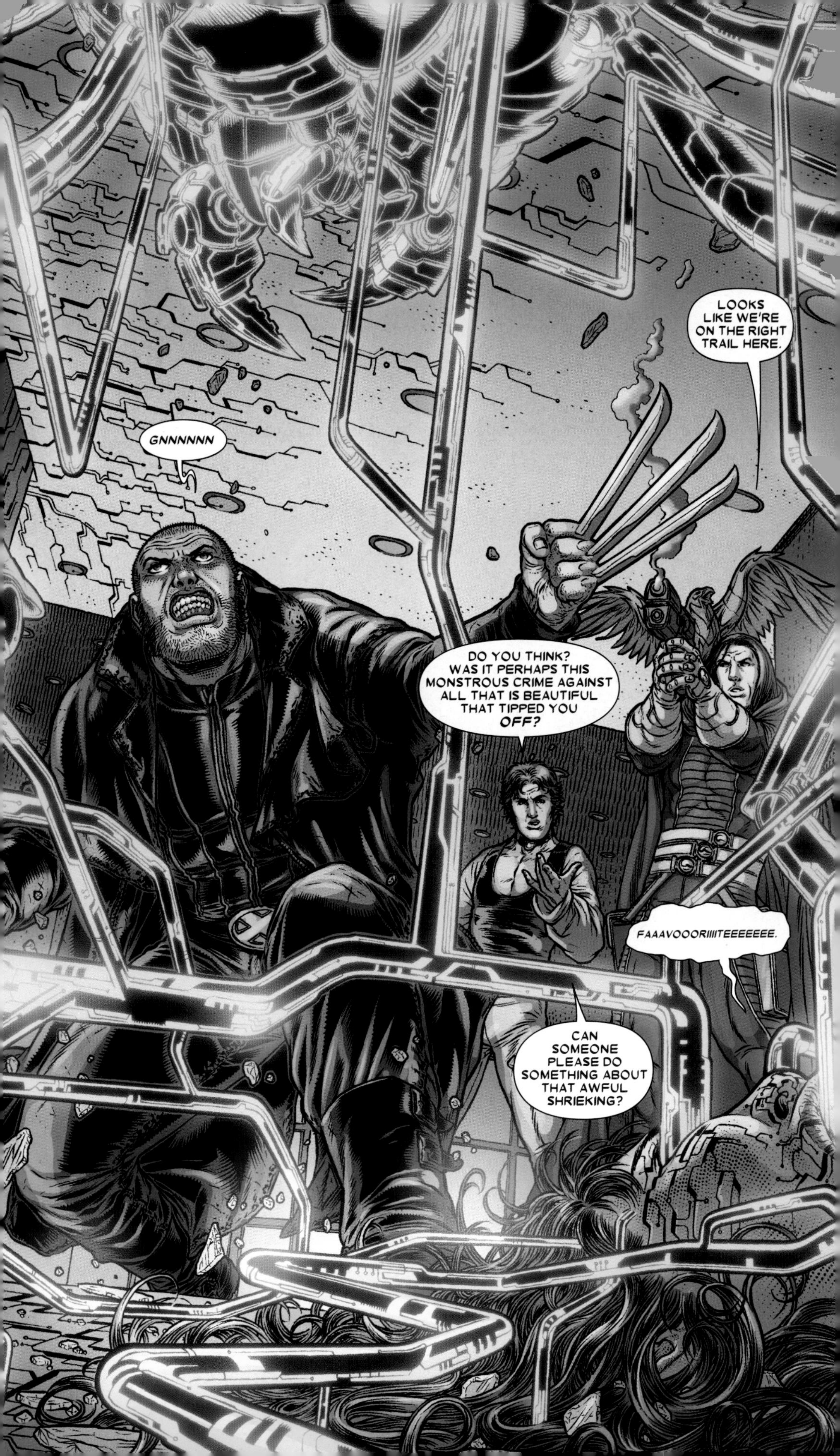
LOOKS LIKE WE'RE ON THE RIGHT TRAIL HERE.
GNNNNNN
DO YOU THINK? WAS IT PERHAPS THIS MONSTROUS CRIME AGAINST ALL THAT IS BEAUTIFUL THAT TIPPED YOU OFF?
FAAAVOOORIIIITEEEEEEE.
CAN SOMEONE PLEASE DO SOMETHING ABOUT THAT AWFUL SHRIEKING?

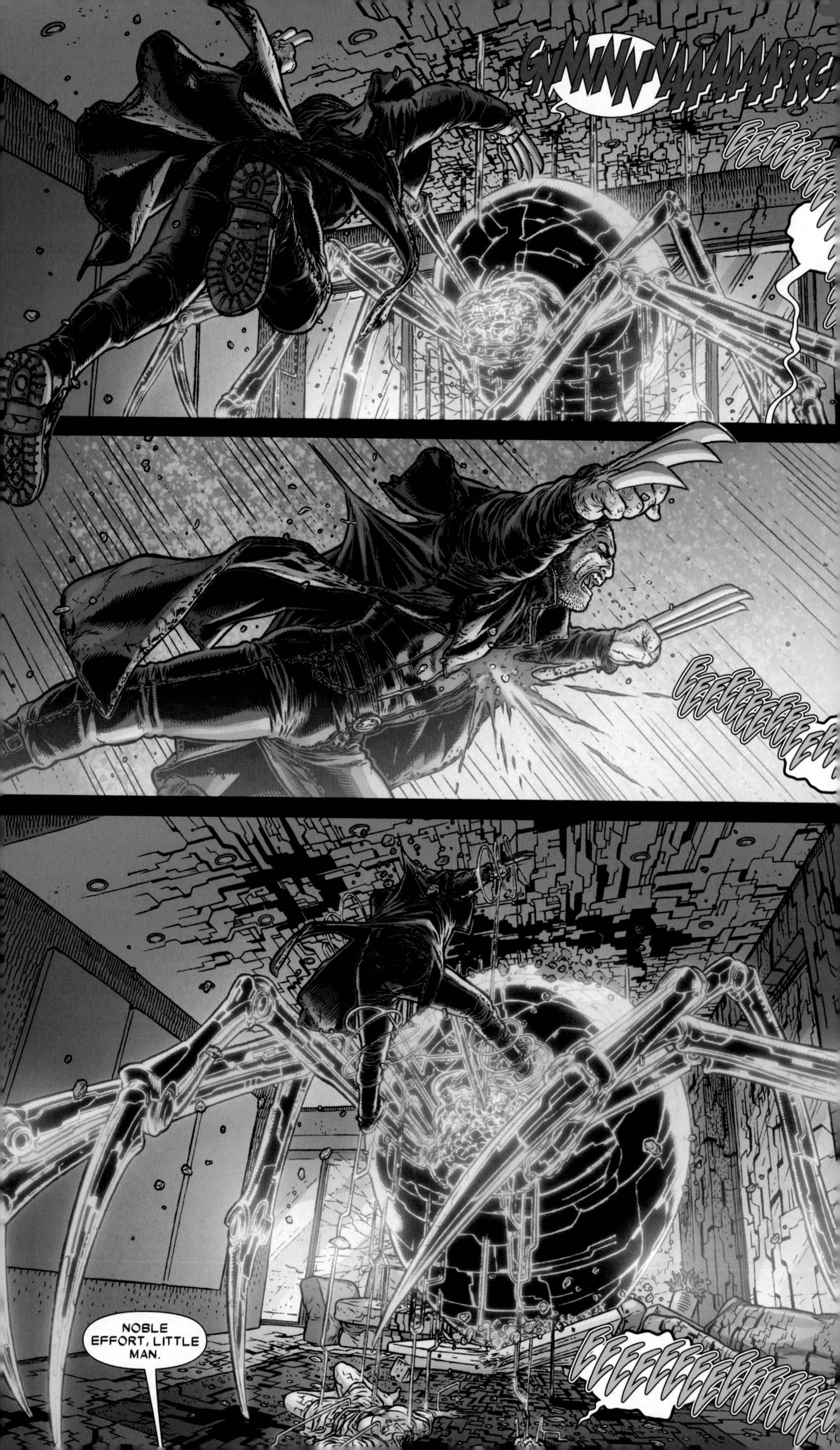
GNNNNNAAAAAARRGH
EEEEEEEEEE
EEEEEEEEEEEEE
NOBLE EFFORT, LITTLE MAN.
EEEEEEEEEEEEEEEE

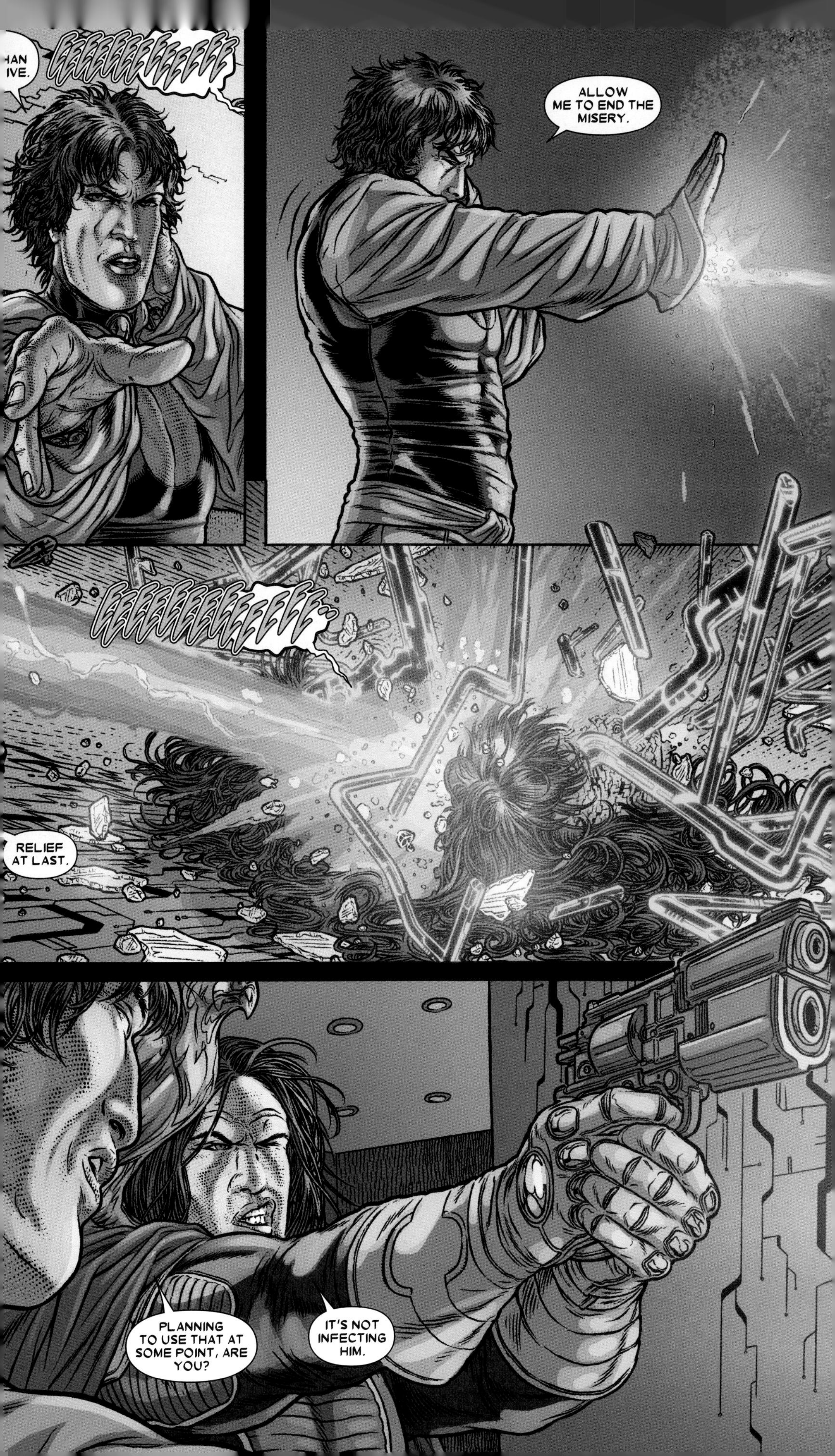

HAN
IVE.
EEEEEEEEEEEEE
ALLOW ME TO END THE MISERY.
EEEEEEEEEEEEEE...
RELIEF AT LAST.
PLANNING TO USE THAT AT SOME POINT, ARE YOU?
IT'S NOT INFECTING HIM.

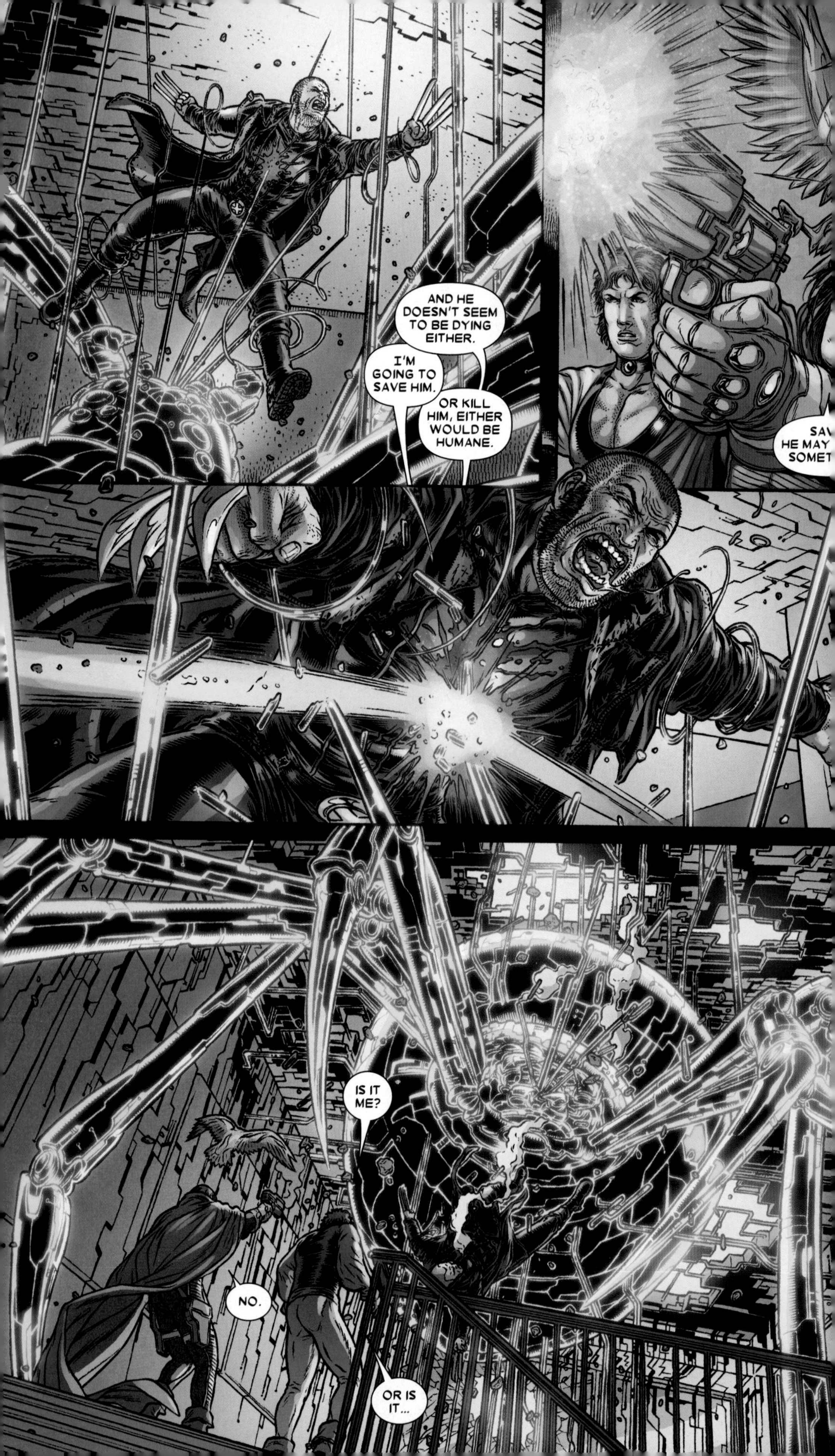
AND HE DOESN'T SEEM TO BE DYING EITHER.
I'M GOING TO SAVE HIM.
OR KILL HIM, EITHER WOULD BE HUMANE.
IS IT ME?
NO.
OR IS IT...

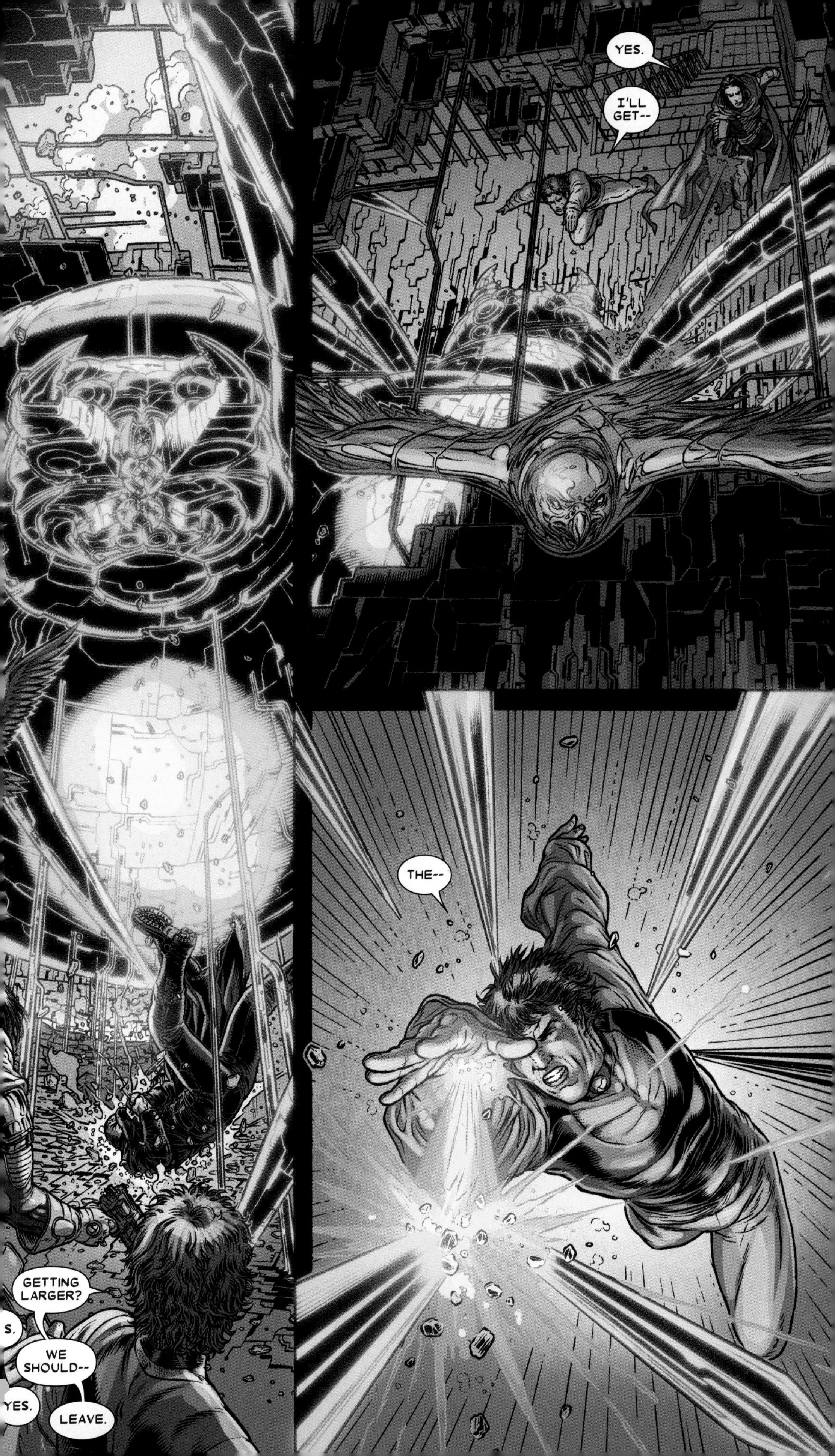
GETTING LARGER?
S.
WE SHOULD--
YES.
LEAVE.
YES.
I'LL GET--
THE--

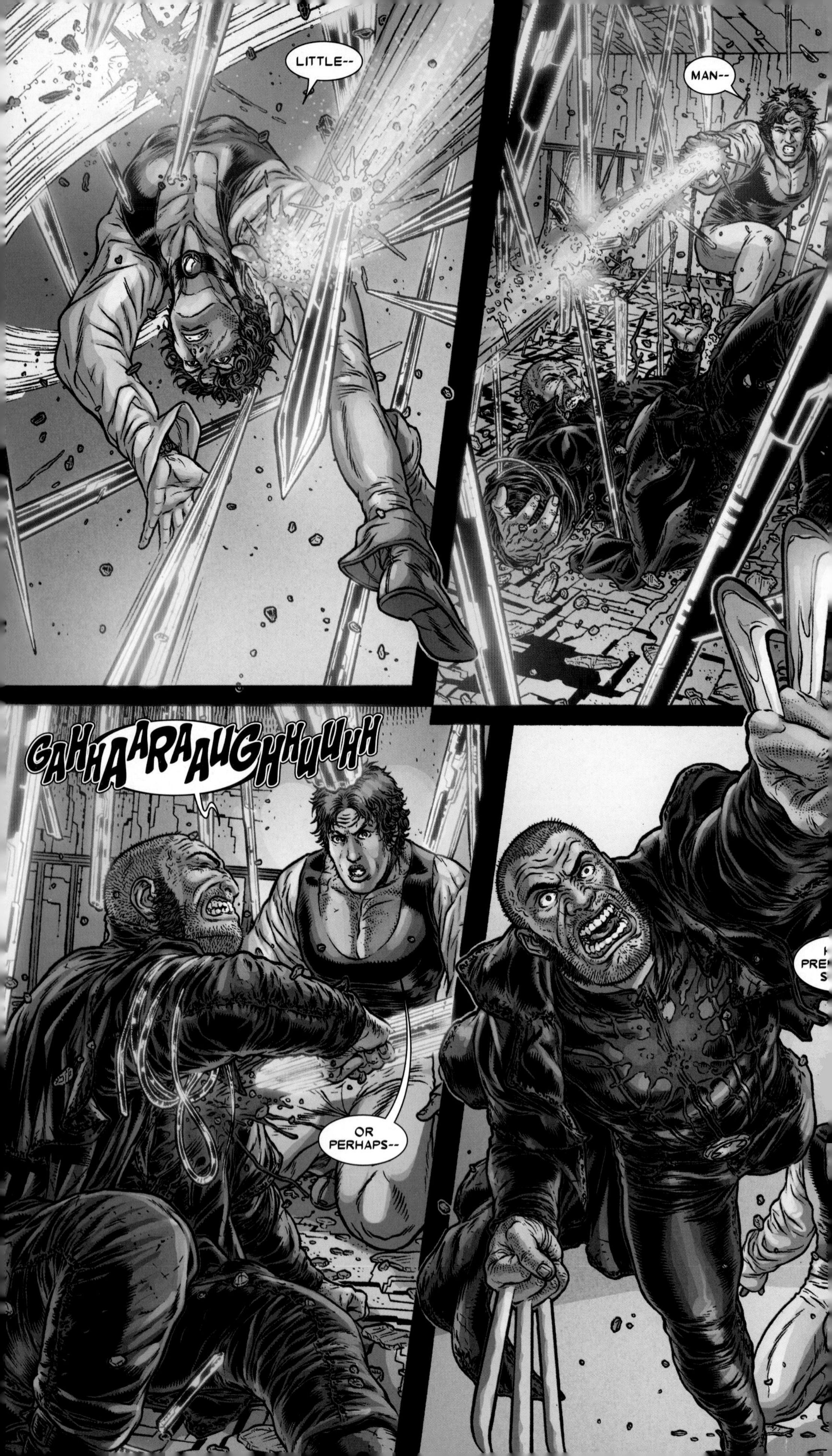
LITTLE--
MAN--
GAHHAARAAUGHHUUHH
OR PERHAPS--

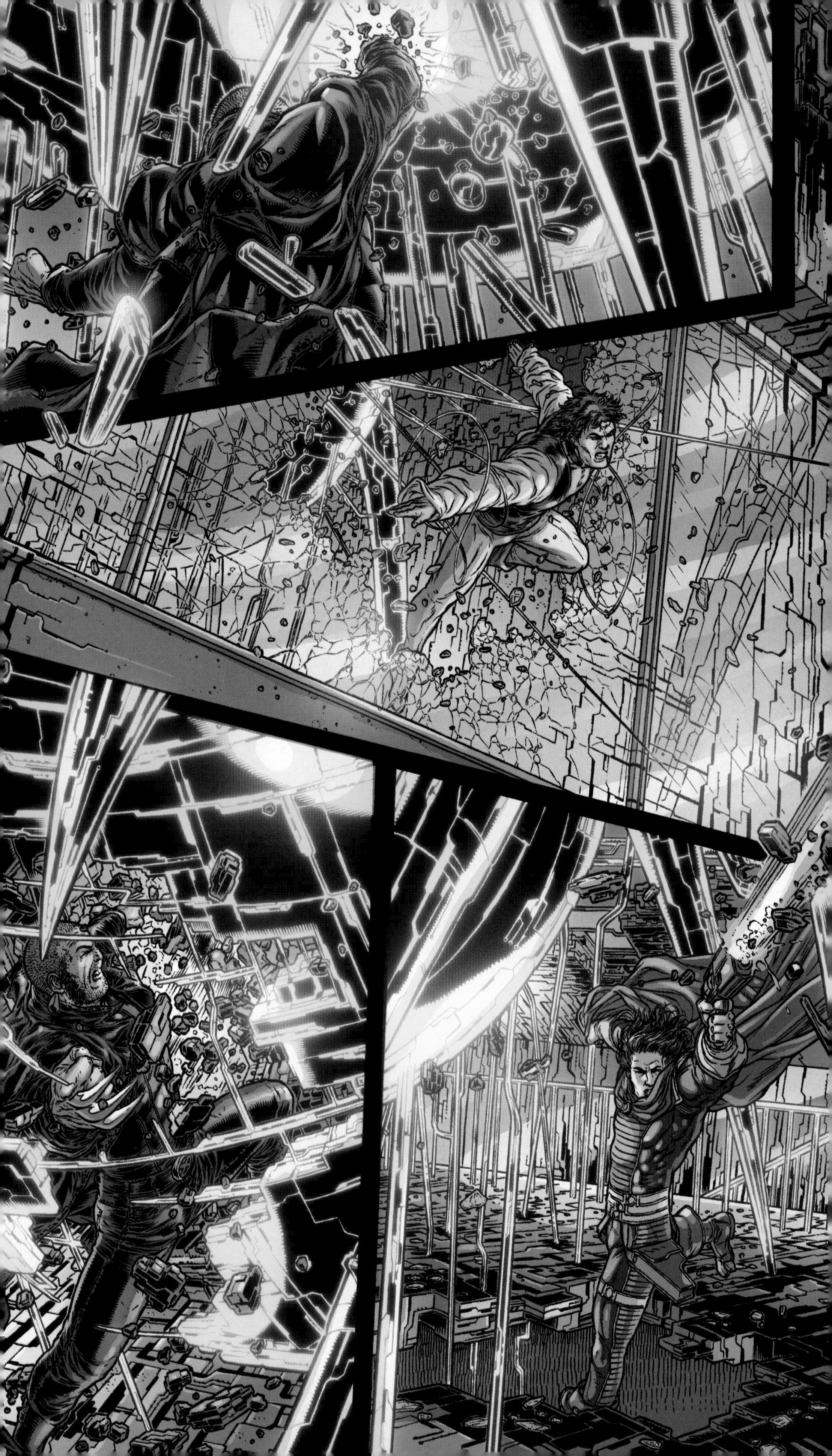

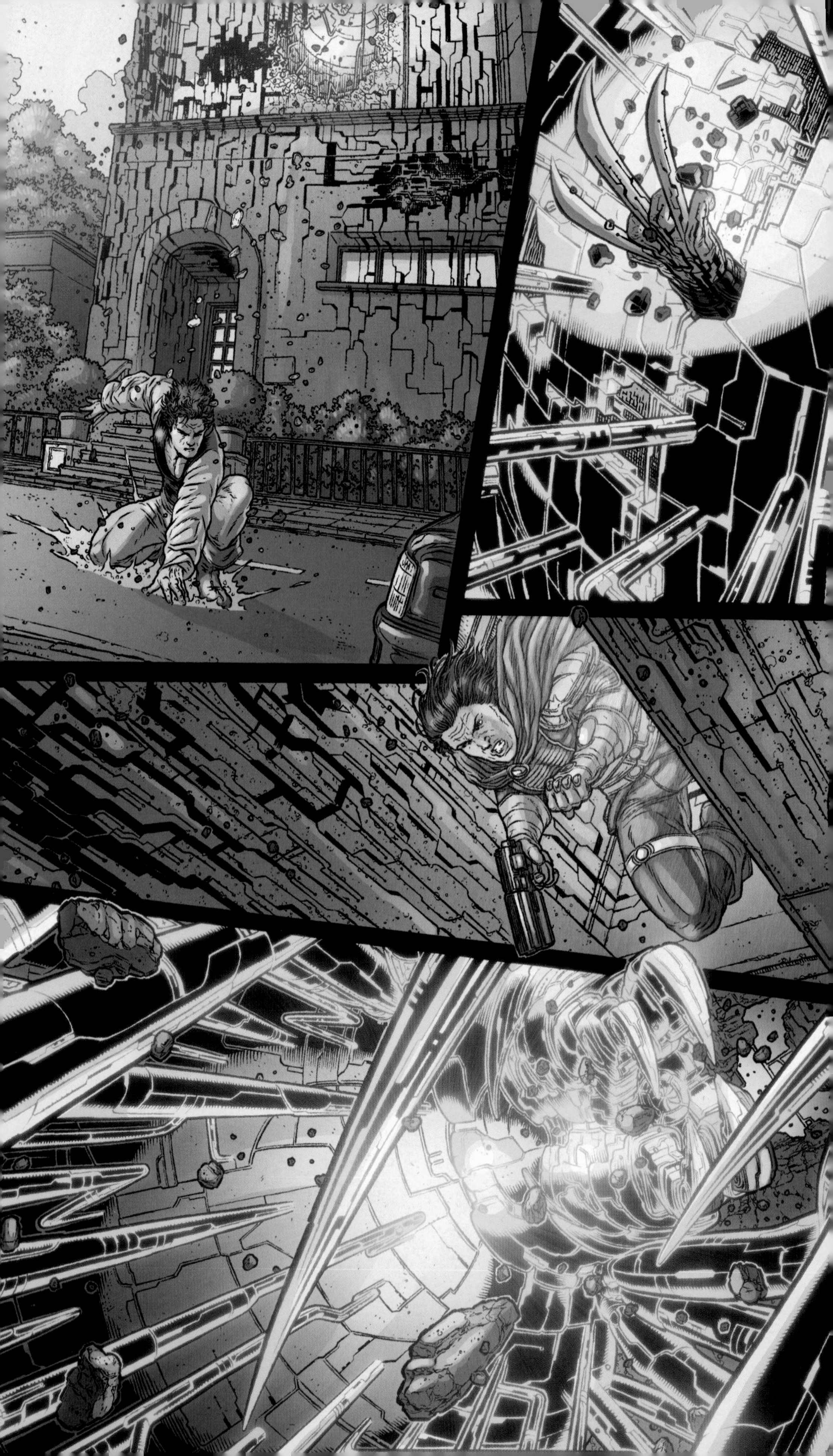

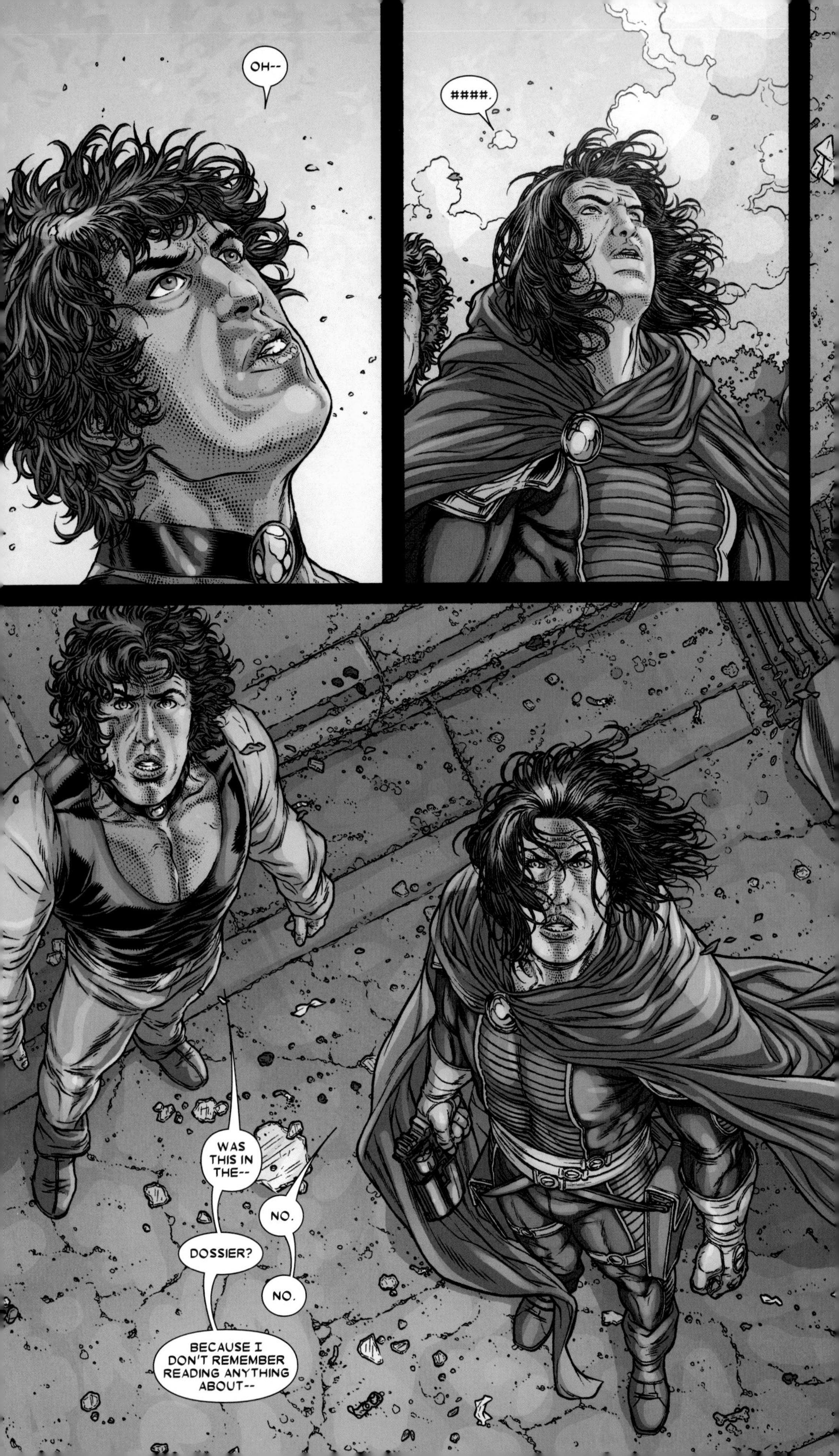
OH--
####.
WAS THIS IN THE--
NO.
DOSSIER?
NO.
BECAUSE I DON'T REMEMBER READING ANYTHING ABOUT--

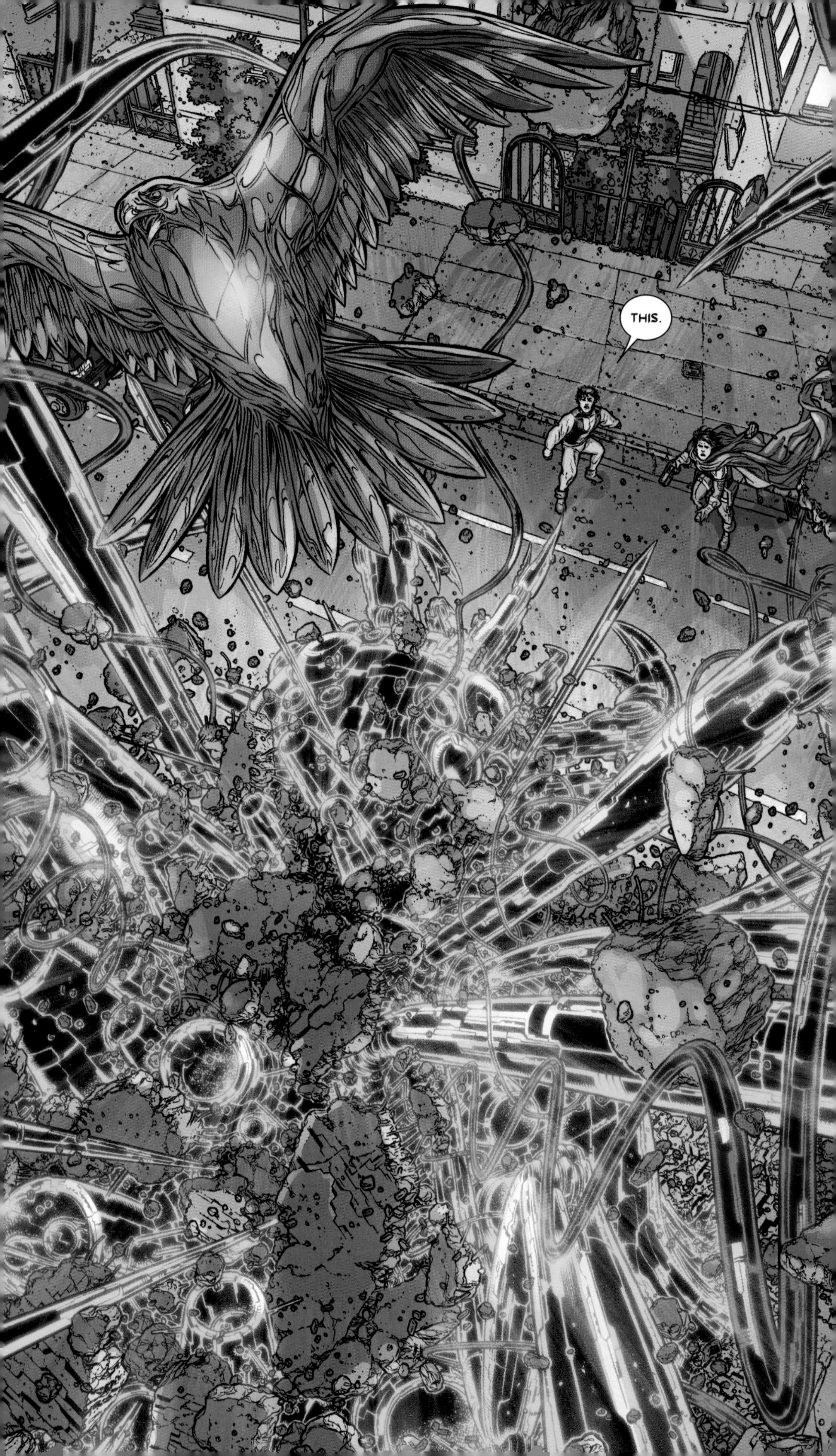
THIS.

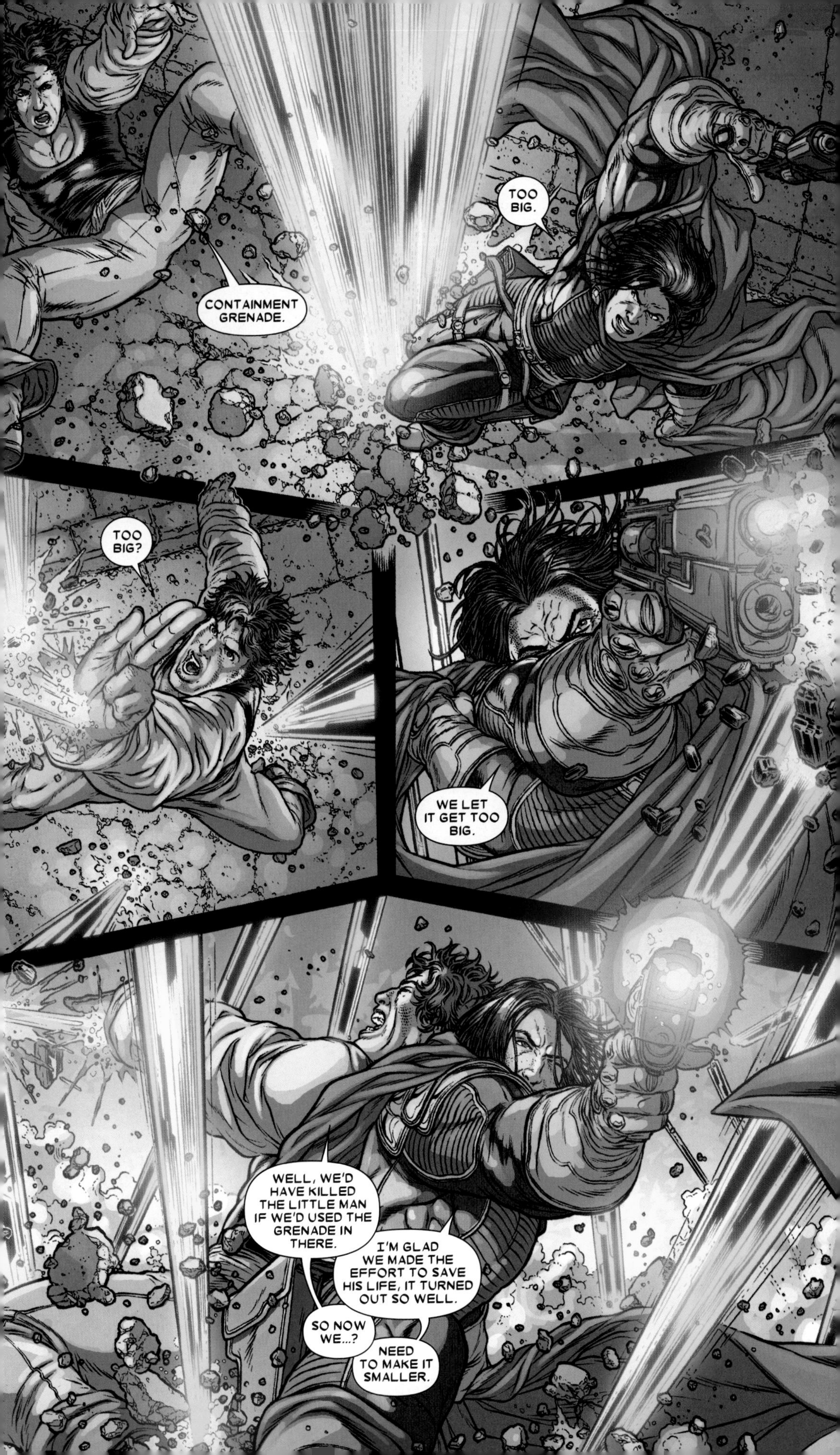
CONTAINMENT GRENADE.
TOO BIG.
TOO BIG?
WE LET IT GET TOO BIG.
WELL, WE'D HAVE KILLED THE LITTLE MAN IF WE'D USED THE GRENADE IN THERE.
I'M GLAD WE MADE THE EFFORT TO SAVE HIS LIFE, IT TURNED OUT SO WELL.
SO NOW WE...?
NEED TO MAKE IT SMALLER.

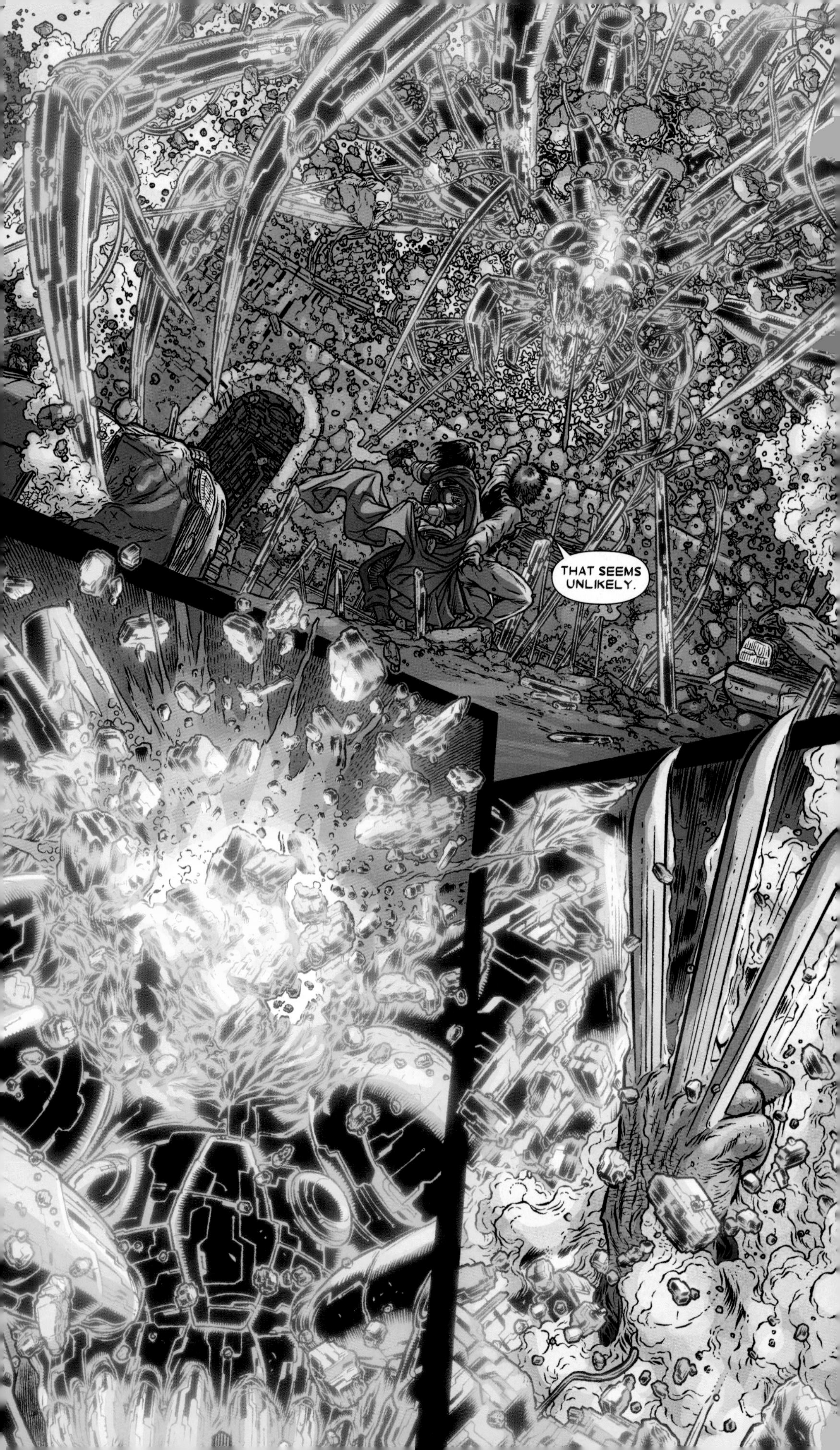
THAT SEEMS UNLIKELY.

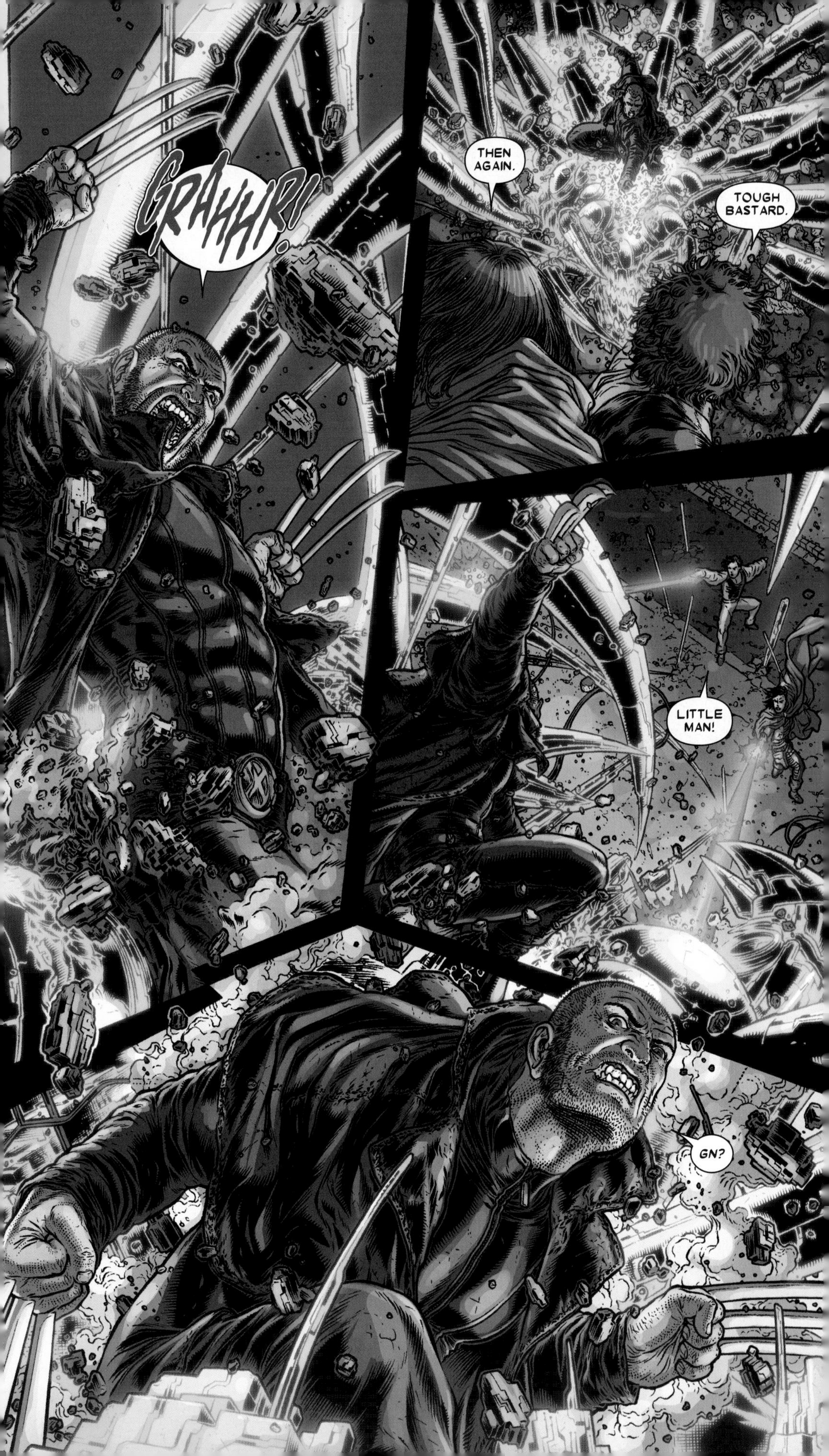
GRAHHR!
THEN AGAIN.
TOUGH BASTARD.
LITTLE MAN!
GN?

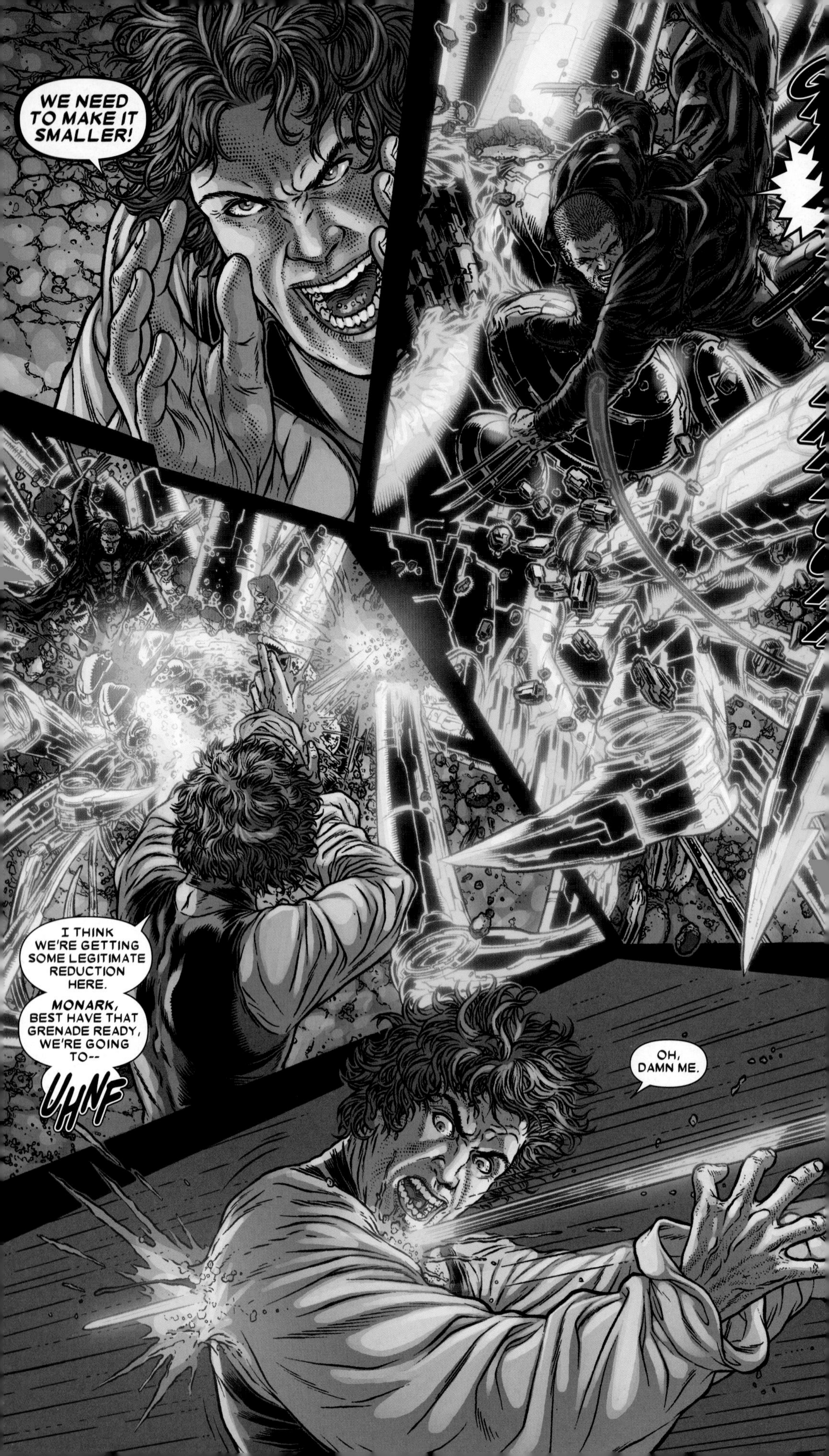

WE NEED TO MAKE IT SMALLER!
I THINK WE'RE GETTING SOME LEGITIMATE REDUCTION HERE.
MONARK, BEST HAVE THAT GRENADE READY, WE'RE GOING TO--
UHNF
OH, DAMN ME.

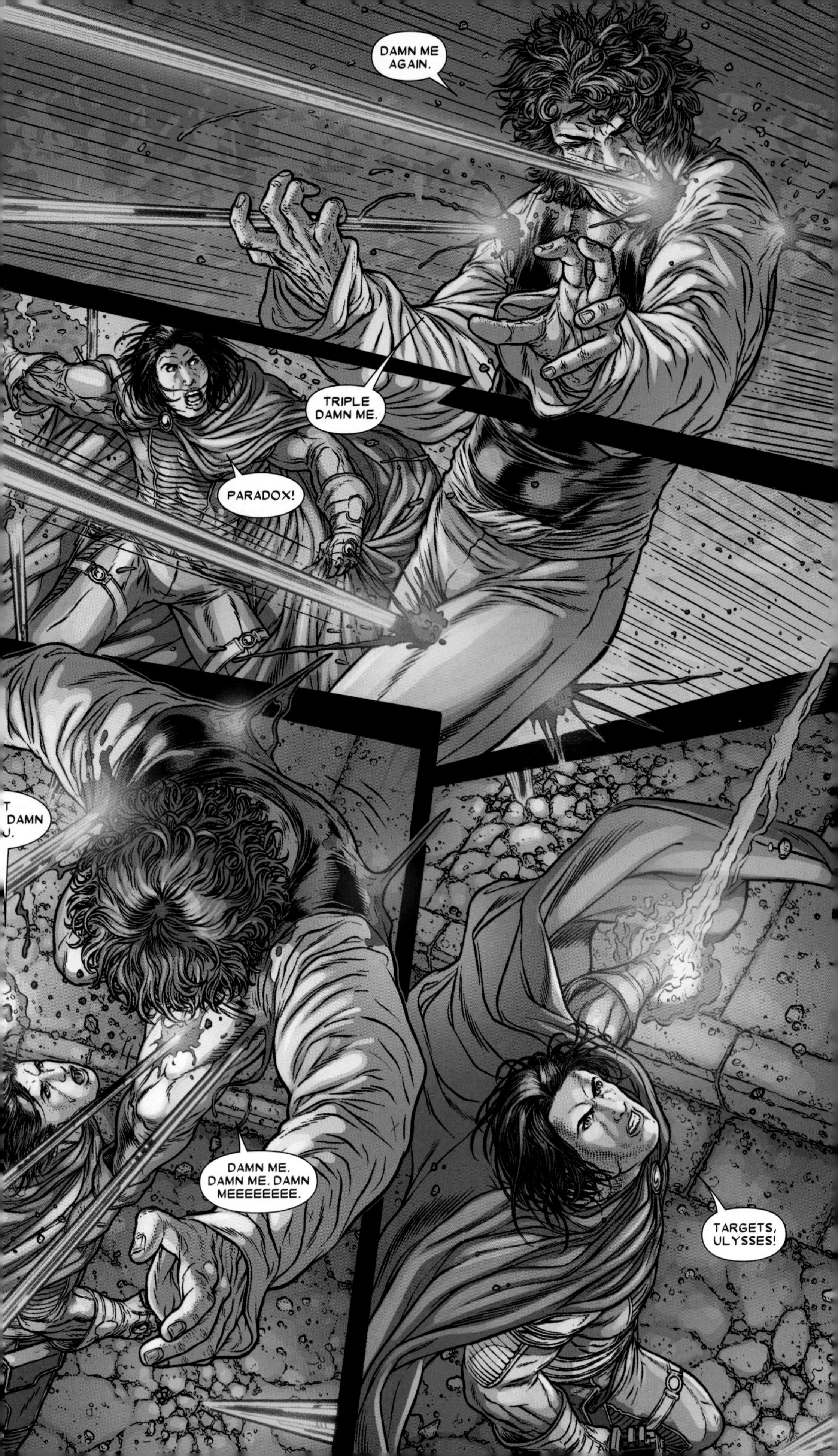
DAMN ME AGAIN.
TRIPLE DAMN ME.
PARADOX!
DAMN ME. DAMN ME. DAMN MEEEEEEEE.
TARGETS, ULYSSES!

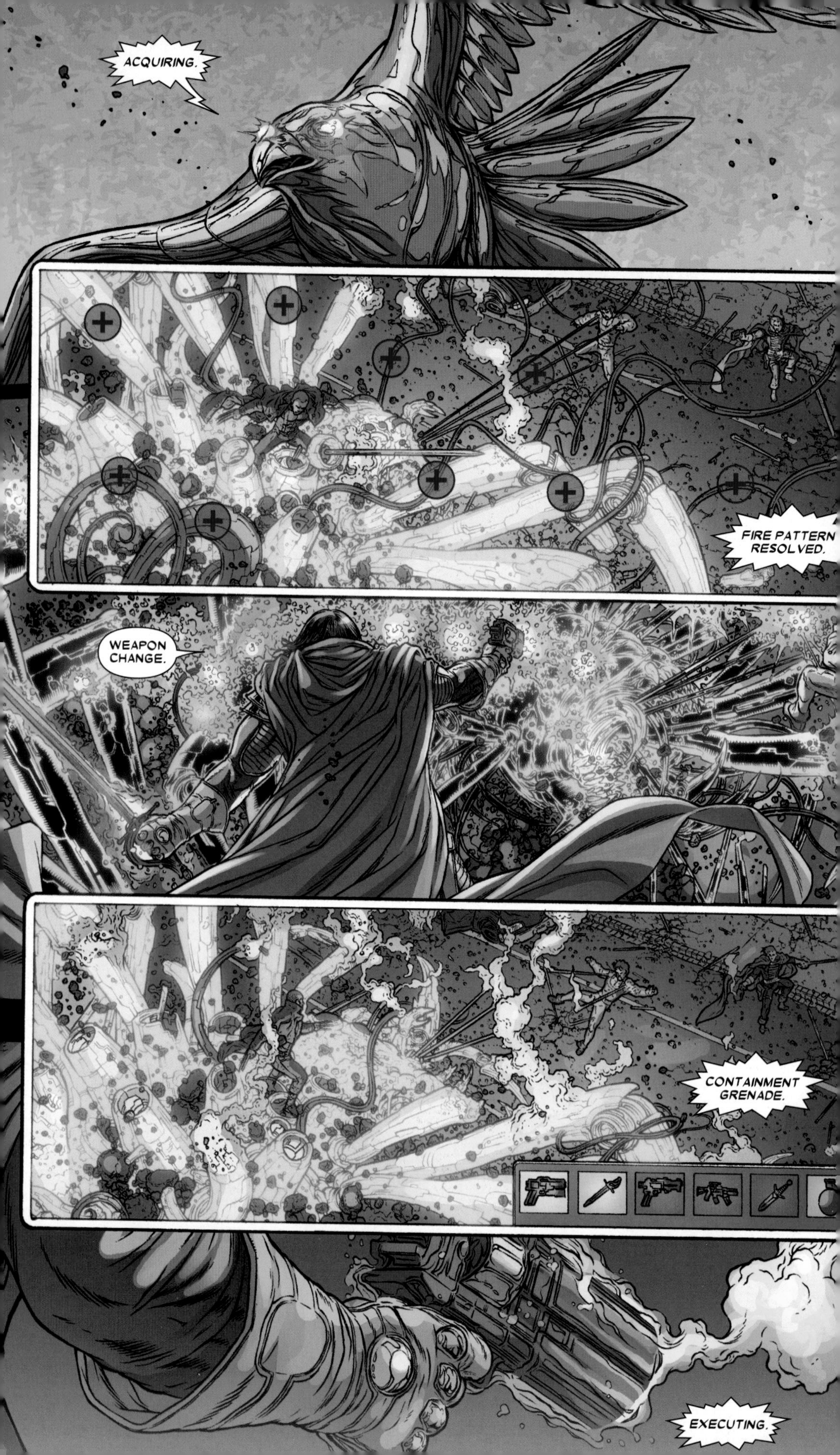
ACQUIRING.
FIRE PATTERN RESOLVED.
WEAPON CHANGE.
CONTAINMENT GRENADE.
EXECUTING.

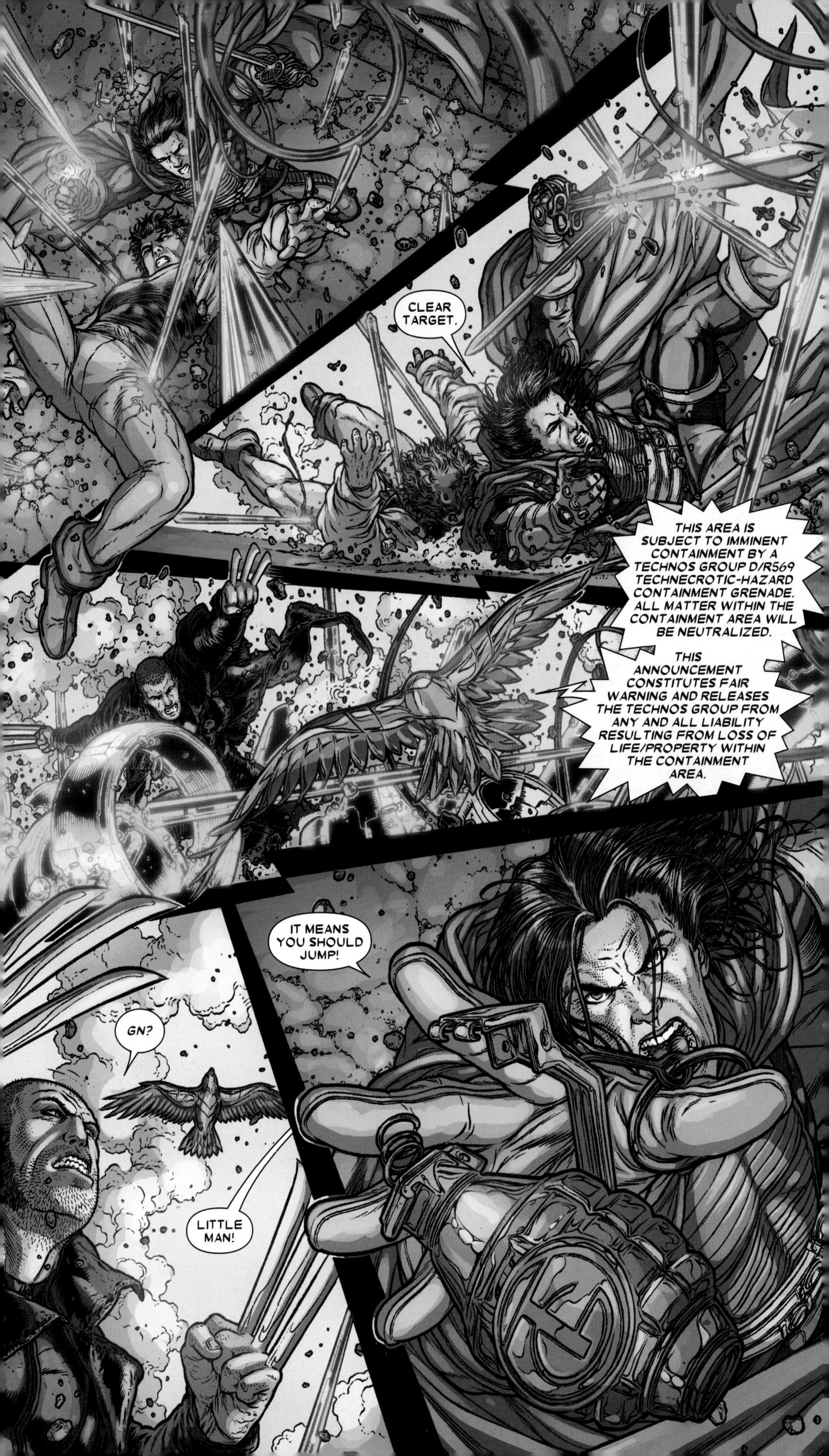
CLEAR TARGET.
THIS AREA IS SUBJECT TO IMMINENT CONTAINMENT BY A TECHNOS GROUP D/R569 TECHNECROTIC-HAZARD CONTAINMENT GRENADE. ALL MATTER WITHIN THE CONTAINMENT AREA WILL BE NEUTRALIZED.
THIS ANNOUNCEMENT CONSTITUTES FAIR WARNING AND RELEASES THE TECHNOS GROUP FROM ANY AND ALL LIABILITY RESULTING FROM LOSS OF LIFE/PROPERTY WITHIN THE CONTAINMENT AREA.
GN?
IT MEANS YOU SHOULD JUMP!
LITTLE MAN!

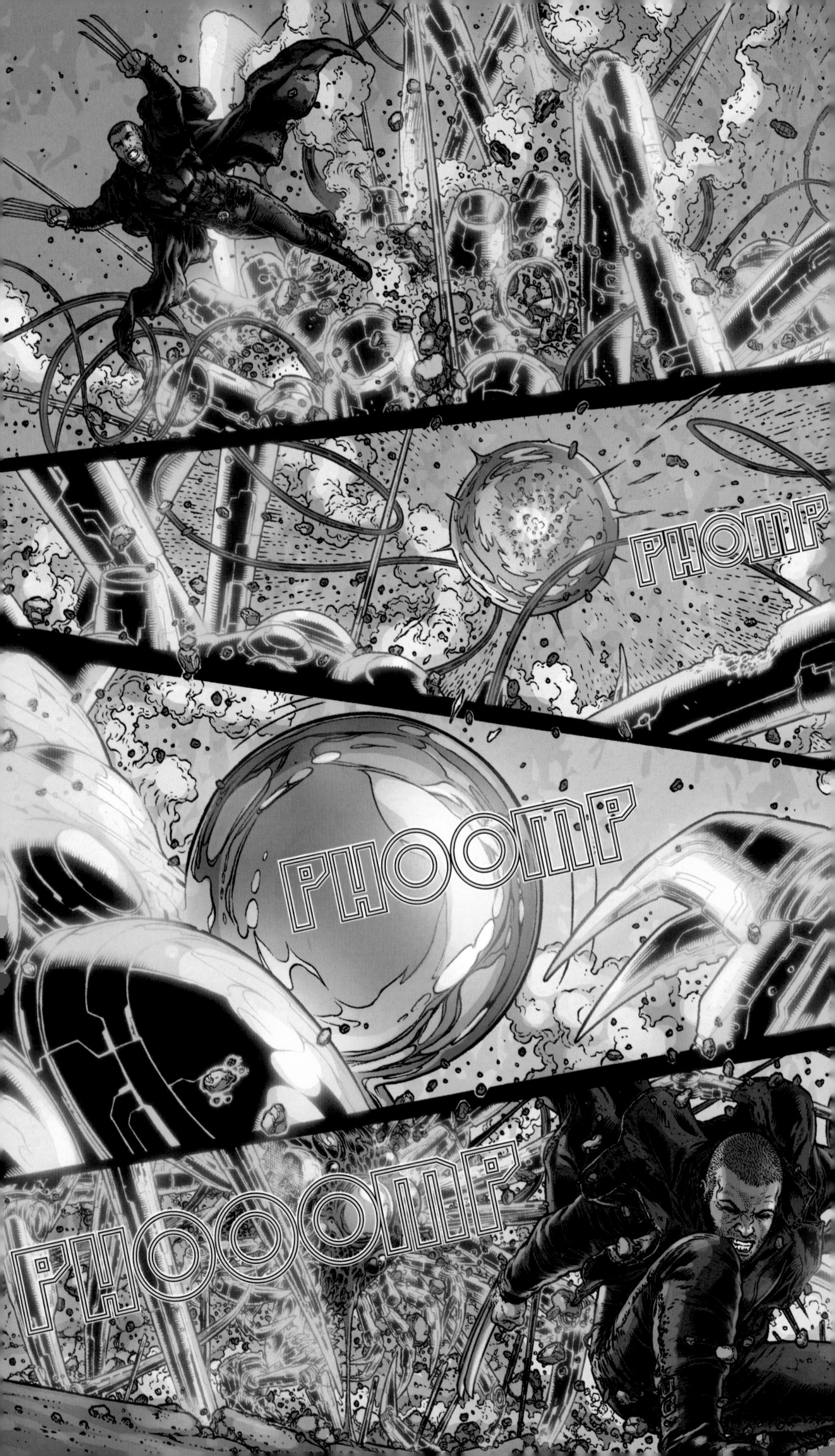
PHOMP
PHOOMP
PHOOOMP

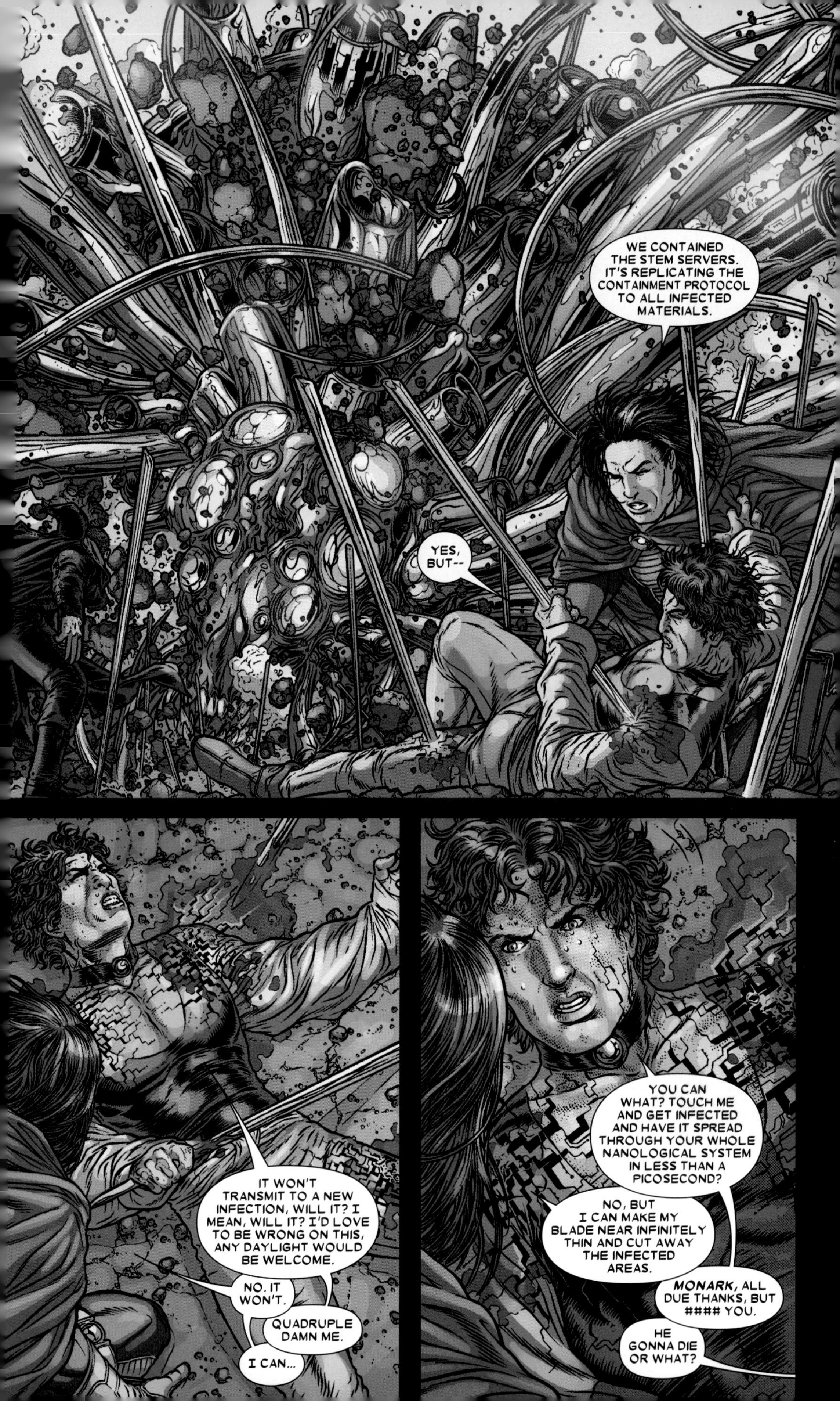
WE CONTAINED THE STEM SERVERS. IT'S REPLICATING THE CONTAINMENT PROTOCOL TO ALL INFECTED MATERIALS.
YES, BUT--
IT WON'T TRANSMIT TO A NEW INFECTION, WILL IT? I MEAN, WILL IT? I'D LOVE TO BE WRONG ON THIS, ANY DAYLIGHT WOULD BE WELCOME.
NO. IT WON'T.
QUADRUPLE DAMN ME.
I CAN...
YOU CAN WHAT? TOUCH ME AND GET INFECTED AND HAVE IT SPREAD THROUGH YOUR WHOLE NANOLOGICAL SYSTEM IN LESS THAN A PICOSECOND?
NO, BUT I CAN MAKE MY BLADE NEAR INFINITELY THIN AND CUT AWAY THE INFECTED AREAS.
MONARK, ALL DUE THANKS, BUT #### YOU.
HE GONNA DIE OR WHAT?

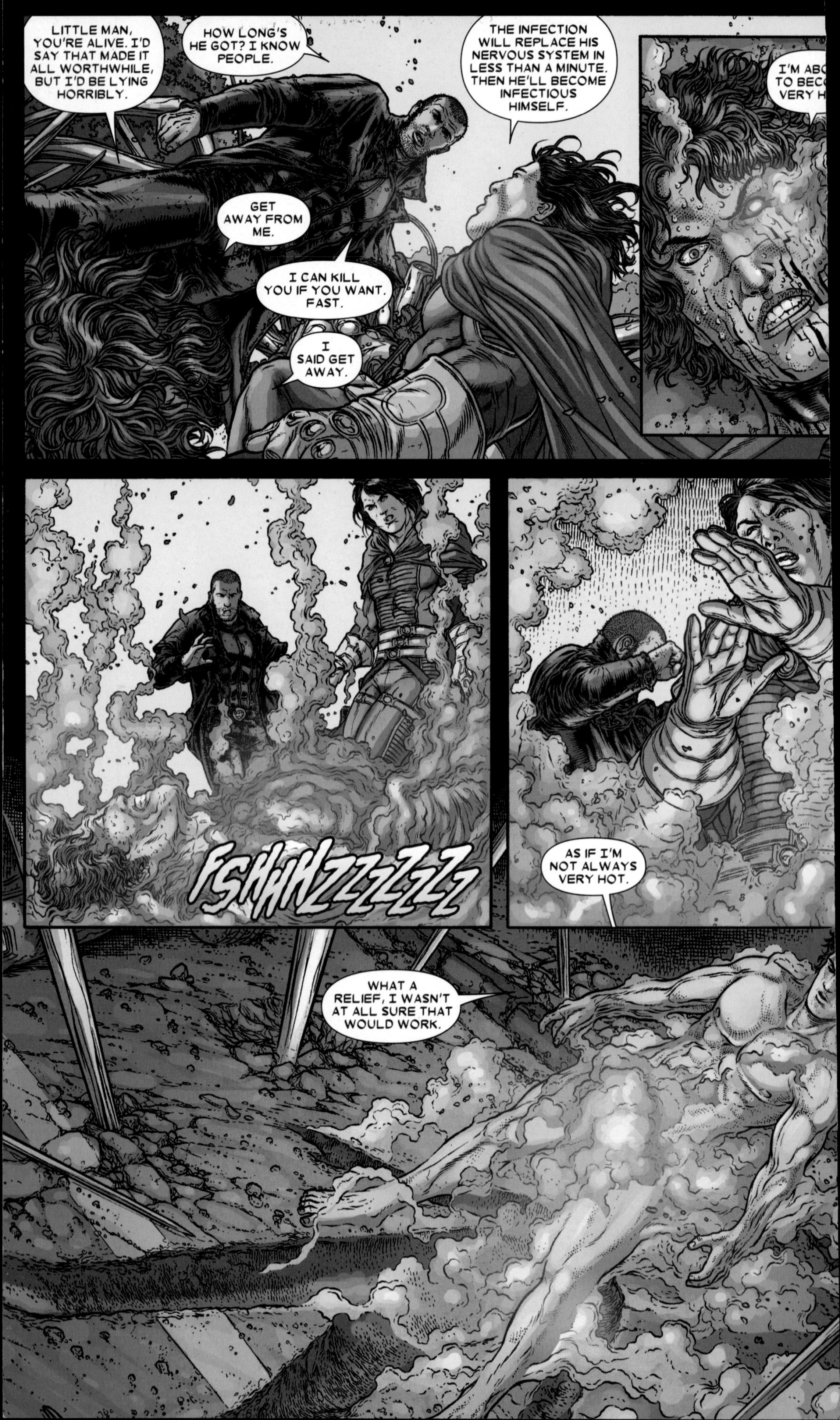
LITTLE MAN, YOU'RE ALIVE. I'D SAY THAT MADE IT ALL WORTHWHILE, BUT I'D BE LYING HORRIBLY.
HOW LONG'S HE GOT? I KNOW PEOPLE.
THE INFECTION WILL REPLACE HIS NERVOUS SYSTEM IN LESS THAN A MINUTE. THEN HE'LL BECOME INFECTIOUS HIMSELF.
GET AWAY FROM ME.
I CAN KILL YOU IF YOU WANT. FAST.
I SAID GET AWAY.
FSHHHZZZZZZZZ
AS IF I'M NOT ALWAYS VERY HOT.
WHAT A RELIEF, I WASN'T AT ALL SURE THAT WOULD WORK.

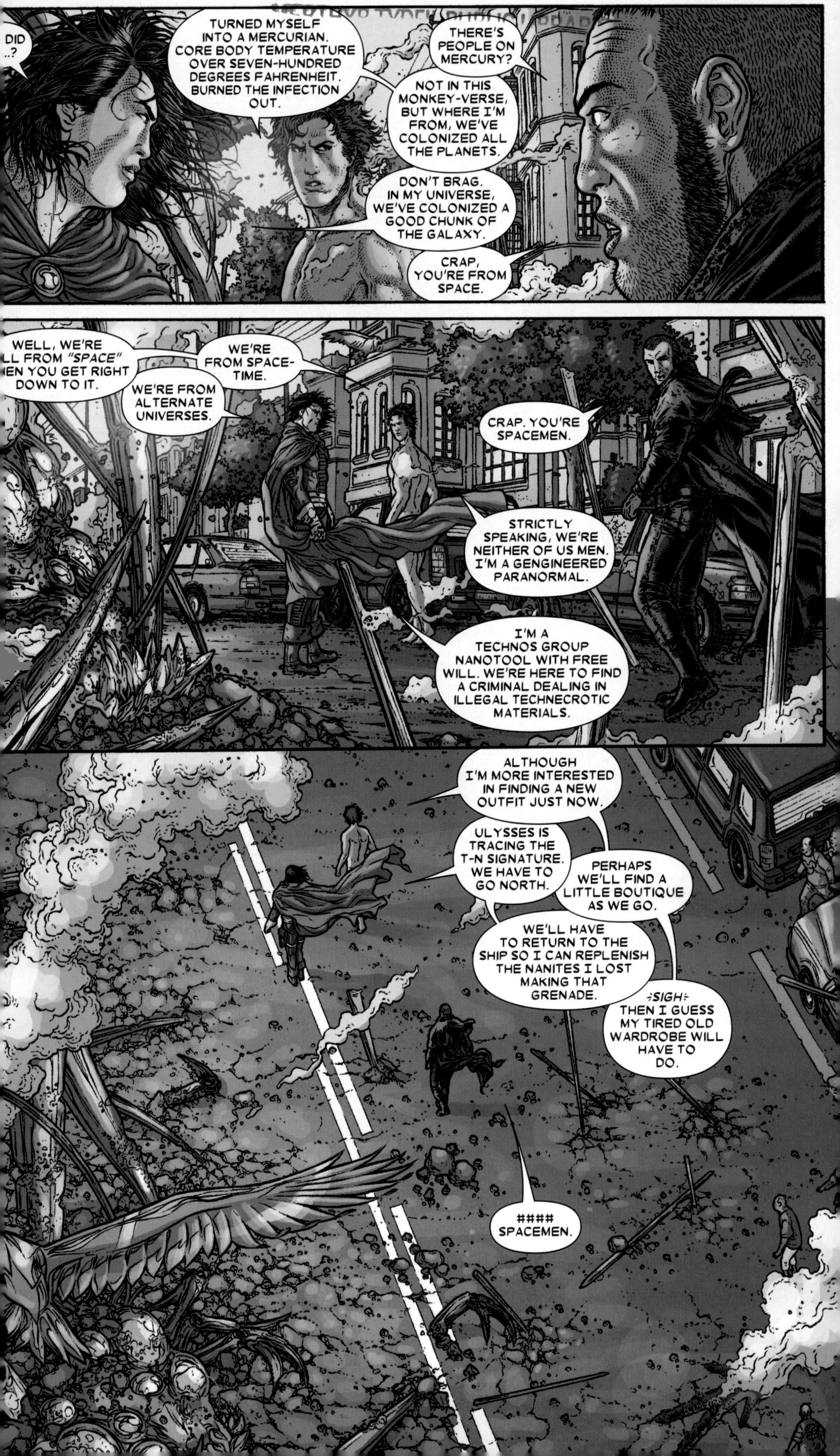
DID ..?
TURNED MYSELF INTO A MERCURIAN. CORE BODY TEMPERATURE OVER SEVEN-HUNDRED DEGREES FAHRENHEIT. BURNED THE INFECTION OUT.
THERE'S PEOPLE ON MERCURY?
NOT IN THIS MONKEY-VERSE, BUT WHERE I'M FROM, WE'VE COLONIZED ALL THE PLANETS.
DON'T BRAG. IN MY UNIVERSE, WE'VE COLONIZED A GOOD CHUNK OF THE GALAXY.
CRAP, YOU'RE FROM SPACE.
WELL, WE'RE LL FROM "SPACE" EN YOU GET RIGHT DOWN TO IT.
WE'RE FROM SPACE-TIME.
WE'RE FROM ALTERNATE UNIVERSES.
CRAP. YOU'RE SPACEMEN.
STRICTLY SPEAKING, WE'RE NEITHER OF US MEN. I'M A GENGINEERED PARANORMAL.
I'M A TECHNOS GROUP NANOTOOL WITH FREE WILL. WE'RE HERE TO FIND A CRIMINAL DEALING IN ILLEGAL TECHNECROTIC MATERIALS.
ALTHOUGH I'M MORE INTERESTED IN FINDING A NEW OUTFIT JUST NOW.
ULYSSES IS TRACING THE T-N SIGNATURE. WE HAVE TO GO NORTH.
PERHAPS WE'LL FIND A LITTLE BOUTIQUE AS WE GO.
WE'LL HAVE TO RETURN TO THE SHIP SO I CAN REPLENISH THE NANITES I LOST MAKING THAT GRENADE.
SIGH
THEN I GUESS MY TIRED OLD WARDROBE WILL HAVE TO DO.
SPACEMEN.

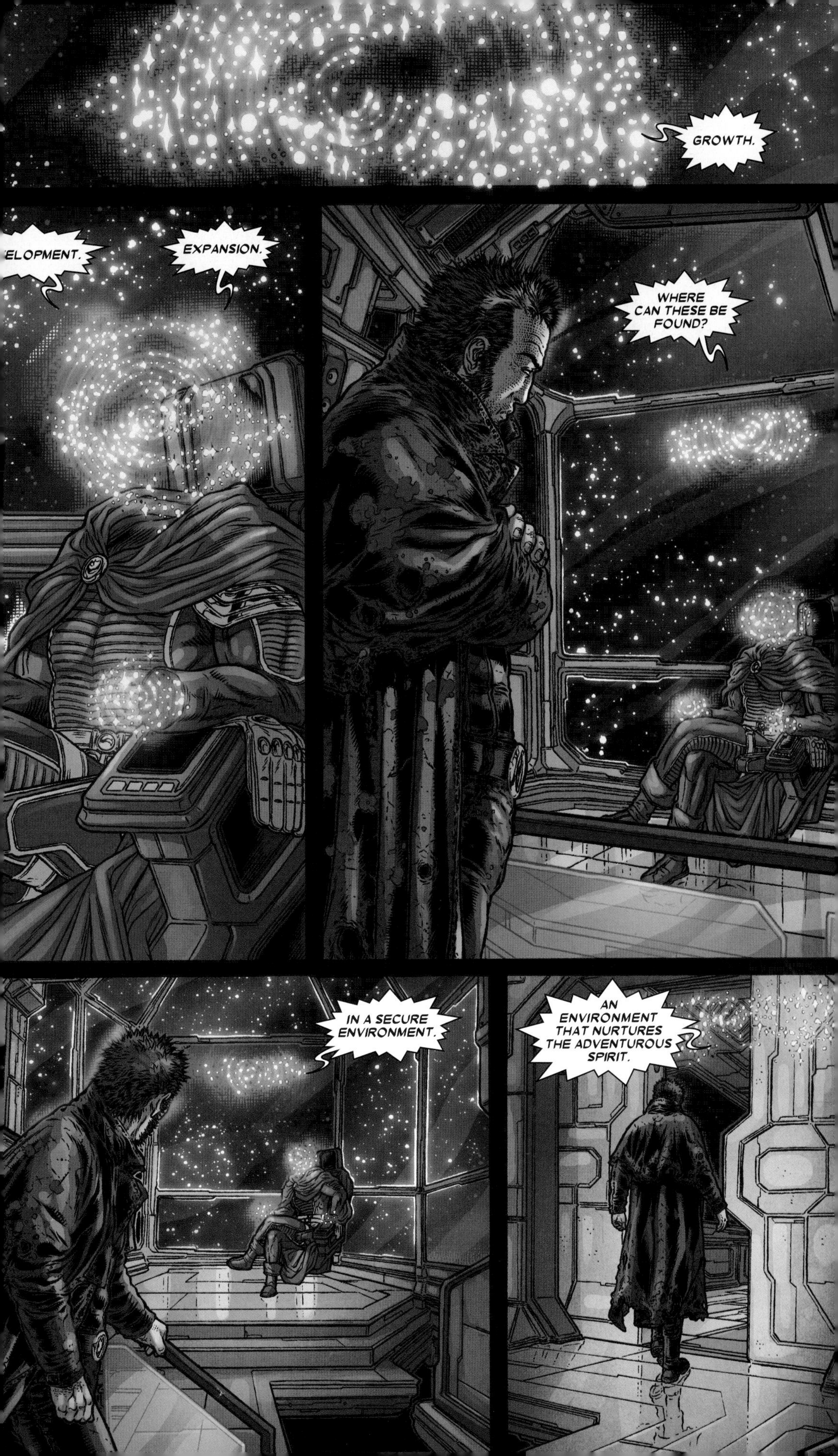
GROWTH.
ELOPMENT.
EXPANSION.
WHERE CAN THESE BE FOUND?
IN A SECURE ENVIRONMENT.
AN ENVIRONMENT THAT NURTURES THE ADVENTUROUS SPIRIT.

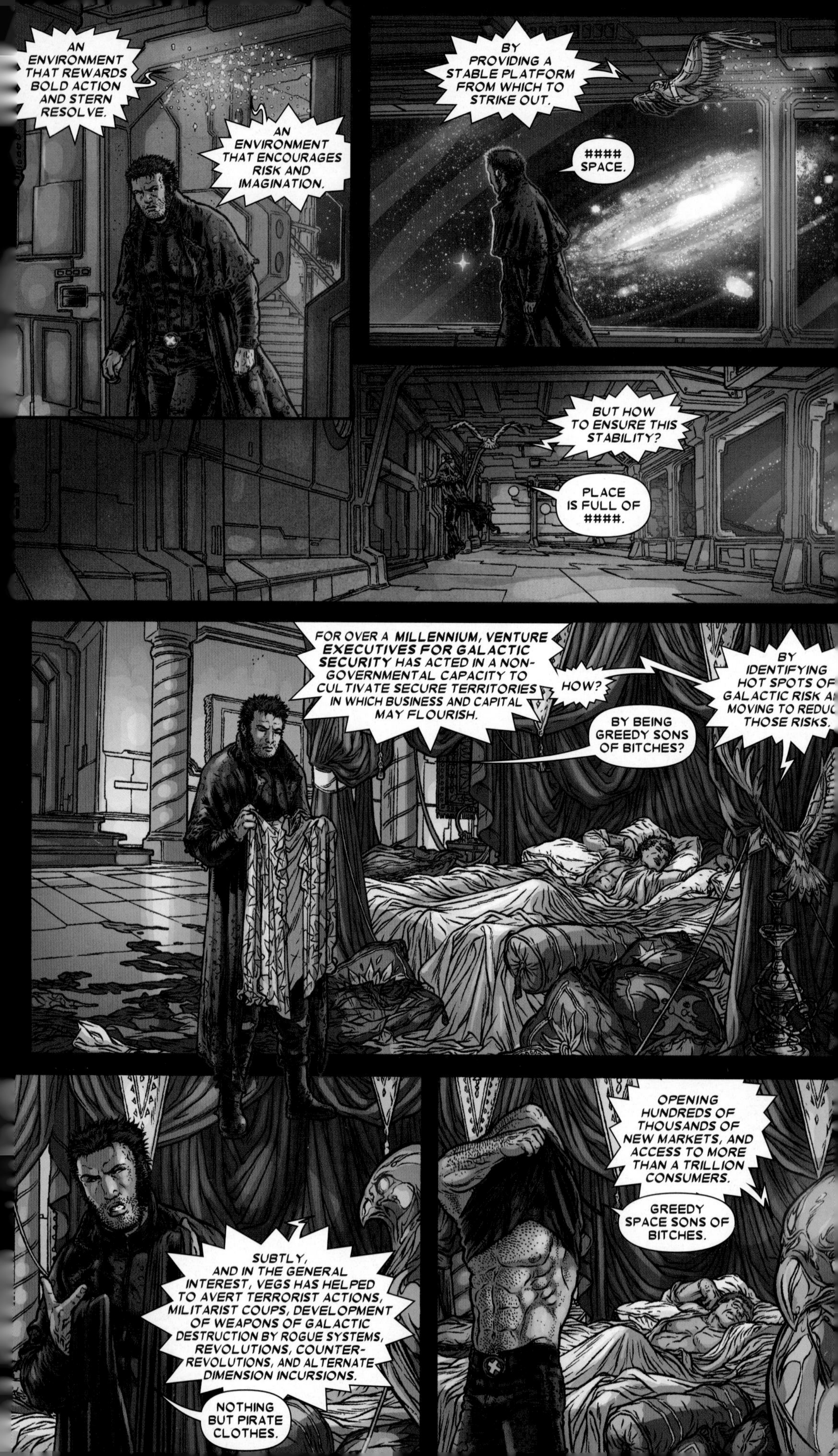
AN ENVIRONMENT THAT REWARDS BOLD ACTION AND STERN RESOLVE.
AN ENVIRONMENT THAT ENCOURAGES RISK AND IMAGINATION.
BY PROVIDING A STABLE PLATFORM FROM WHICH TO STRIKE OUT.
SPACE.
BUT HOW TO ENSURE THIS STABILITY?
PLACE IS FULL OF ####.
FOR OVER A MILLENNIUM, VENTURE EXECUTIVES FOR GALACTIC SECURITY HAS ACTED IN A NON-GOVERNMENTAL CAPACITY TO CULTIVATE SECURE TERRITORIES IN WHICH BUSINESS AND CAPITAL MAY FLOURISH.
HOW?
BY IDENTIFYING HOT SPOTS OF GALACTIC RISK A MOVING TO REDUC THOSE RISKS.
BY BEING GREEDY SONS OF BITCHES?
SUBTLY, AND IN THE GENERAL INTEREST, VEGS HAS HELPED TO AVERT TERRORIST ACTIONS, MILITARIST COUPS, DEVELOPMENT OF WEAPONS OF GALACTIC DESTRUCTION BY ROGUE SYSTEMS, REVOLUTIONS, COUNTER-REVOLUTIONS, AND ALTERNATE DIMENSION INCURSIONS.
NOTHING BUT PIRATE CLOTHES.
OPENING HUNDREDS OF THOUSANDS OF NEW MARKETS, AND ACCESS TO MORE THAN A TRILLION CONSUMERS.
GREEDY SPACE SONS OF BITCHES.

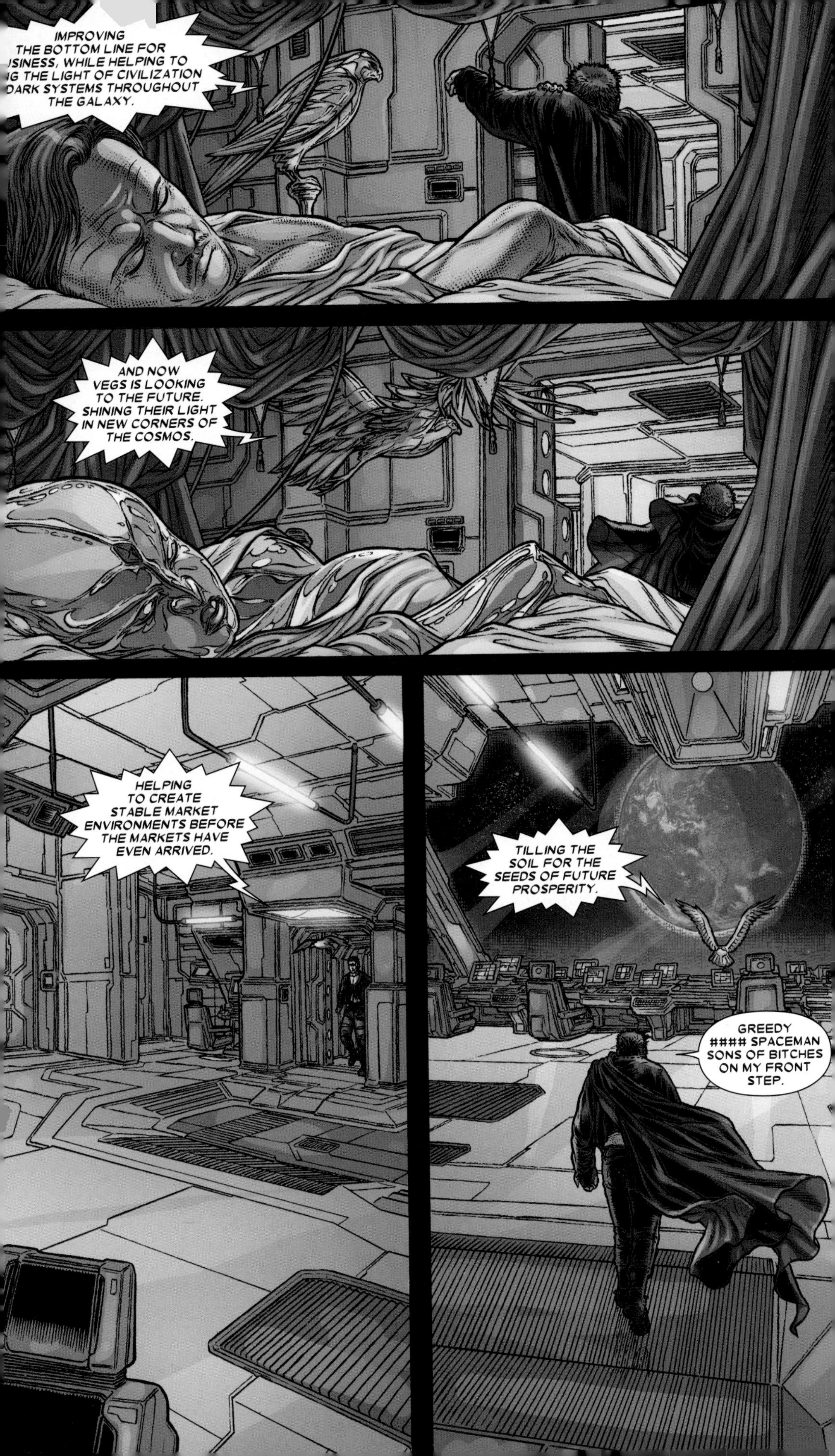
IMPROVING THE BOTTOM LINE FOR USINESS, WHILE HELPING TO G THE LIGHT OF CIVILIZATION DARK SYSTEMS THROUGHOUT THE GALAXY.
AND NOW VEGS IS LOOKING TO THE FUTURE. SHINING THEIR LIGHT IN NEW CORNERS OF THE COSMOS.
HELPING TO CREATE STABLE MARKET ENVIRONMENTS BEFORE THE MARKETS HAVE EVEN ARRIVED.
TILLING THE SOIL FOR THE SEEDS OF FUTURE PROSPERITY.
GREEDY #### SPACEMAN SONS OF BITCHES ON MY FRONT STEP.

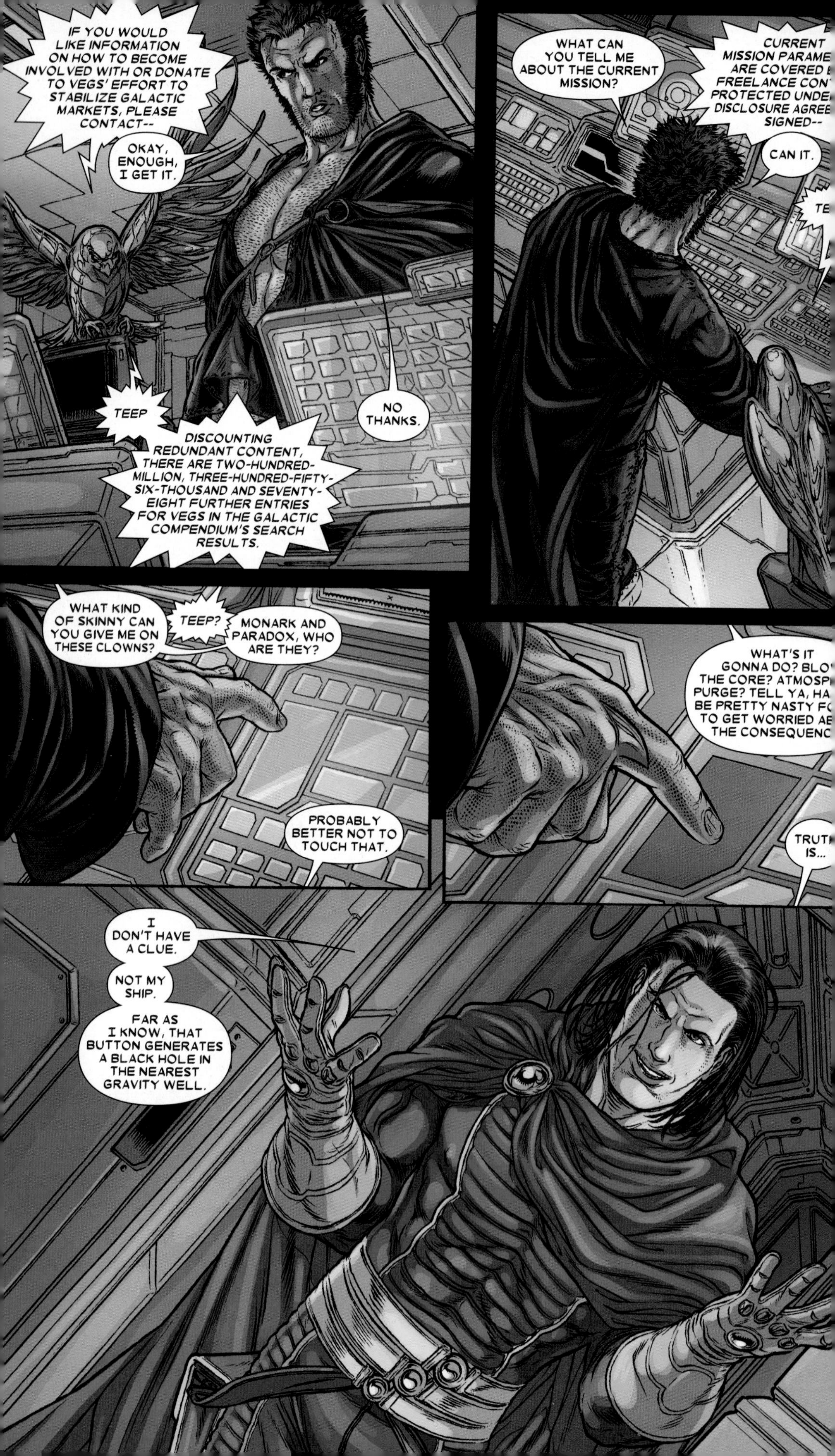

IF YOU WOULD LIKE INFORMATION ON HOW TO BECOME INVOLVED WITH OR DONATE TO VEGS' EFFORT TO STABILIZE GALACTIC MARKETS, PLEASE CONTACT--
OKAY, ENOUGH, I GET IT.
TEEP
DISCOUNTING REDUNDANT CONTENT, THERE ARE TWO-HUNDRED-MILLION, THREE-HUNDRED-FIFTY-SIX-THOUSAND AND SEVENTY-EIGHT FURTHER ENTRIES FOR VEGS IN THE GALACTIC COMPENDIUM'S SEARCH RESULTS.
NO THANKS.
WHAT CAN YOU TELL ME ABOUT THE CURRENT MISSION?
CURRENT MISSION PARAME ARE COVERED FREELANCE CON PROTECTED UNDE DISCLOSURE AGREE SIGNED--
CAN IT.
TE
WHAT KIND OF SKINNY CAN YOU GIVE ME ON THESE CLOWNS?
TEEP?
MONARK AND PARADOX, WHO ARE THEY?
PROBABLY BETTER NOT TO TOUCH THAT.
WHAT'S IT GONNA DO? BLO THE CORE? ATMOSP PURGE? TELL YA, HA BE PRETTY NASTY F TO GET WORRIED A THE CONSEQUEN
TRUT IS...
I DON'T HAVE A CLUE.
NOT MY SHIP.
FAR AS I KNOW, THAT BUTTON GENERATES A BLACK HOLE IN THE NEAREST GRAVITY WELL.

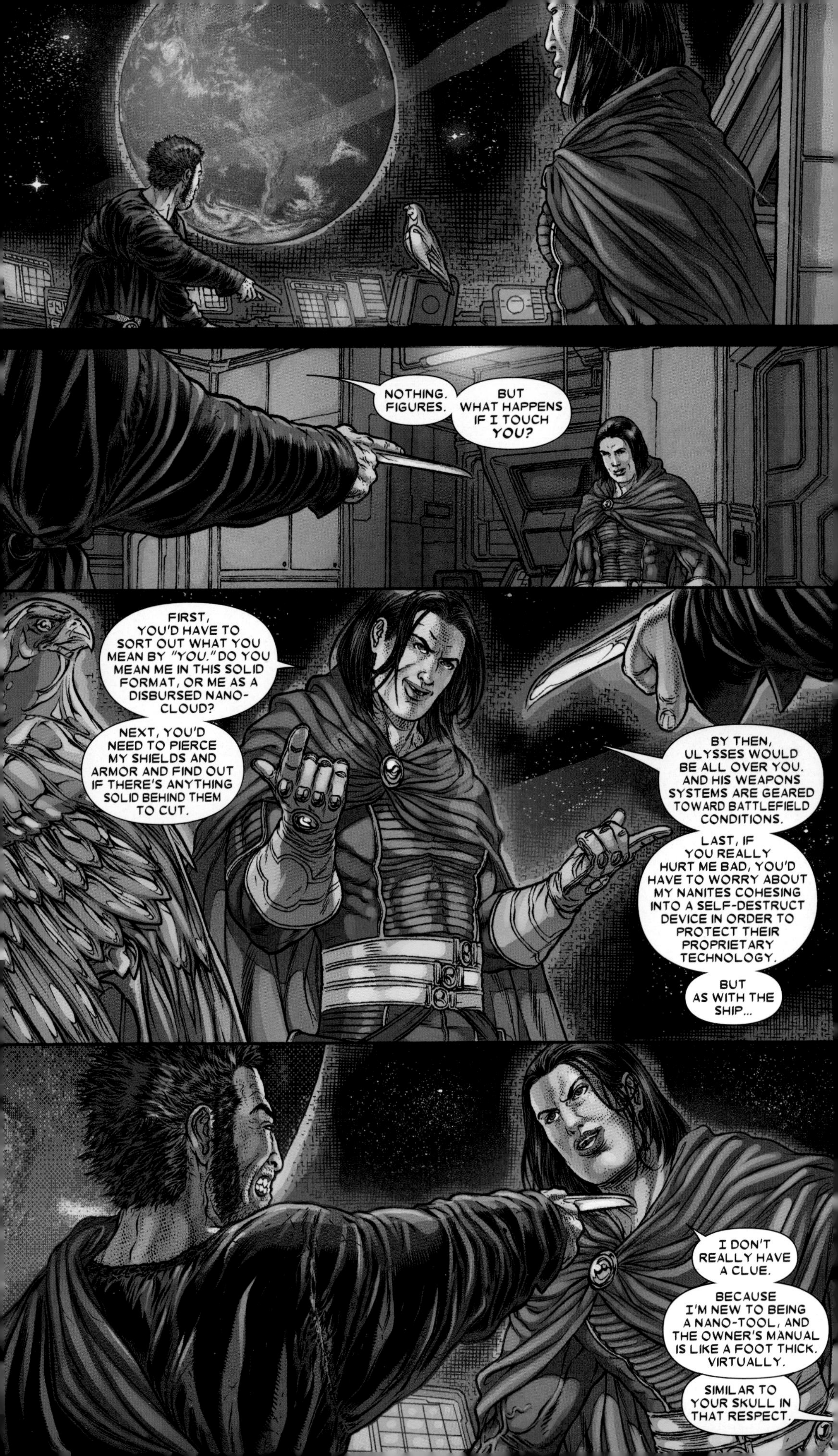
NOTHING. FIGURES.
BUT WHAT HAPPENS IF I TOUCH *YOU?*
FIRST, YOU'D HAVE TO SORT OUT WHAT YOU MEAN BY *"YOU."* DO YOU MEAN ME IN THIS SOLID FORMAT, OR ME AS A DISBURSED NANO-CLOUD?
NEXT, YOU'D NEED TO PIERCE MY SHIELDS AND ARMOR AND FIND OUT IF THERE'S ANYTHING SOLID BEHIND THEM TO CUT.
BY THEN, ULYSSES WOULD BE ALL OVER YOU. AND HIS WEAPONS SYSTEMS ARE GEARED TOWARD BATTLEFIELD CONDITIONS.
LAST, IF YOU REALLY HURT ME BAD, YOU'D HAVE TO WORRY ABOUT MY NANITES COHESING INTO A SELF-DESTRUCT DEVICE IN ORDER TO PROTECT THEIR PROPRIETARY TECHNOLOGY.
BUT AS WITH THE SHIP...
I DON'T REALLY HAVE A CLUE.
BECAUSE I'M NEW TO BEING A NANO-TOOL, AND THE OWNER'S MANUAL IS LIKE A FOOT THICK. VIRTUALLY.
SIMILAR TO YOUR SKULL IN THAT RESPECT.

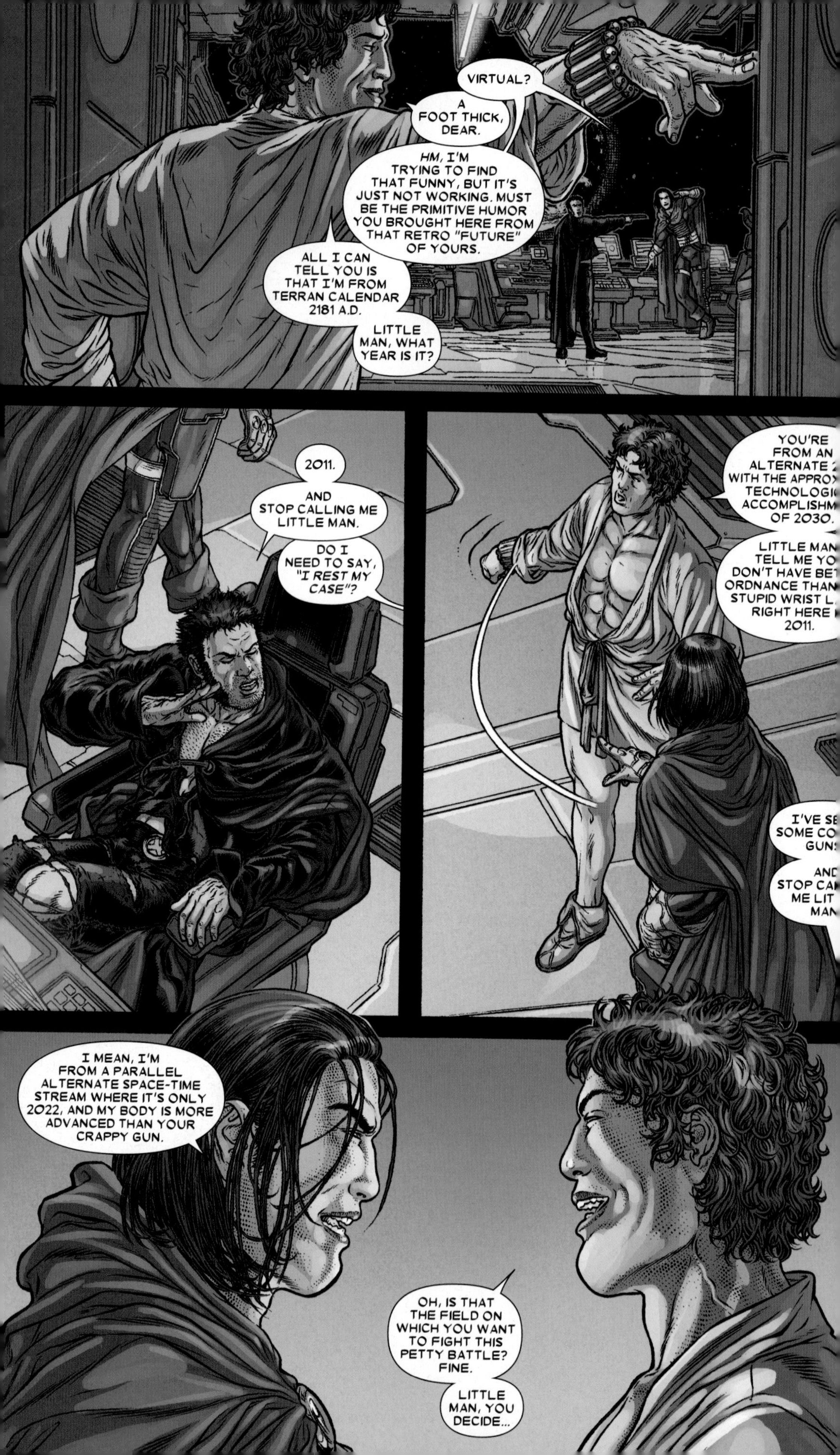

VIRTUAL?
A FOOT THICK, DEAR.
HM, I'M TRYING TO FIND THAT FUNNY, BUT IT'S JUST NOT WORKING. MUST BE THE PRIMITIVE HUMOR YOU BROUGHT HERE FROM THAT RETRO "FUTURE" OF YOURS.
ALL I CAN TELL YOU IS THAT I'M FROM TERRAN CALENDAR 2181 A.D.
LITTLE MAN, WHAT YEAR IS IT?
2011.
AND STOP CALLING ME LITTLE MAN.
DO I NEED TO SAY, *"I REST MY CASE"*?
YOU'RE FROM AN ALTERNATE WITH THE APPROX TECHNOLOGI ACCOMPLISHM OF 2030.
LITTLE MAN TELL ME YO DON'T HAVE BE ORDNANCE THAN STUPID WRIST RIGHT HERE 2011.
I'VE SE SOME CO GUNS
AND STOP CA ME LIT MAN
I MEAN, I'M FROM A PARALLEL ALTERNATE SPACE-TIME STREAM WHERE IT'S ONLY 2022, AND MY BODY IS MORE ADVANCED THAN YOUR CRAPPY GUN.
OH, IS THAT THE FIELD ON WHICH YOU WANT TO FIGHT THIS PETTY BATTLE? FINE.
LITTLE MAN, YOU DECIDE...

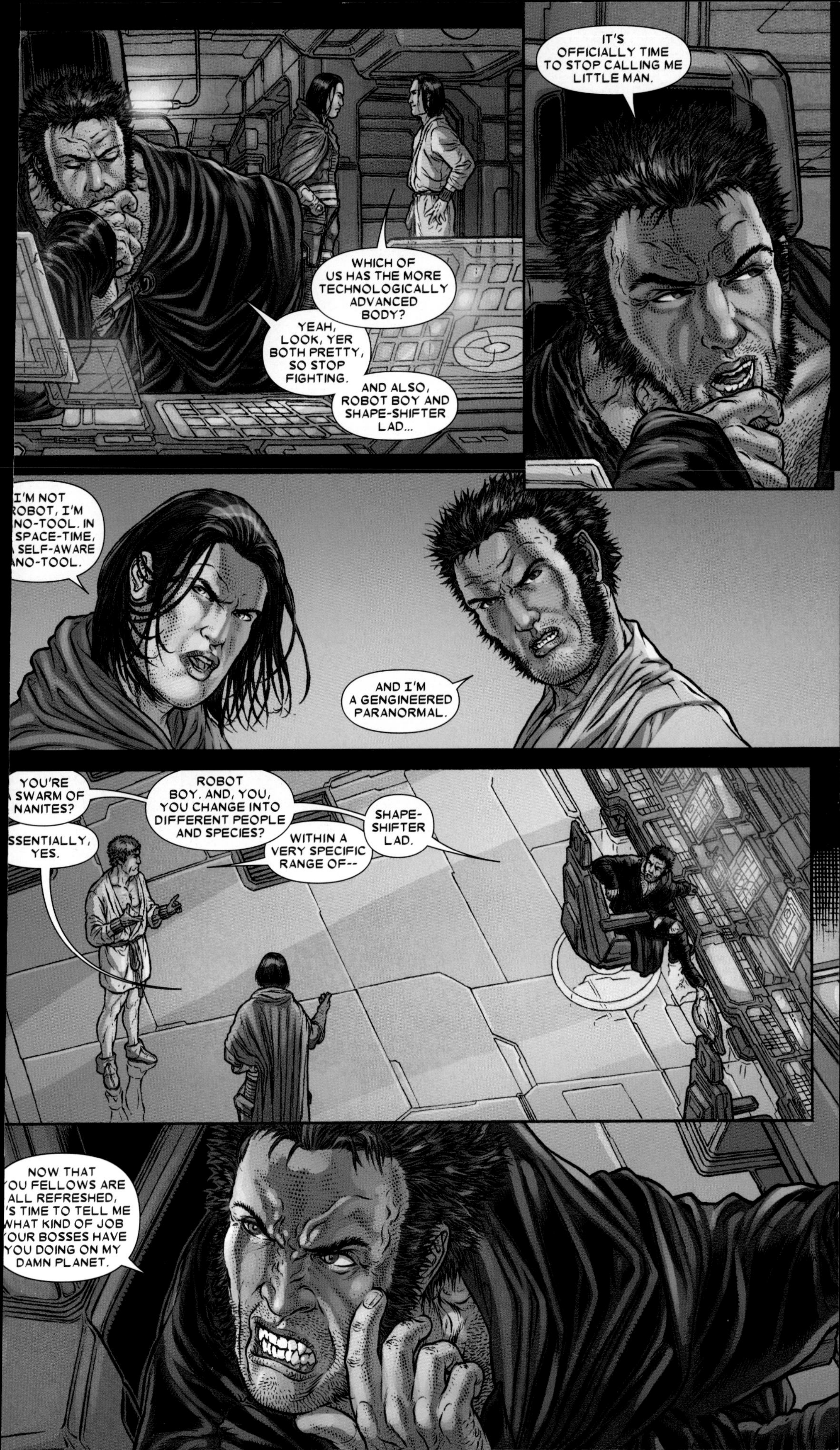
WHICH OF US HAS THE MORE TECHNOLOGICALLY ADVANCED BODY?
YEAH, LOOK, YER BOTH PRETTY, SO STOP FIGHTING.
AND ALSO, ROBOT BOY AND SHAPE-SHIFTER LAD...
IT'S OFFICIALLY TIME TO STOP CALLING ME LITTLE MAN.
I'M NOT ROBOT, I'M NO-TOOL. IN SPACE-TIME, SELF-AWARE ANO-TOOL.
AND I'M A GENGINEERED PARANORMAL.
YOU'RE SWARM OF NANITES?
SSENTIALLY, YES.
ROBOT BOY. AND, YOU, YOU CHANGE INTO DIFFERENT PEOPLE AND SPECIES?
WITHIN A VERY SPECIFIC RANGE OF--
SHAPE-SHIFTER LAD.
NOW THAT OU FELLOWS ARE ALL REFRESHED, 'S TIME TO TELL ME WHAT KIND OF JOB YOUR BOSSES HAVE YOU DOING ON MY DAMN PLANET.

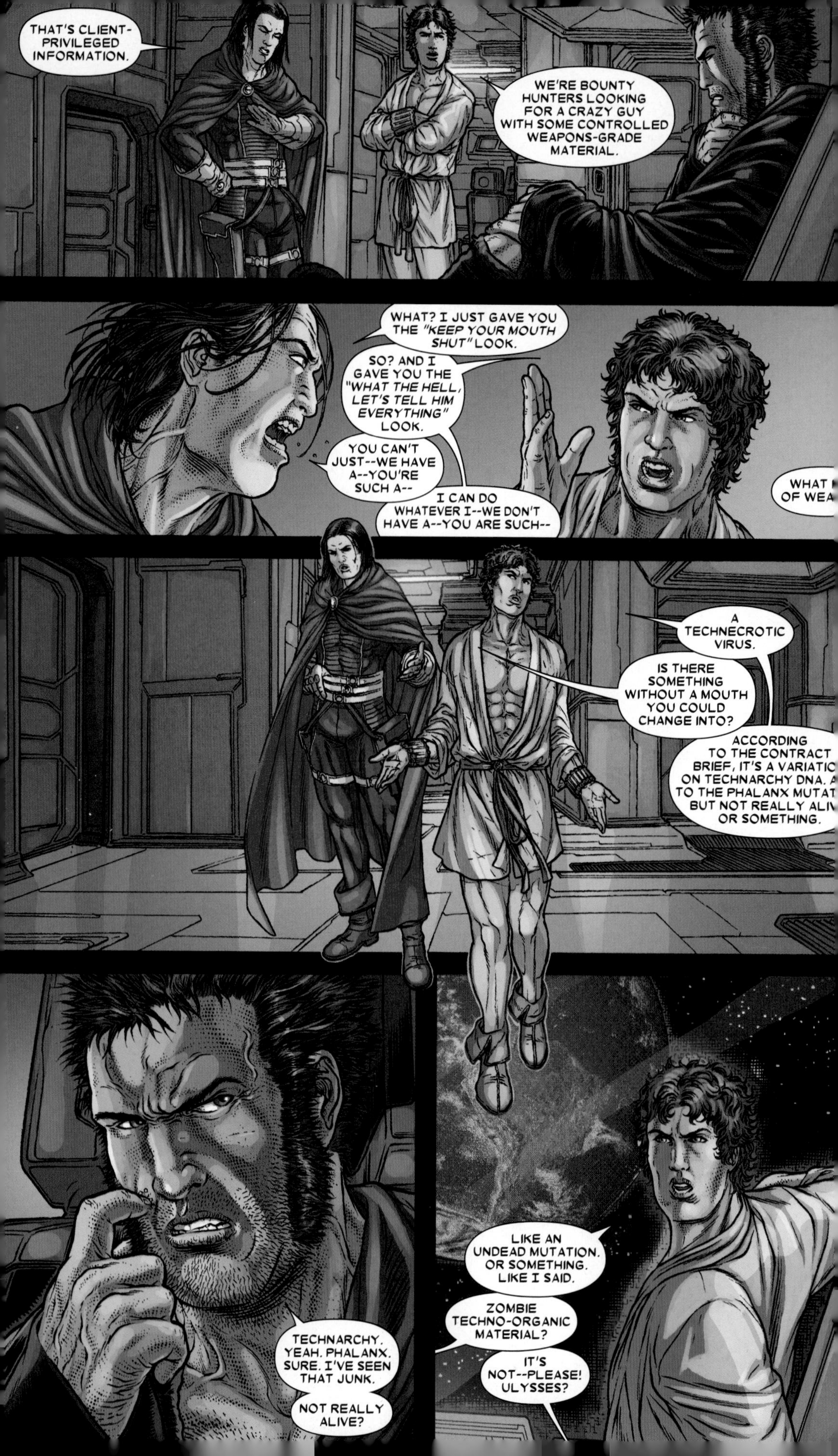
THAT'S CLIENT-PRIVILEGED INFORMATION.
WE'RE BOUNTY HUNTERS LOOKING FOR A CRAZY GUY WITH SOME CONTROLLED WEAPONS-GRADE MATERIAL.
WHAT? I JUST GAVE YOU THE "KEEP YOUR MOUTH SHUT" LOOK.
SO? AND I GAVE YOU THE "WHAT THE HELL, LET'S TELL HIM EVERYTHING" LOOK.
YOU CAN'T JUST--WE HAVE A--YOU'RE SUCH A--
I CAN DO WHATEVER I--WE DON'T HAVE A--YOU ARE SUCH--
A TECHNECROTIC VIRUS.
IS THERE SOMETHING WITHOUT A MOUTH YOU COULD CHANGE INTO?
TECHNARCHY. YEAH. PHALANX. SURE. I'VE SEEN THAT JUNK.
NOT REALLY ALIVE?
LIKE AN UNDEAD MUTATION. OR SOMETHING. LIKE I SAID.
ZOMBIE TECHNO-ORGANIC MATERIAL?
IT'S NOT--PLEASE! ULYSSES?

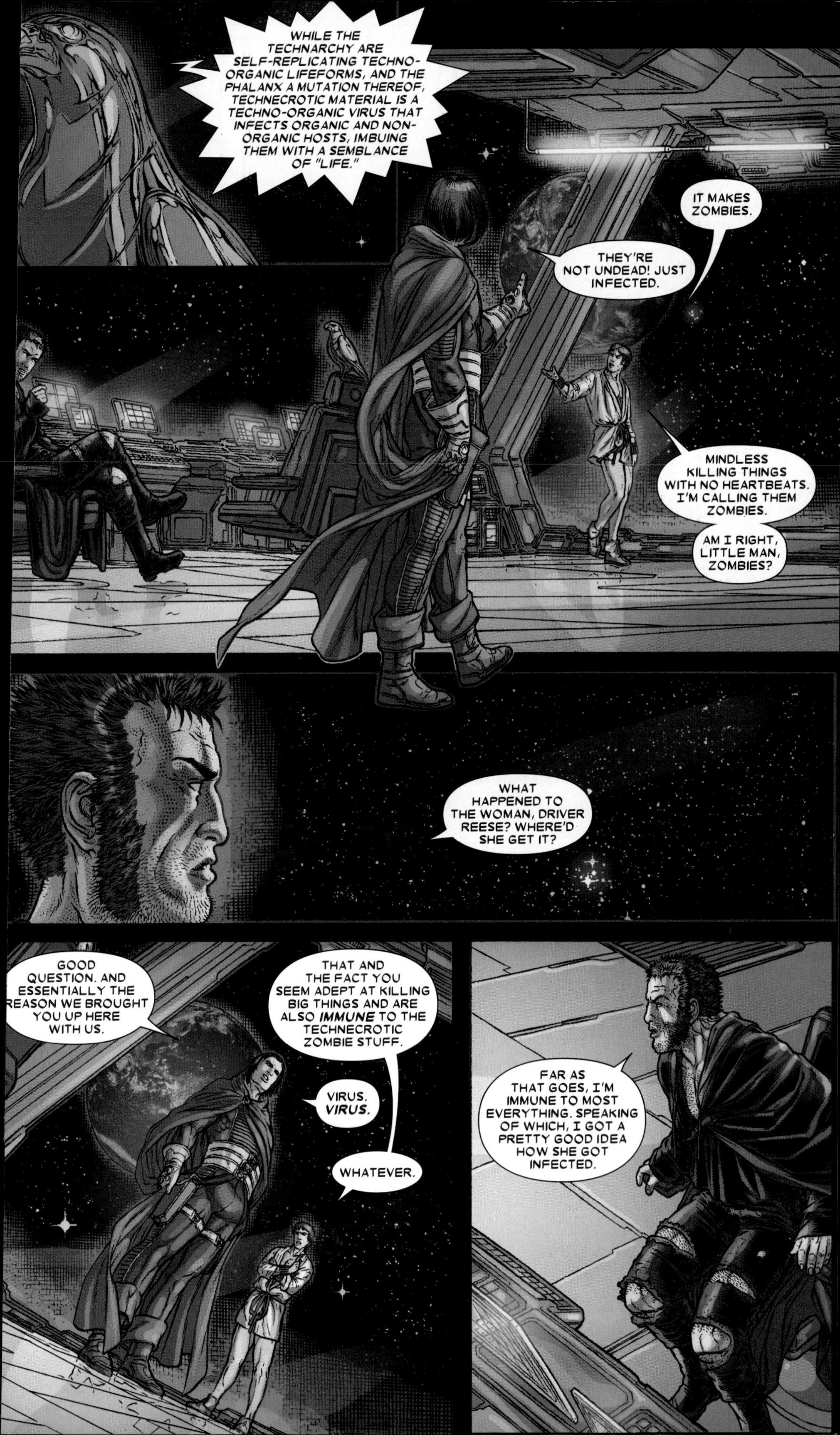
WHILE THE TECHNARCHY ARE SELF-REPLICATING TECHNO-ORGANIC LIFEFORMS, AND THE PHALANX A MUTATION THEREOF, TECHNECROTIC MATERIAL IS A TECHNO-ORGANIC VIRUS THAT INFECTS ORGANIC AND NON-ORGANIC HOSTS, IMBUING THEM WITH A SEMBLANCE OF "LIFE."
IT MAKES ZOMBIES.
THEY'RE NOT UNDEAD! JUST INFECTED.
MINDLESS KILLING THINGS WITH NO HEARTBEATS. I'M CALLING THEM ZOMBIES.
AM I RIGHT, LITTLE MAN, ZOMBIES?
WHAT HAPPENED TO THE WOMAN, DRIVER REESE? WHERE'D SHE GET IT?
GOOD QUESTION. AND ESSENTIALLY THE REASON WE BROUGHT YOU UP HERE WITH US.
THAT AND THE FACT YOU SEEM ADEPT AT KILLING BIG THINGS AND ARE ALSO IMMUNE TO THE TECHNECROTIC ZOMBIE STUFF.
VIRUS. VIRUS.
WHATEVER.
FAR AS THAT GOES, I'M IMMUNE TO MOST EVERYTHING. SPEAKING OF WHICH, I GOT A PRETTY GOOD IDEA HOW SHE GOT INFECTED.

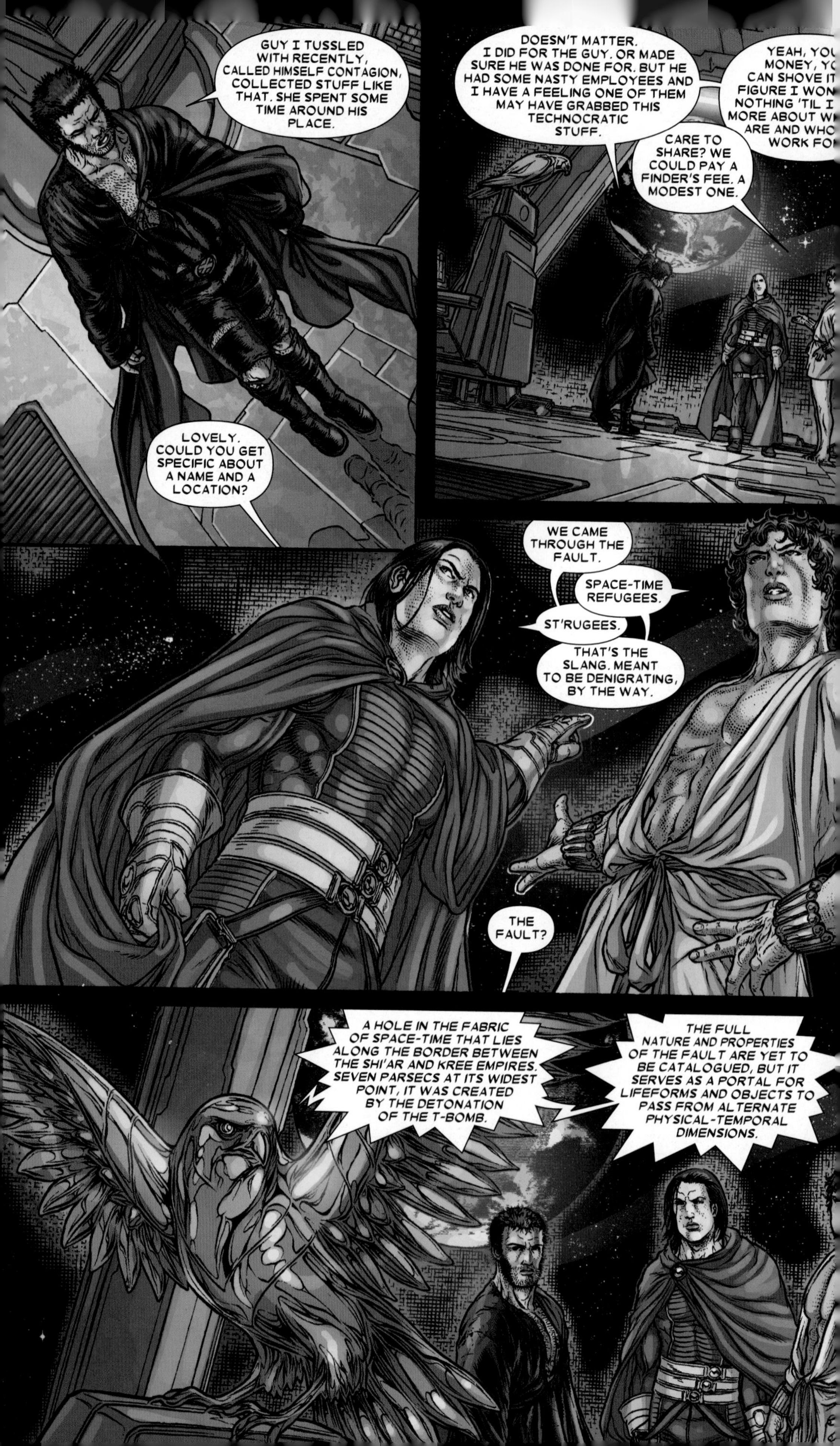
GUY I TUSSLED WITH RECENTLY, CALLED HIMSELF CONTAGION, COLLECTED STUFF LIKE THAT. SHE SPENT SOME TIME AROUND HIS PLACE.
LOVELY. COULD YOU GET SPECIFIC ABOUT A NAME AND A LOCATION?
DOESN'T MATTER. I DID FOR THE GUY. OR MADE SURE HE WAS DONE FOR. BUT HE HAD SOME NASTY EMPLOYEES AND I HAVE A FEELING ONE OF THEM MAY HAVE GRABBED THIS TECHNOCRATIC STUFF.
CARE TO SHARE? WE COULD PAY A FINDER'S FEE. A MODEST ONE.
YEAH, YOU... MONEY, YO... CAN SHOVE IT... FIGURE I WON... NOTHING 'TIL I... MORE ABOUT WH... ARE AND WHO... WORK FO...
WE CAME THROUGH THE FAULT.
SPACE-TIME REFUGEES.
ST'RUGEES.
THAT'S THE SLANG. MEANT TO BE DENIGRATING, BY THE WAY.
THE FAULT?
A HOLE IN THE FABRIC OF SPACE-TIME THAT LIES ALONG THE BORDER BETWEEN THE SHI'AR AND KREE EMPIRES. SEVEN PARSECS AT ITS WIDEST POINT, IT WAS CREATED BY THE DETONATION OF THE T-BOMB.
THE FULL NATURE AND PROPERTIES OF THE FAULT ARE YET TO BE CATALOGUED, BUT IT SERVES AS A PORTAL FOR LIFEFORMS AND OBJECTS TO PASS FROM ALTERNATE PHYSICAL-TEMPORAL DIMENSIONS.

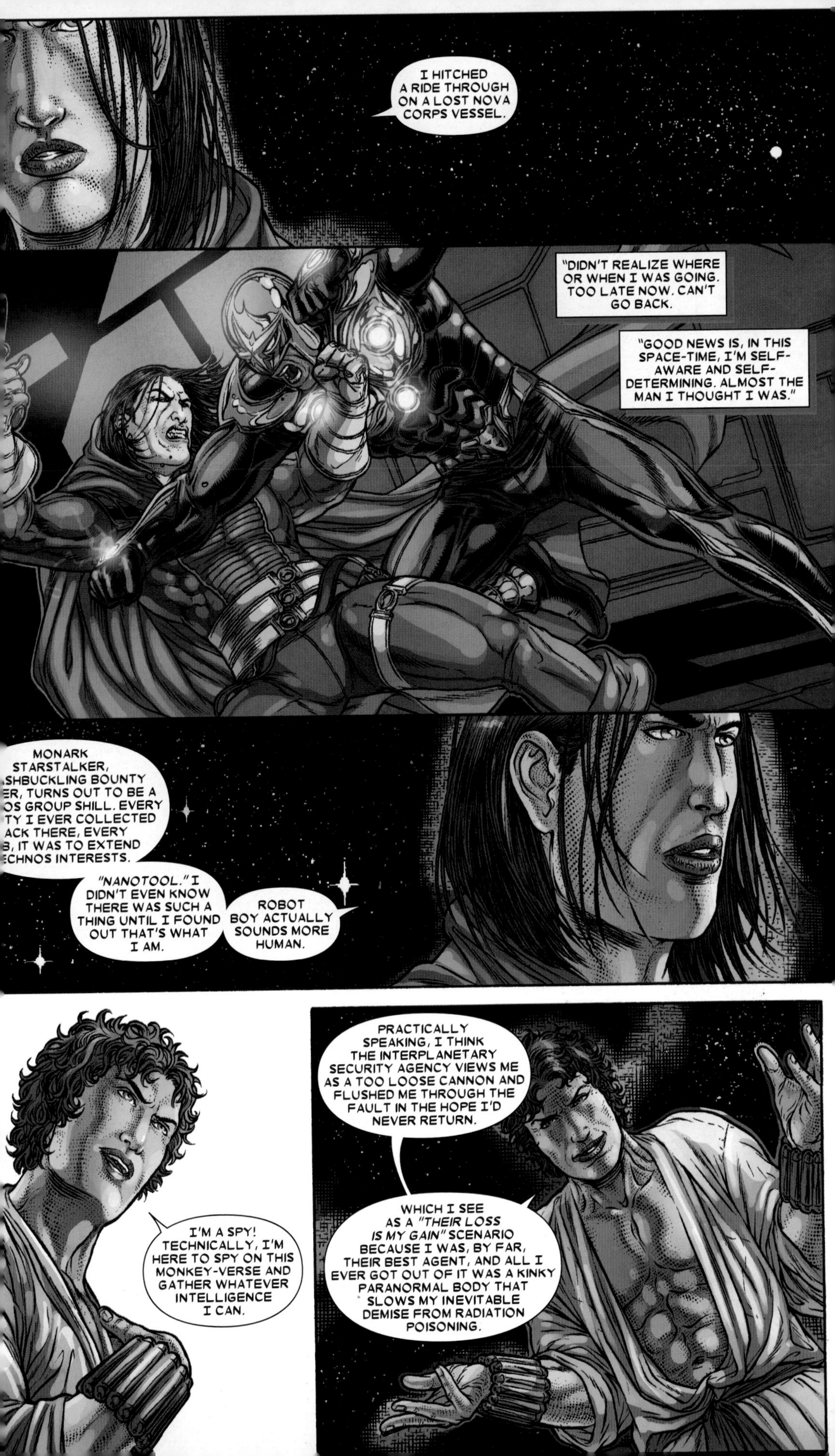
I HITCHED A RIDE THROUGH ON A LOST NOVA CORPS VESSEL.
"DIDN'T REALIZE WHERE OR WHEN I WAS GOING. TOO LATE NOW. CAN'T GO BACK.
"GOOD NEWS IS, IN THIS SPACE-TIME, I'M SELF-AWARE AND SELF-DETERMINING. ALMOST THE MAN I THOUGHT I WAS."
MONARK STARSTALKER, SHBUCKLING BOUNTY ER, TURNS OUT TO BE A OS GROUP SHILL. EVERY TY I EVER COLLECTED ACK THERE, EVERY B, IT WAS TO EXTEND ECHNOS INTERESTS.
"NANOTOOL." I DIDN'T EVEN KNOW THERE WAS SUCH A THING UNTIL I FOUND OUT THAT'S WHAT I AM.
ROBOT BOY ACTUALLY SOUNDS MORE HUMAN.
I'M A SPY! TECHNICALLY, I'M HERE TO SPY ON THIS MONKEY-VERSE AND GATHER WHATEVER INTELLIGENCE I CAN.
PRACTICALLY SPEAKING, I THINK THE INTERPLANETARY SECURITY AGENCY VIEWS ME AS A TOO LOOSE CANNON AND FLUSHED ME THROUGH THE FAULT IN THE HOPE I'D NEVER RETURN.
WHICH I SEE AS A "THEIR LOSS IS MY GAIN" SCENARIO BECAUSE I WAS, BY FAR, THEIR BEST AGENT, AND ALL I EVER GOT OUT OF IT WAS A KINKY PARANORMAL BODY THAT SLOWS MY INEVITABLE DEMISE FROM RADIATION POISONING.

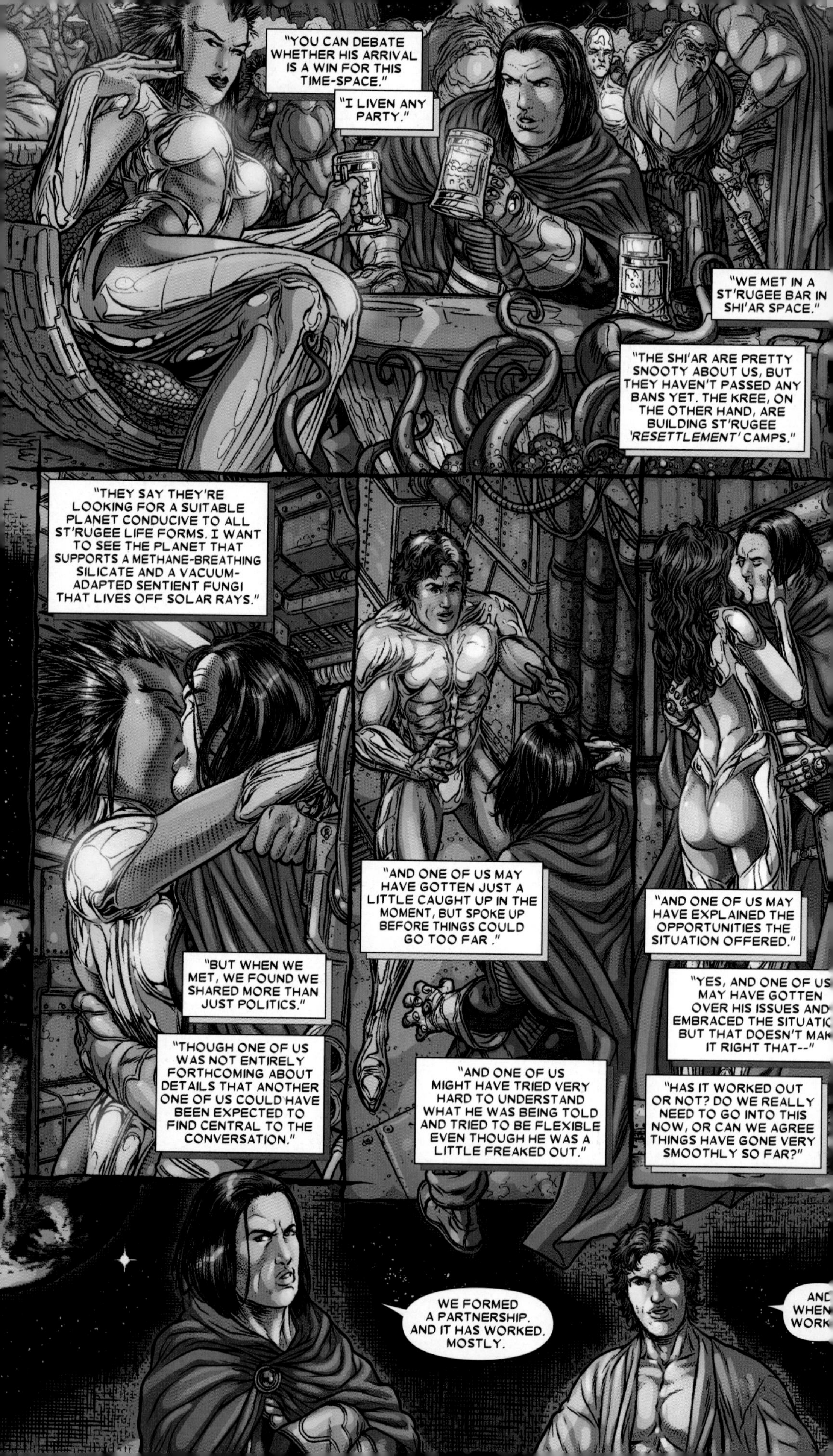
"YOU CAN DEBATE WHETHER HIS ARRIVAL IS A WIN FOR THIS TIME-SPACE."
"I LIVEN ANY PARTY."
"WE MET IN A ST'RUGEE BAR IN SHI'AR SPACE."
"THE SHI'AR ARE PRETTY SNOOTY ABOUT US, BUT THEY HAVEN'T PASSED ANY BANS YET. THE KREE, ON THE OTHER HAND, ARE BUILDING ST'RUGEE 'RESETTLEMENT' CAMPS."
"THEY SAY THEY'RE LOOKING FOR A SUITABLE PLANET CONDUCIVE TO ALL ST'RUGEE LIFE FORMS. I WANT TO SEE THE PLANET THAT SUPPORTS A METHANE-BREATHING SILICATE AND A VACUUM-ADAPTED SENTIENT FUNGI THAT LIVES OFF SOLAR RAYS."
"BUT WHEN WE MET, WE FOUND WE SHARED MORE THAN JUST POLITICS."
"THOUGH ONE OF US WAS NOT ENTIRELY FORTHCOMING ABOUT DETAILS THAT ANOTHER ONE OF US COULD HAVE BEEN EXPECTED TO FIND CENTRAL TO THE CONVERSATION."
"AND ONE OF US MAY HAVE GOTTEN JUST A LITTLE CAUGHT UP IN THE MOMENT, BUT SPOKE UP BEFORE THINGS COULD GO TOO FAR."
"AND ONE OF US MIGHT HAVE TRIED VERY HARD TO UNDERSTAND WHAT HE WAS BEING TOLD AND TRIED TO BE FLEXIBLE EVEN THOUGH HE WAS A LITTLE FREAKED OUT."
"AND ONE OF US MAY HAVE EXPLAINED THE OPPORTUNITIES THE SITUATION OFFERED."
"YES, AND ONE OF US MAY HAVE GOTTEN OVER HIS ISSUES AND EMBRACED THE SITUATI BUT THAT DOESN'T MA IT RIGHT THAT--"
"HAS IT WORKED OUT OR NOT? DO WE REALLY NEED TO GO INTO THIS NOW, OR CAN WE AGREE THINGS HAVE GONE VERY SMOOTHLY SO FAR?"
WE FORMED A PARTNERSHIP. AND IT HAS WORKED. MOSTLY.
AN WHEN WORK

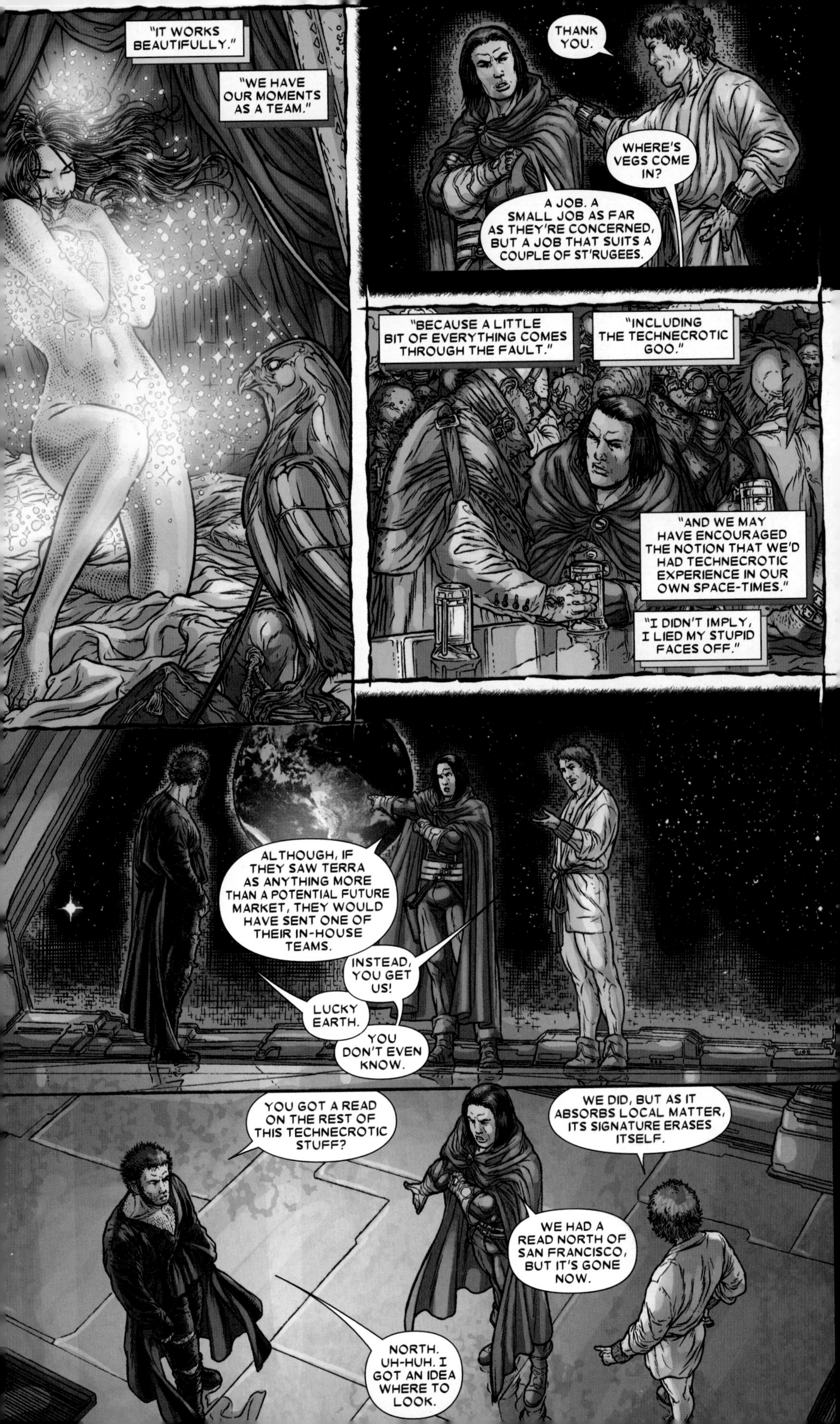

"IT WORKS BEAUTIFULLY."
"WE HAVE OUR MOMENTS AS A TEAM."
THANK YOU.
WHERE'S VEGS COME IN?
A JOB. A SMALL JOB AS FAR AS THEY'RE CONCERNED, BUT A JOB THAT SUITS A COUPLE OF ST'RUGEES.
"BECAUSE A LITTLE BIT OF EVERYTHING COMES THROUGH THE FAULT."
"INCLUDING THE TECHNECROTIC GOO."
"AND WE MAY HAVE ENCOURAGED THE NOTION THAT WE'D HAD TECHNECROTIC EXPERIENCE IN OUR OWN SPACE-TIMES."
"I DIDN'T IMPLY, I LIED MY STUPID FACES OFF."
ALTHOUGH, IF THEY SAW TERRA AS ANYTHING MORE THAN A POTENTIAL FUTURE MARKET, THEY WOULD HAVE SENT ONE OF THEIR IN-HOUSE TEAMS.
INSTEAD, YOU GET US!
LUCKY EARTH.
YOU DON'T EVEN KNOW.
YOU GOT A READ ON THE REST OF THIS TECHNECROTIC STUFF?
WE DID, BUT AS IT ABSORBS LOCAL MATTER, ITS SIGNATURE ERASES ITSELF.
WE HAD A READ NORTH OF SAN FRANCISCO, BUT IT'S GONE NOW.
NORTH. UH-HUH. I GOT AN IDEA WHERE TO LOOK.

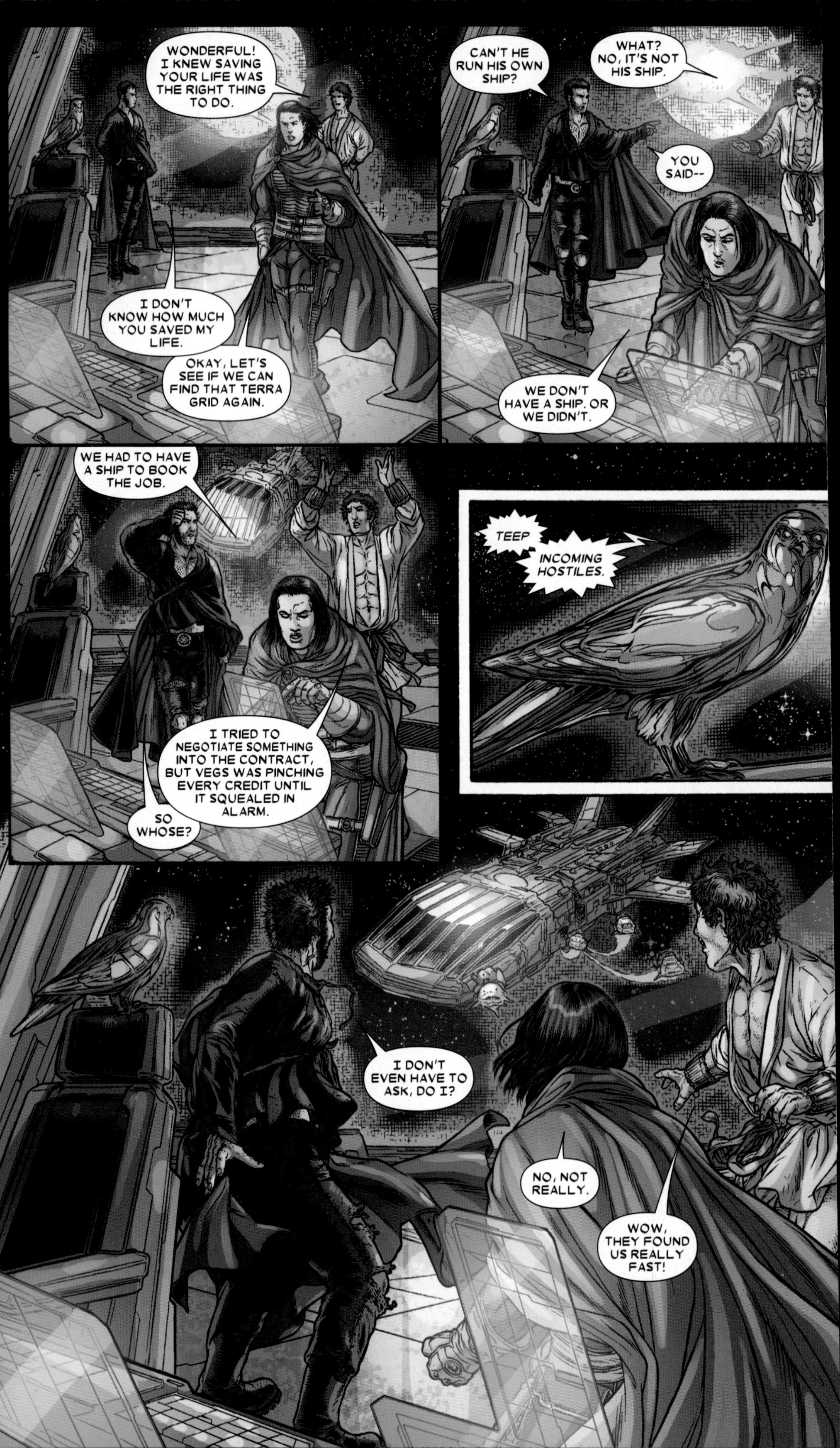
WONDERFUL! I KNEW SAVING YOUR LIFE WAS THE RIGHT THING TO DO.
I DON'T KNOW HOW MUCH YOU SAVED MY LIFE.
OKAY, LET'S SEE IF WE CAN FIND THAT TERRA GRID AGAIN.
CAN'T HE RUN HIS OWN SHIP?
WHAT? NO, IT'S NOT HIS SHIP.
YOU SAID--
WE DON'T HAVE A SHIP. OR WE DIDN'T.
WE HAD TO HAVE A SHIP TO BOOK THE JOB.
I TRIED TO NEGOTIATE SOMETHING INTO THE CONTRACT, BUT VEGS WAS PINCHING EVERY CREDIT UNTIL IT SQUEALED IN ALARM.
SO WHOSE?
TEEP
INCOMING HOSTILES.
I DON'T EVEN HAVE TO ASK, DO I?
NO, NOT REALLY.
WOW, THEY FOUND US REALLY FAST!

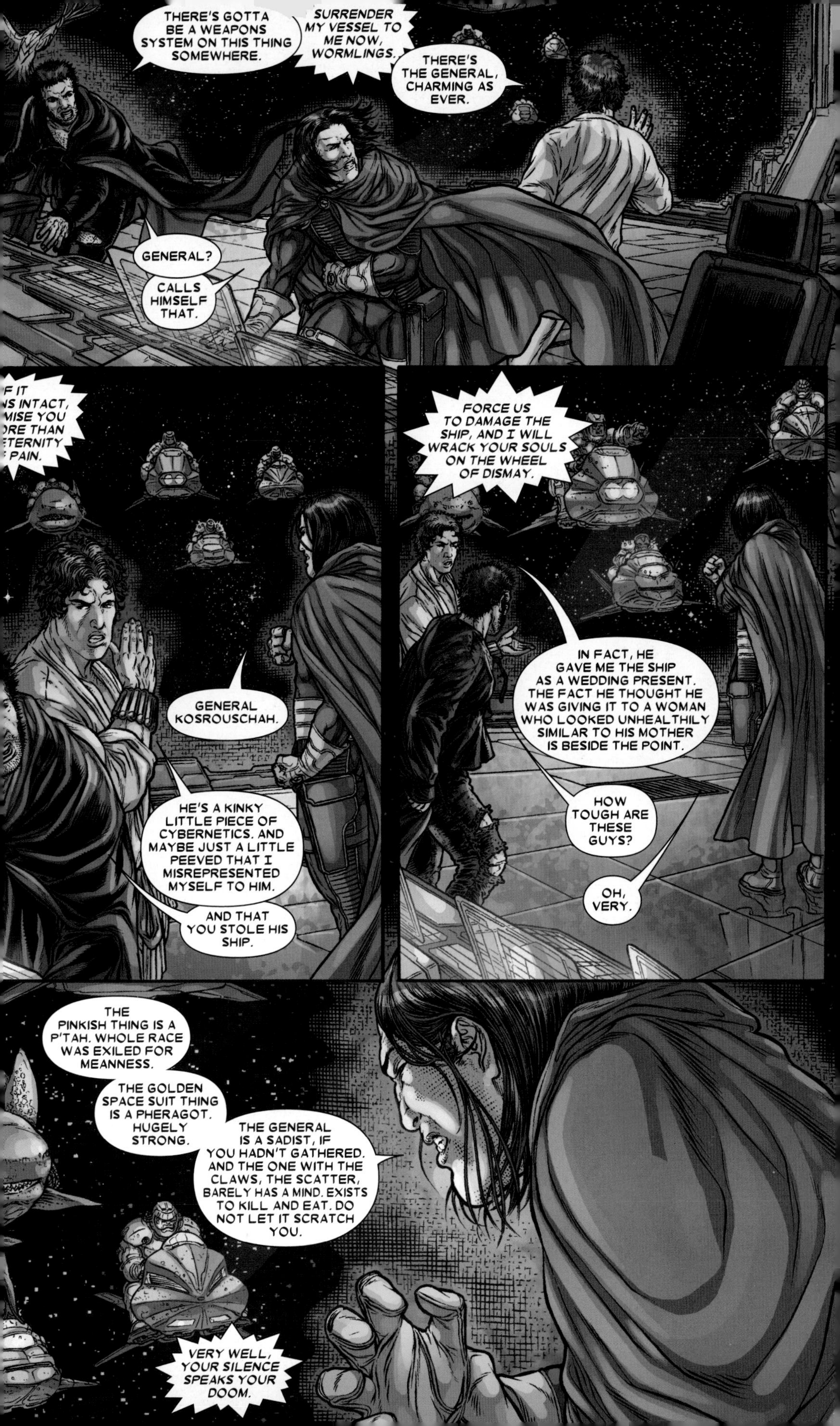
THERE'S GOTTA BE A WEAPONS SYSTEM ON THIS THING SOMEWHERE.
SURRENDER MY VESSEL TO ME NOW, WORMLINGS.
THERE'S THE GENERAL, CHARMING AS EVER.
GENERAL?
CALLS HIMSELF THAT.
F IT NS INTACT, MISE YOU ORE THAN ETERNITY F PAIN.
GENERAL KOSROUSCHAH.
HE'S A KINKY LITTLE PIECE OF CYBERNETICS. AND MAYBE JUST A LITTLE PEEVED THAT I MISREPRESENTED MYSELF TO HIM.
AND THAT YOU STOLE HIS SHIP.
FORCE US TO DAMAGE THE SHIP, AND I WILL WRACK YOUR SOULS ON THE WHEEL OF DISMAY.
IN FACT, HE GAVE ME THE SHIP AS A WEDDING PRESENT. THE FACT HE THOUGHT HE WAS GIVING IT TO A WOMAN WHO LOOKED UNHEALTHILY SIMILAR TO HIS MOTHER IS BESIDE THE POINT.
HOW TOUGH ARE THESE GUYS?
OH, VERY.
THE PINKISH THING IS A P'TAH. WHOLE RACE WAS EXILED FOR MEANNESS.
THE GOLDEN SPACE SUIT THING IS A PHERAGOT. HUGELY STRONG.
THE GENERAL IS A SADIST, IF YOU HADN'T GATHERED. AND THE ONE WITH THE CLAWS, THE SCATTER, BARELY HAS A MIND. EXISTS TO KILL AND EAT. DO NOT LET IT SCRATCH YOU.
VERY WELL, YOUR SILENCE SPEAKS YOUR DOOM.

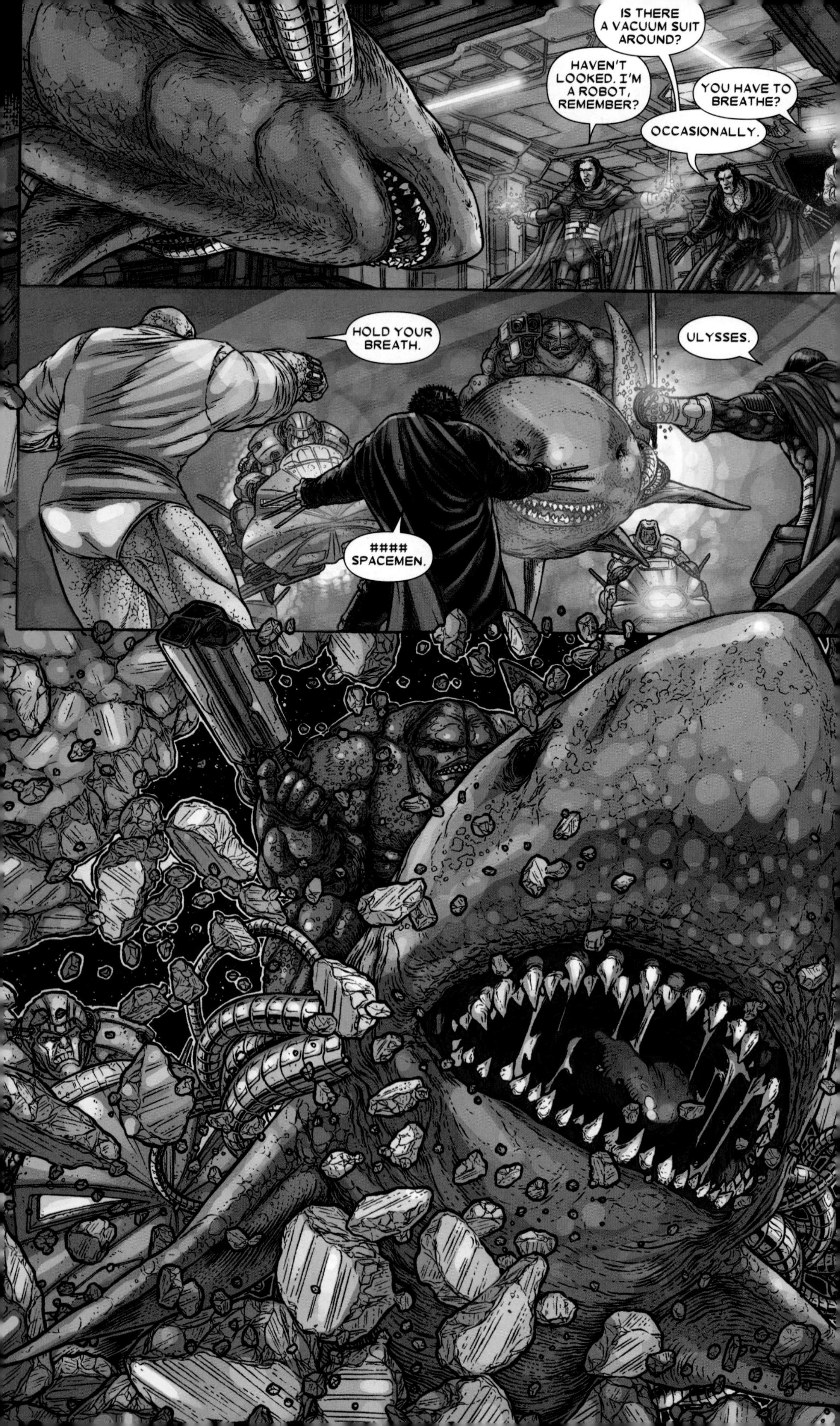
IS THERE A VACUUM SUIT AROUND?
HAVEN'T LOOKED. I'M A ROBOT, REMEMBER?
YOU HAVE TO BREATHE?
OCCASIONALLY.
HOLD YOUR BREATH.
ULYSSES.
SPACEMEN.

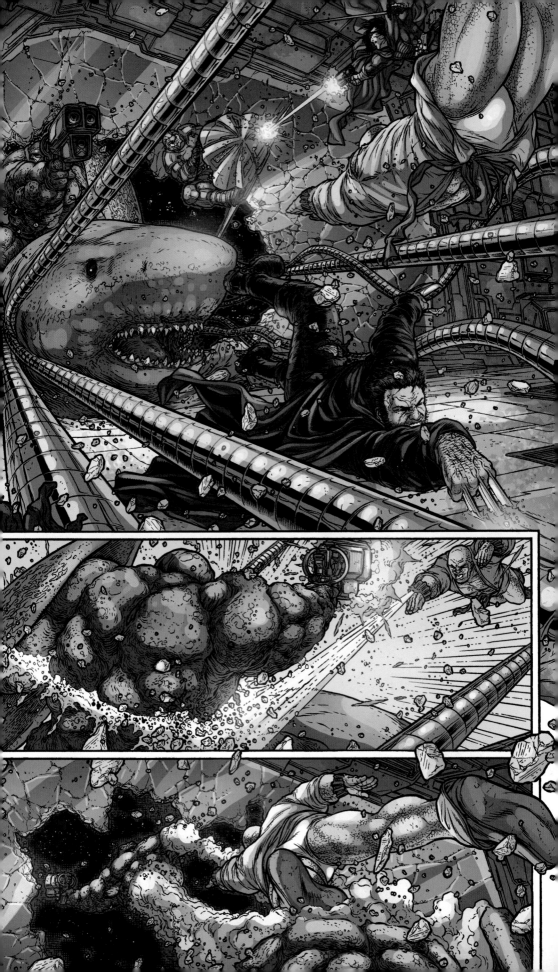

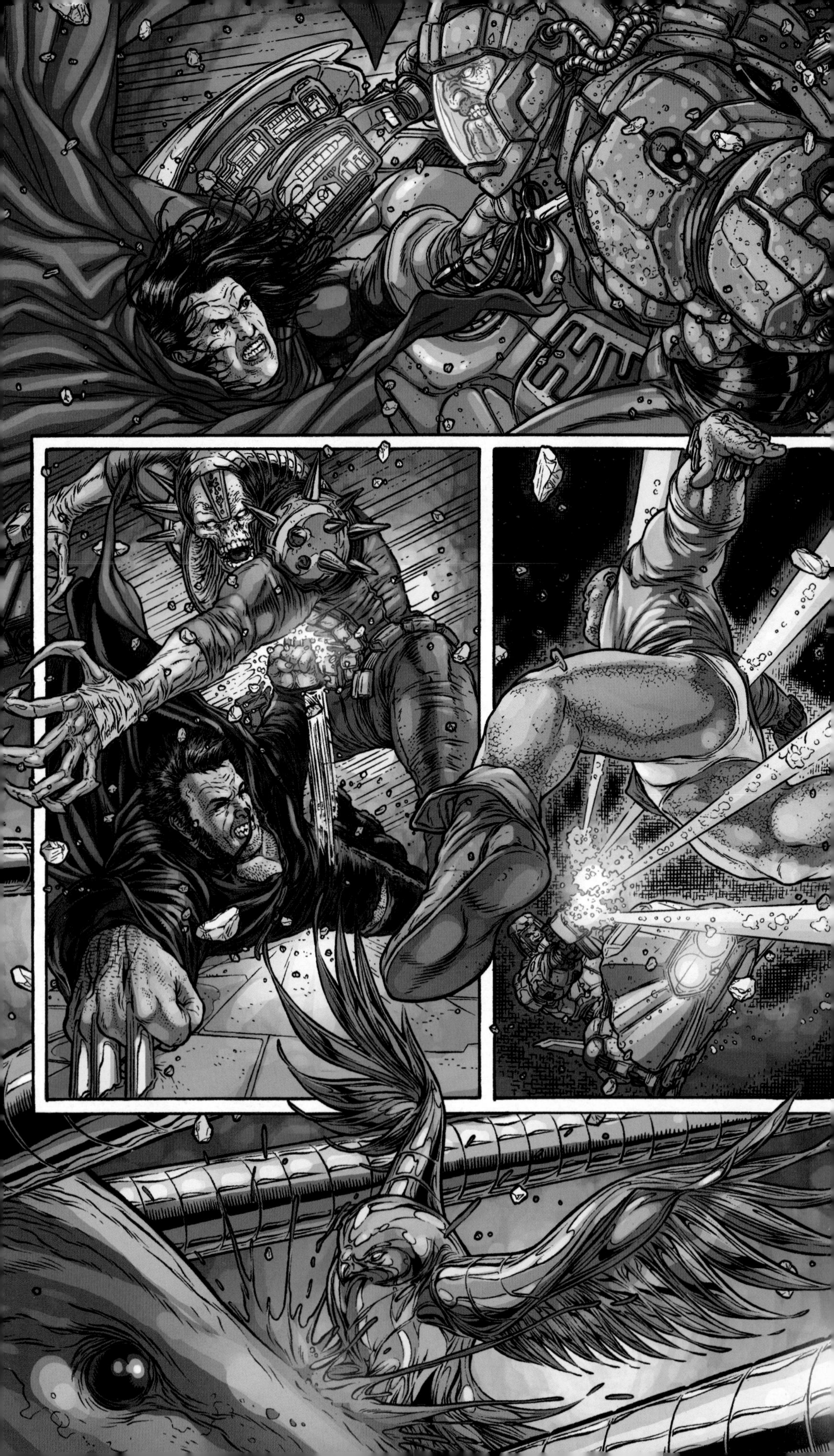

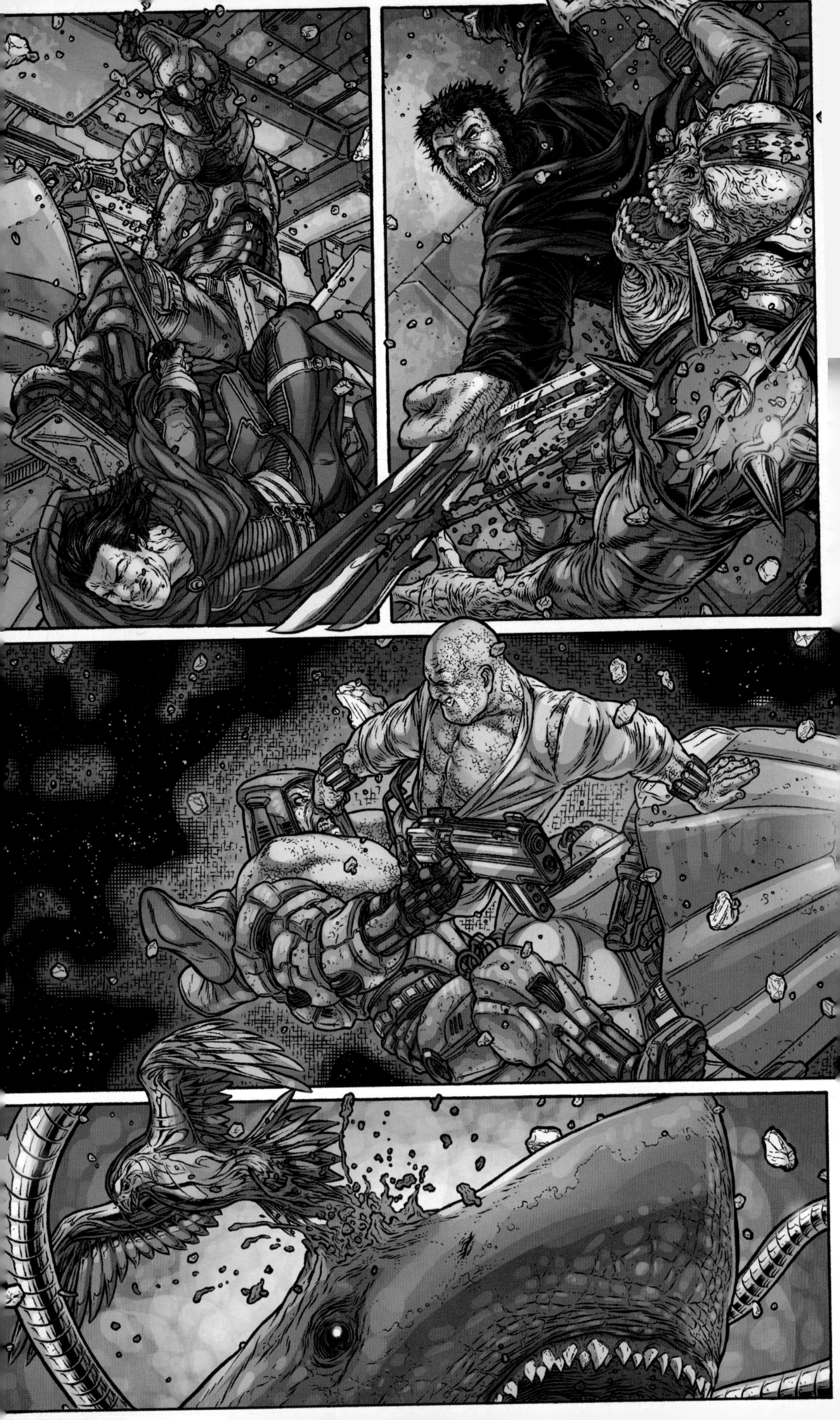

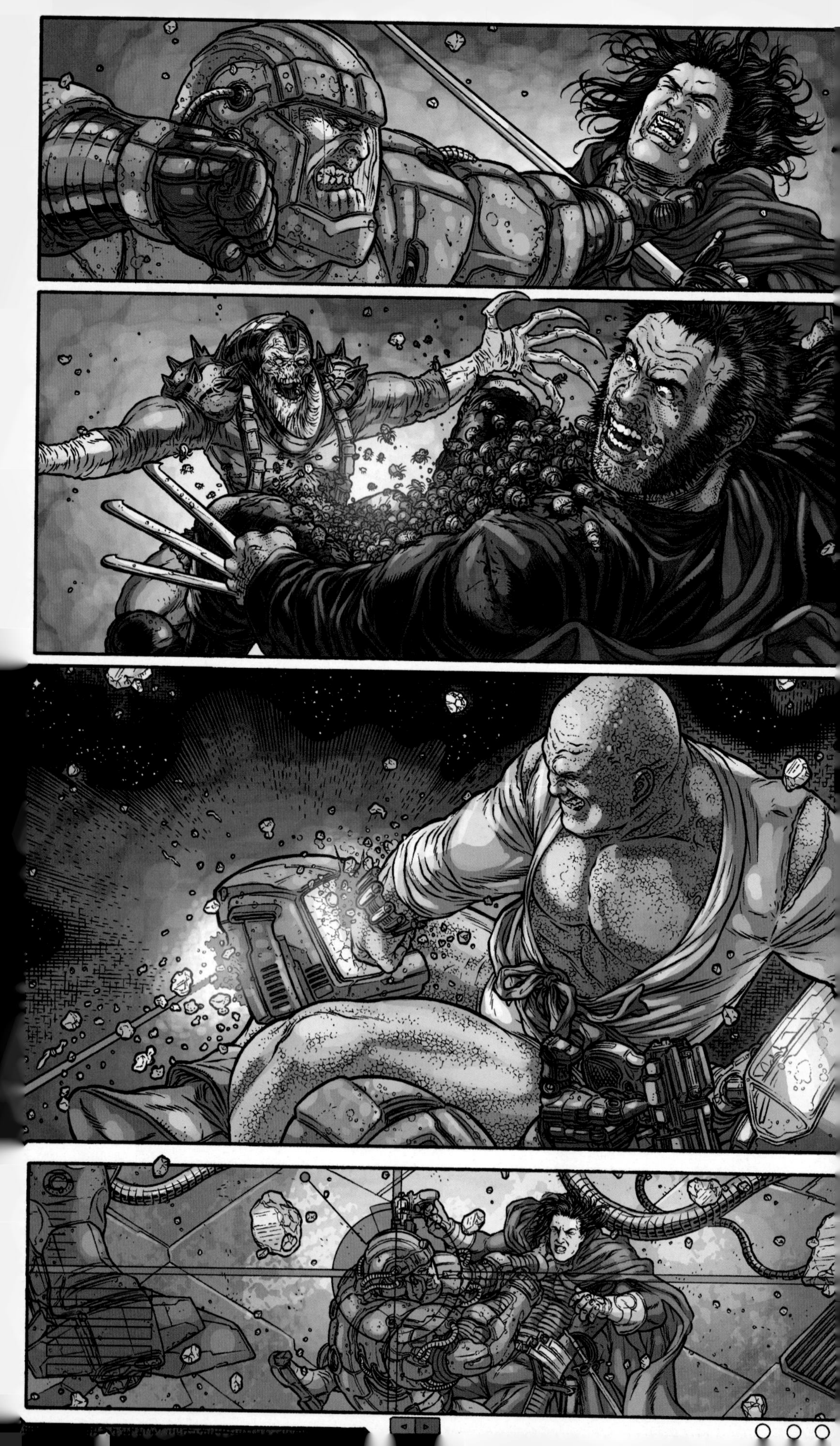

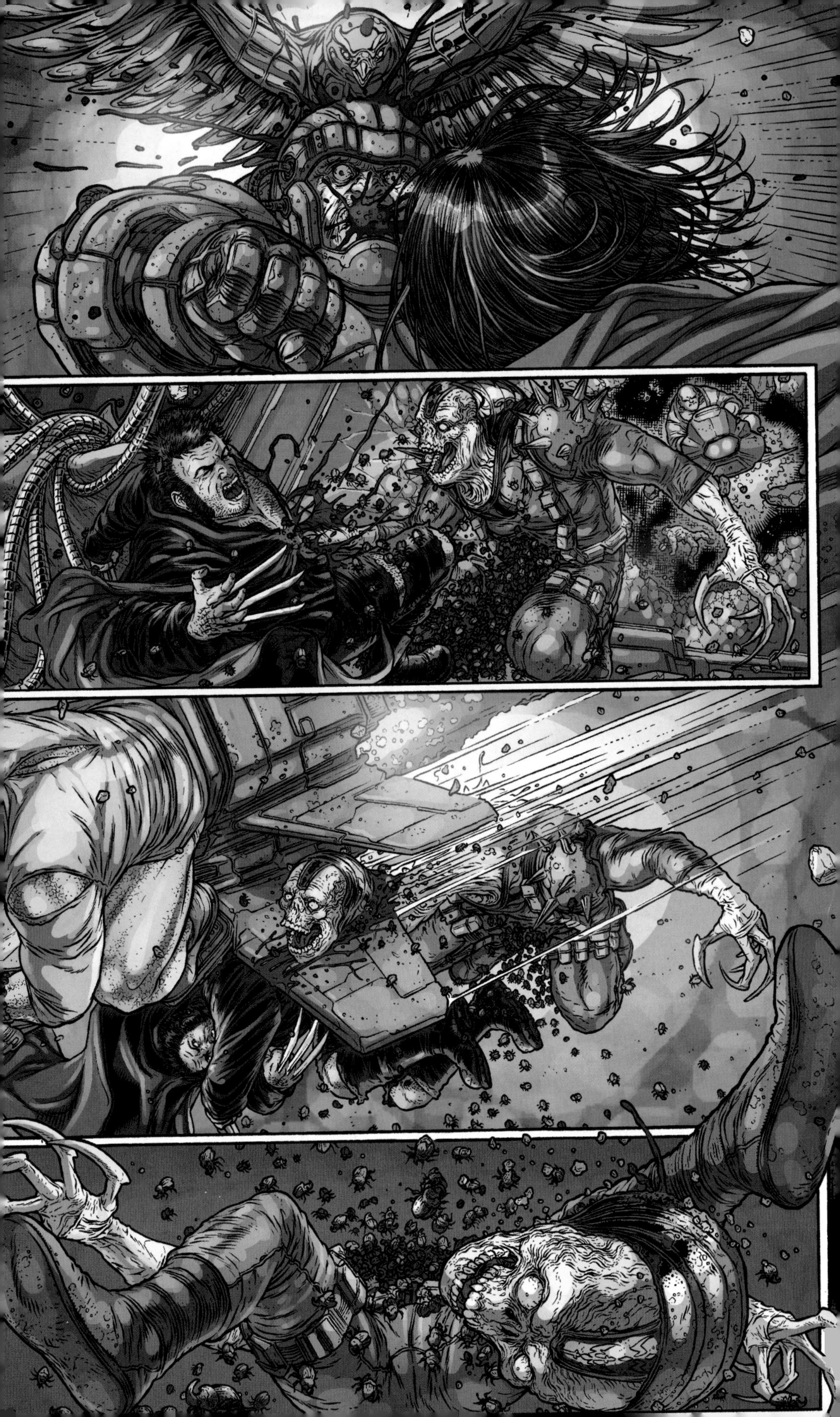

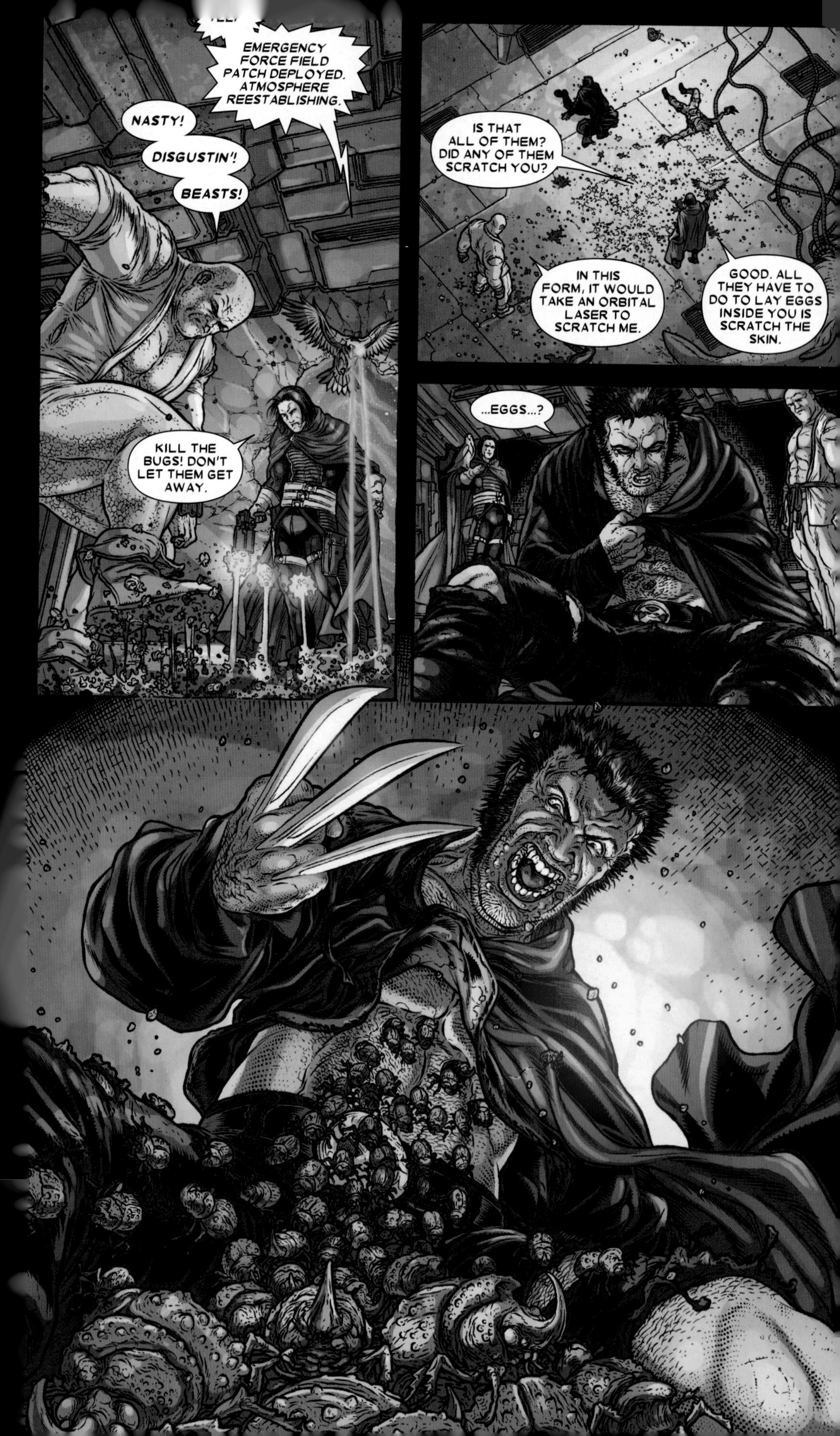
EMERGENCY FORCE FIELD PATCH DEPLOYED. ATMOSPHERE REESTABLISHING.
NASTY!
DISGUSTIN'!
BEASTS!
KILL THE BUGS! DON'T LET THEM GET AWAY.
IS THAT ALL OF THEM? DID ANY OF THEM SCRATCH YOU?
IN THIS FORM, IT WOULD TAKE AN ORBITAL LASER TO SCRATCH ME.
GOOD. ALL THEY HAVE TO DO TO LAY EGGS INSIDE YOU IS SCRATCH THE SKIN.
...EGGS...?

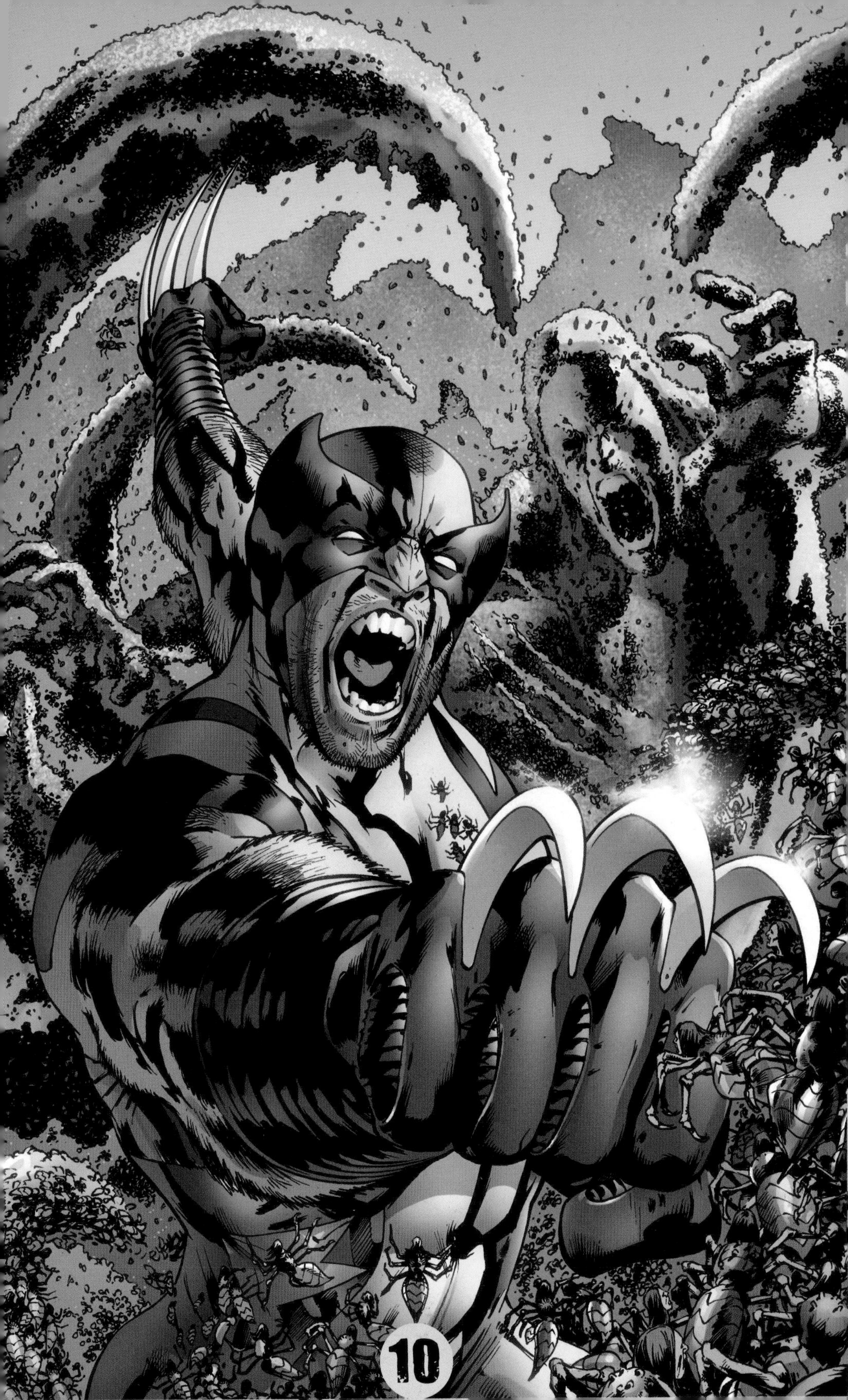
10

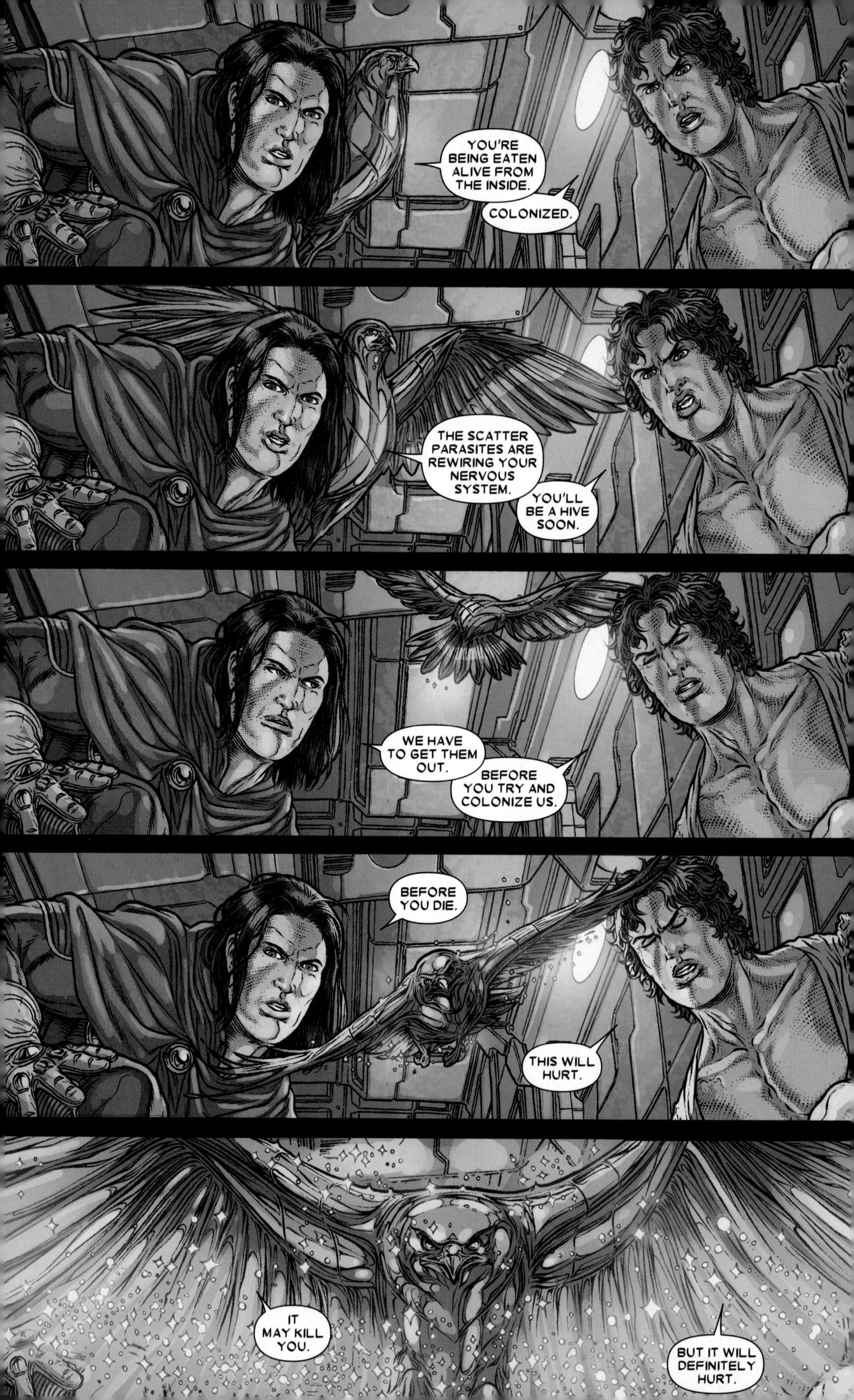
YOU'RE BEING EATEN ALIVE FROM THE INSIDE.
COLONIZED.
THE SCATTER PARASITES ARE REWIRING YOUR NERVOUS SYSTEM.
YOU'LL BE A HIVE SOON.
WE HAVE TO GET THEM OUT.
BEFORE YOU TRY AND COLONIZE US.
BEFORE YOU DIE.
THIS WILL HURT.
IT MAY KILL YOU.
BUT IT WILL DEFINITELY HURT.

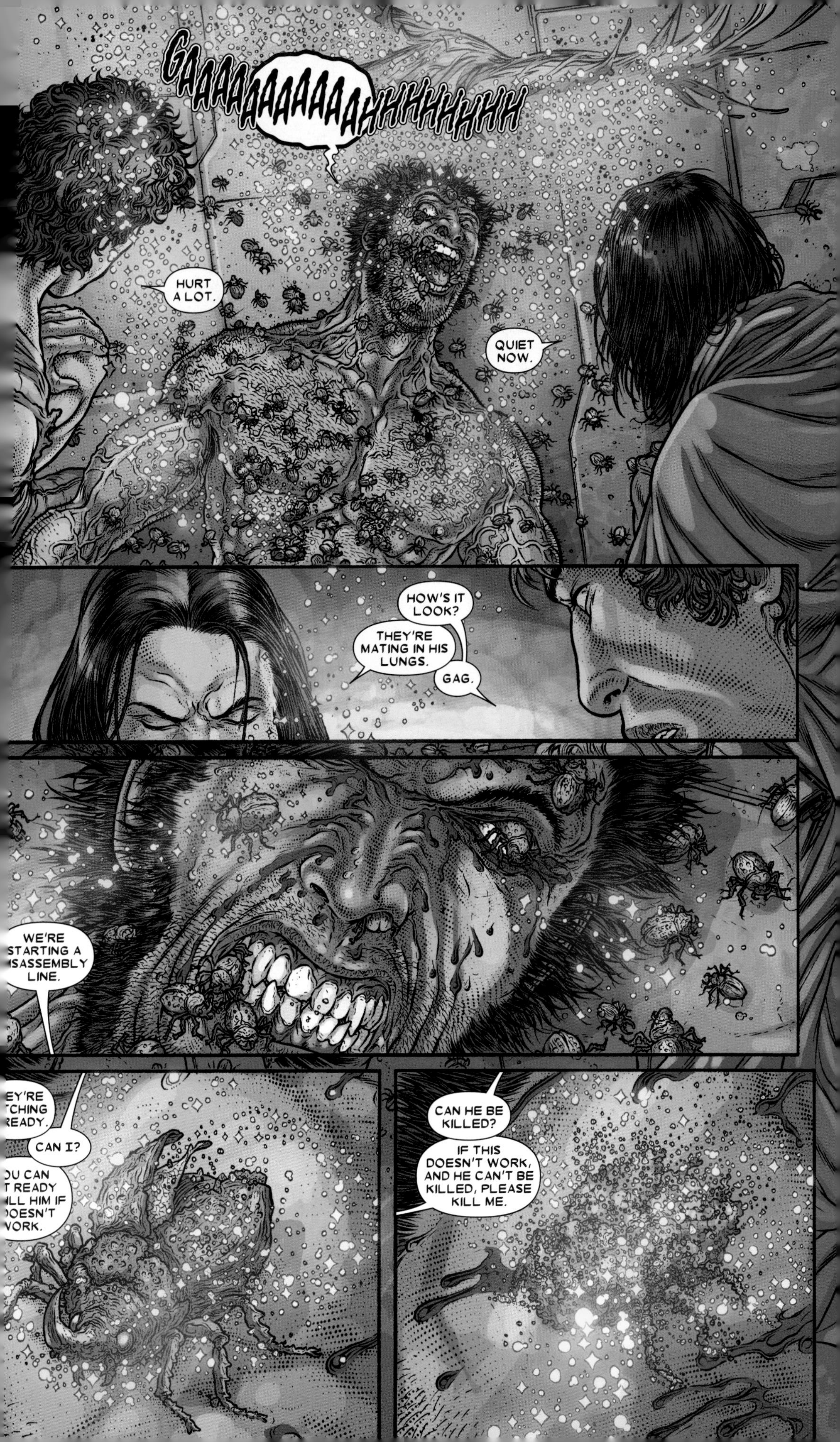
GAAAAAAAAAAHHHHHHHH
HURT A LOT.
QUIET NOW.
HOW'S IT LOOK?
THEY'RE MATING IN HIS LUNGS.
GAG.
WE'RE STARTING A ISASSEMBLY LINE.
EY'RE TCHING READY.
CAN I?
OU CAN T READY ILL HIM IF OESN'T VORK.
CAN HE BE KILLED?
IF THIS DOESN'T WORK, AND HE CAN'T BE KILLED, PLEASE KILL ME.

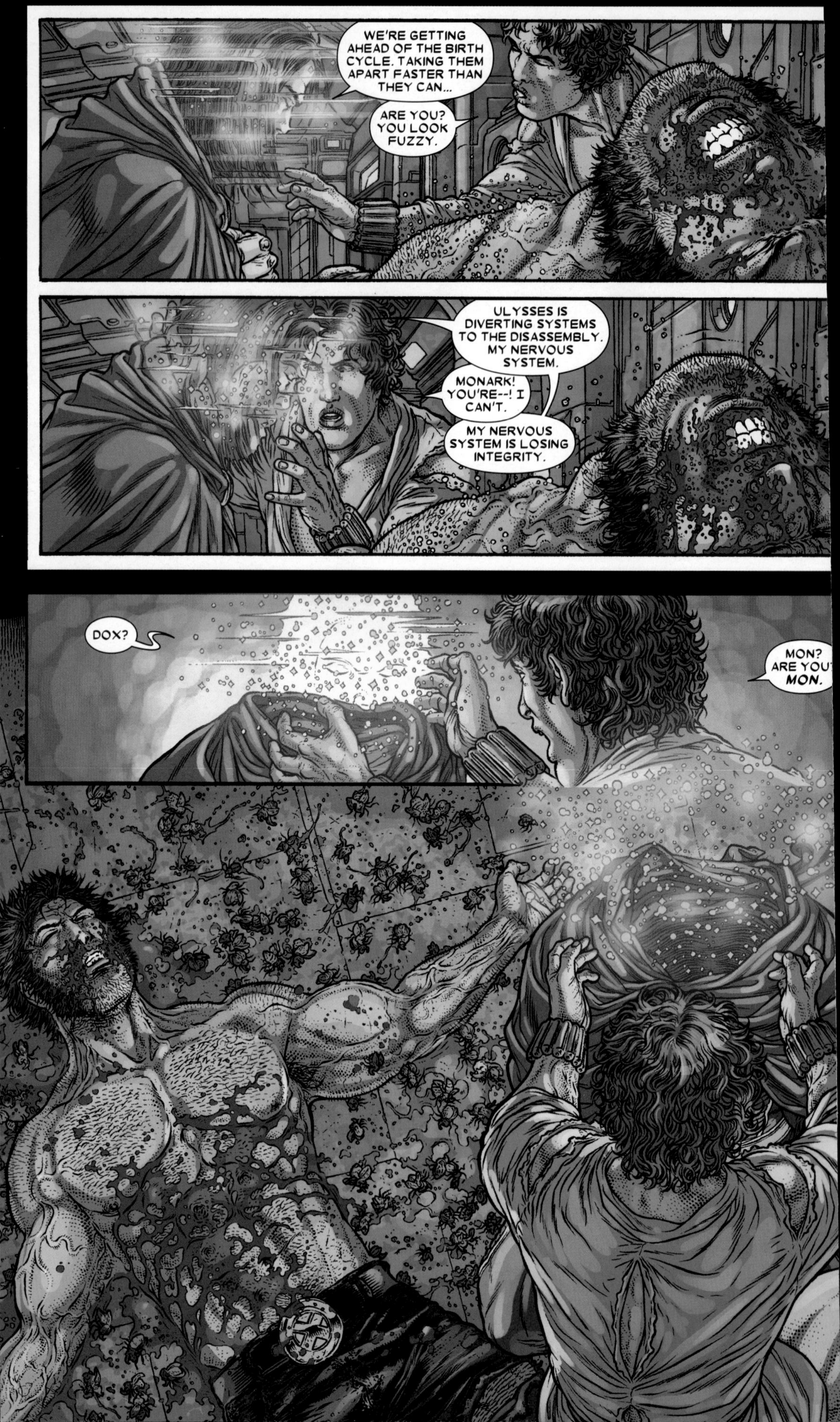
WE'RE GETTING AHEAD OF THE BIRTH CYCLE. TAKING THEM APART FASTER THAN THEY CAN...
ARE YOU? YOU LOOK FUZZY.
ULYSSES IS DIVERTING SYSTEMS TO THE DISASSEMBLY. MY NERVOUS SYSTEM.
MONARK! YOU'RE--! I CAN'T.
MY NERVOUS SYSTEM IS LOSING INTEGRITY.
DOX?
MON? ARE YOU
MON.

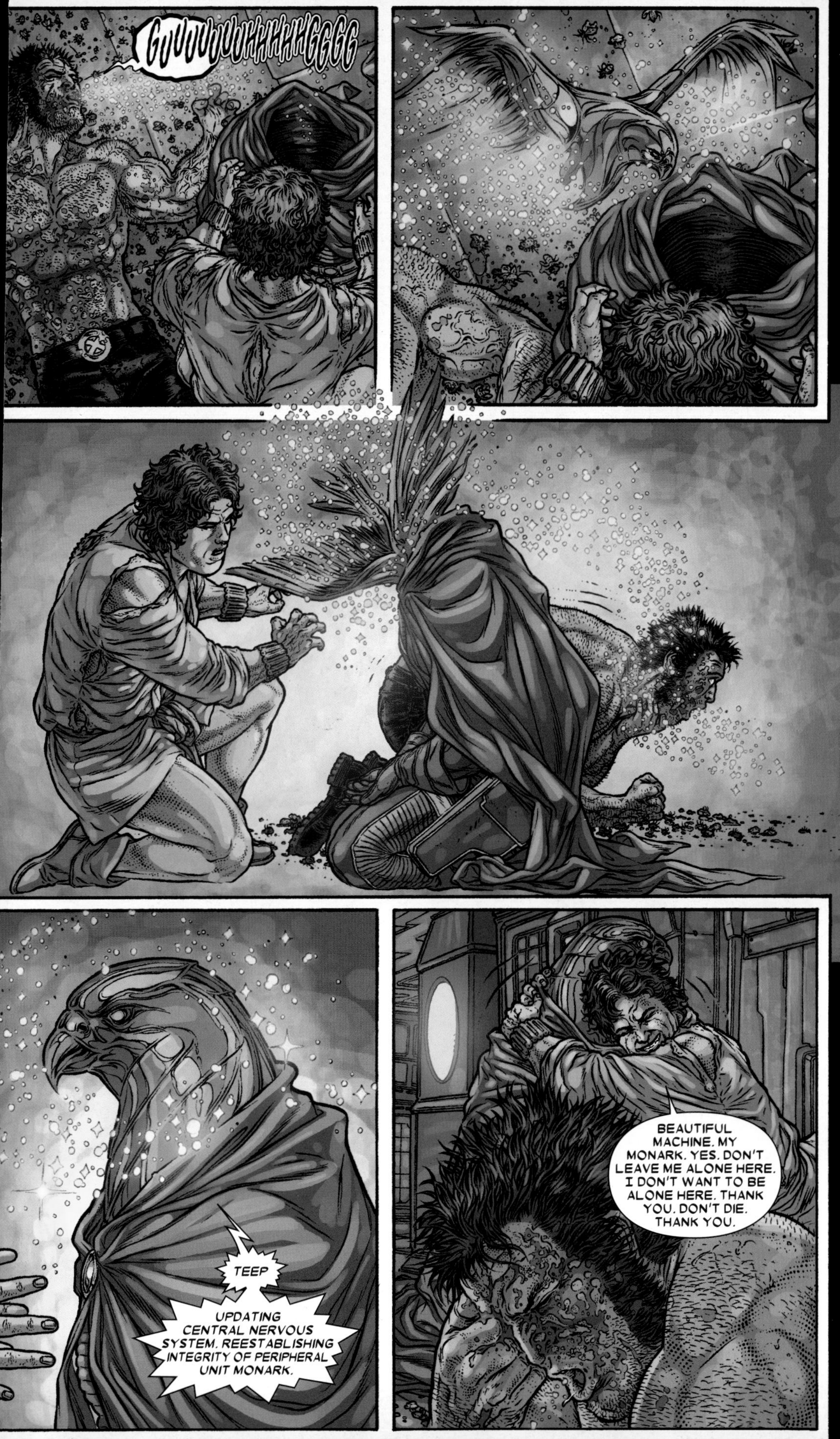
GUUUUUUUHHHHHGGGG
TEEP
UPDATING CENTRAL NERVOUS SYSTEM. REESTABLISHING INTEGRITY OF PERIPHERAL UNIT MONARK.
BEAUTIFUL MACHINE. MY MONARK. YES. DON'T LEAVE ME ALONE HERE. I DON'T WANT TO BE ALONE HERE. THANK YOU. DON'T DIE. THANK YOU.

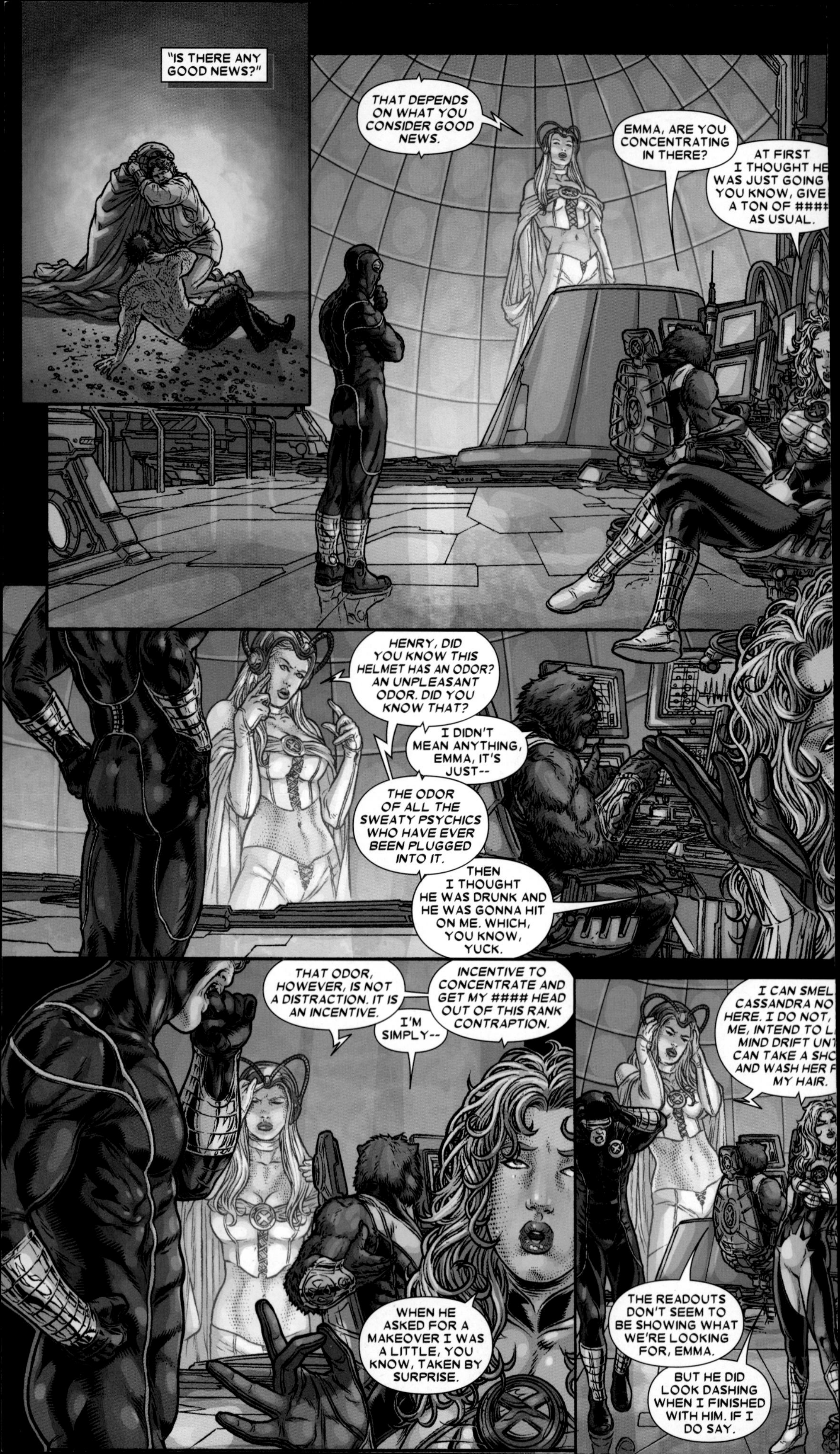
"IS THERE ANY GOOD NEWS?"
THAT DEPENDS ON WHAT YOU CONSIDER GOOD NEWS.
EMMA, ARE YOU CONCENTRATING IN THERE?
AT FIRST I THOUGHT HE WAS JUST GOING YOU KNOW, GIVE A TON OF #### AS USUAL.
HENRY, DID YOU KNOW THIS HELMET HAS AN ODOR? AN UNPLEASANT ODOR. DID YOU KNOW THAT?
I DIDN'T MEAN ANYTHING, EMMA, IT'S JUST--
THE ODOR OF ALL THE SWEATY PSYCHICS WHO HAVE EVER BEEN PLUGGED INTO IT.
THEN I THOUGHT HE WAS DRUNK AND HE WAS GONNA HIT ON ME. WHICH, YOU KNOW, YUCK.
THAT ODOR, HOWEVER, IS NOT A DISTRACTION. IT IS AN INCENTIVE.
I'M SIMPLY--
INCENTIVE TO CONCENTRATE AND GET MY #### HEAD OUT OF THIS RANK CONTRAPTION.
WHEN HE ASKED FOR A MAKEOVER I WAS A LITTLE, YOU KNOW, TAKEN BY SURPRISE.
THE READOUTS DON'T SEEM TO BE SHOWING WHAT WE'RE LOOKING FOR, EMMA.
BUT HE DID LOOK DASHING WHEN I FINISHED WITH HIM. IF I DO SAY.

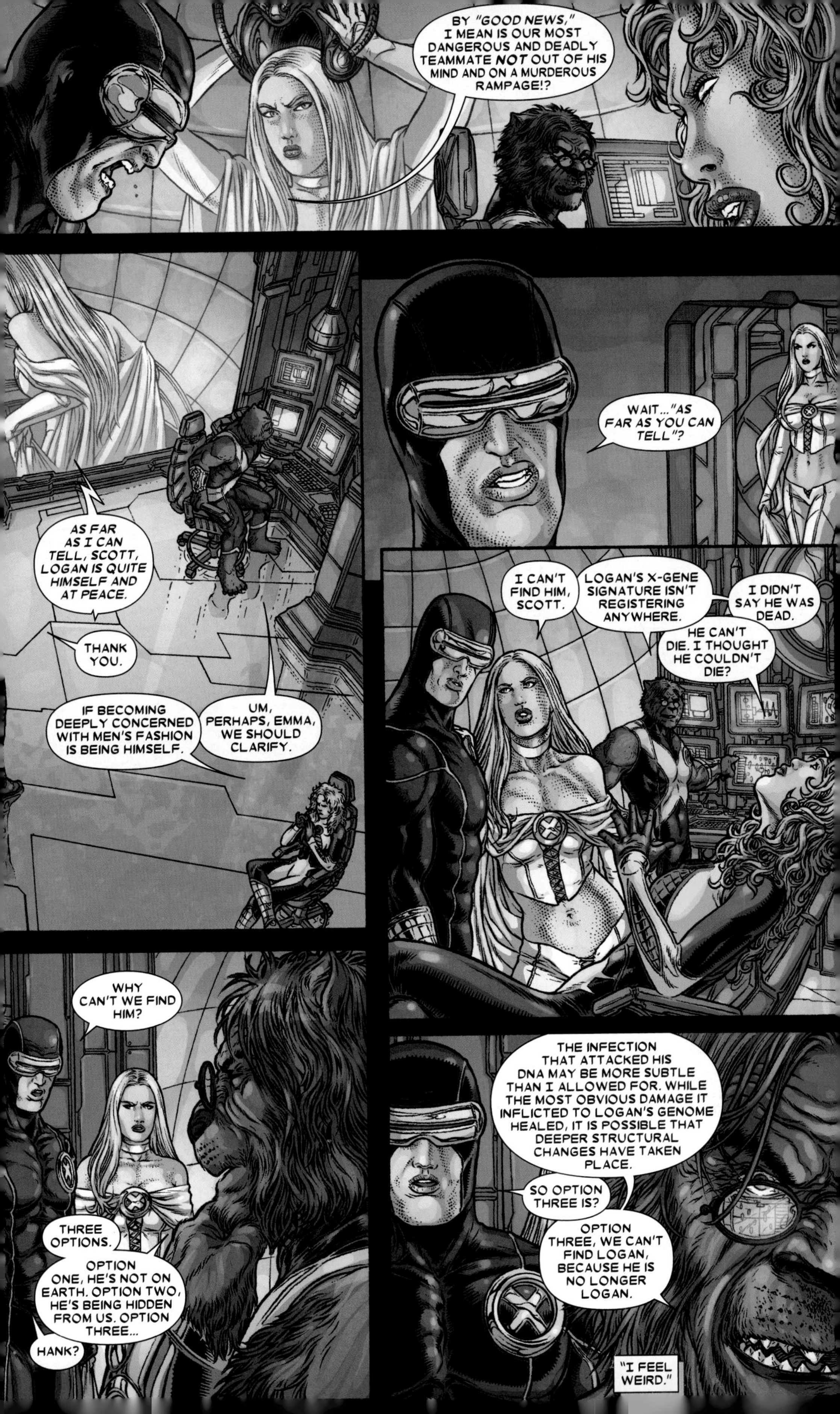
BY "GOOD NEWS," I MEAN IS OUR MOST DANGEROUS AND DEADLY TEAMMATE NOT OUT OF HIS MIND AND ON A MURDEROUS RAMPAGE!?
AS FAR AS I CAN TELL, SCOTT, LOGAN IS QUITE HIMSELF AND AT PEACE.
THANK YOU.
IF BECOMING DEEPLY CONCERNED WITH MEN'S FASHION IS BEING HIMSELF.
UM, PERHAPS, EMMA, WE SHOULD CLARIFY.
WAIT..."AS FAR AS YOU CAN TELL"?
I CAN'T FIND HIM, SCOTT.
LOGAN'S X-GENE SIGNATURE ISN'T REGISTERING ANYWHERE.
I DIDN'T SAY HE WAS DEAD.
HE CAN'T DIE. I THOUGHT HE COULDN'T DIE?
WHY CAN'T WE FIND HIM?
THREE OPTIONS.
OPTION ONE, HE'S NOT ON EARTH. OPTION TWO, HE'S BEING HIDDEN FROM US. OPTION THREE...
HANK?
THE INFECTION THAT ATTACKED HIS DNA MAY BE MORE SUBTLE THAN I ALLOWED FOR. WHILE THE MOST OBVIOUS DAMAGE IT INFLICTED TO LOGAN'S GENOME HEALED, IT IS POSSIBLE THAT DEEPER STRUCTURAL CHANGES HAVE TAKEN PLACE.
SO OPTION THREE IS?
OPTION THREE, WE CAN'T FIND LOGAN, BECAUSE HE IS NO LONGER LOGAN.
"I FEEL WEIRD."

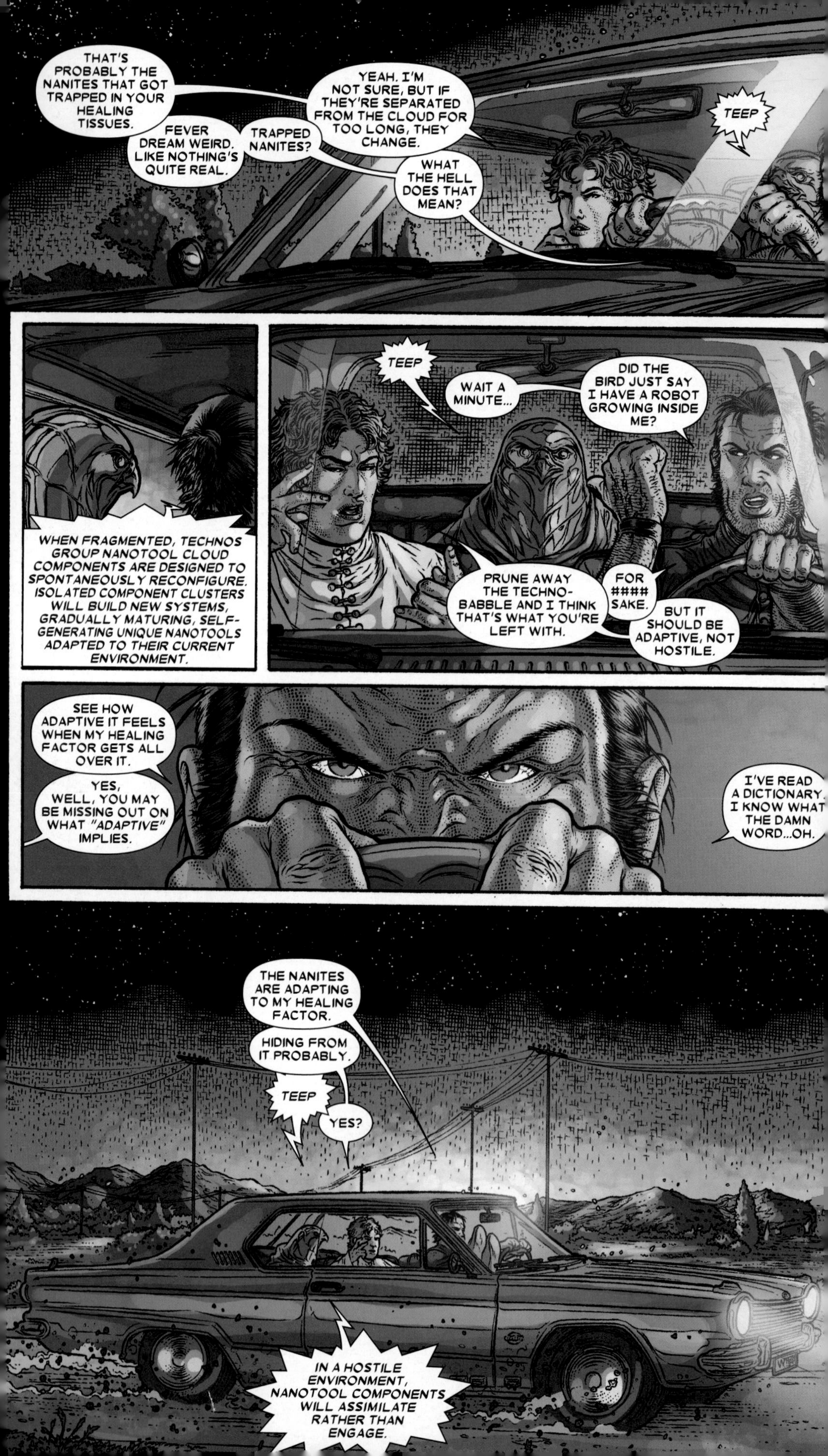
THAT'S PROBABLY THE NANITES THAT GOT TRAPPED IN YOUR HEALING TISSUES.
FEVER DREAM WEIRD. LIKE NOTHING'S QUITE REAL.
YEAH. I'M NOT SURE, BUT IF THEY'RE SEPARATED FROM THE CLOUD FOR TOO LONG, THEY CHANGE.
TRAPPED NANITES?
WHAT THE HELL DOES THAT MEAN?
TEEP
WHEN FRAGMENTED, TECHNOS GROUP NANOTOOL CLOUD COMPONENTS ARE DESIGNED TO SPONTANEOUSLY RECONFIGURE. ISOLATED COMPONENT CLUSTERS WILL BUILD NEW SYSTEMS, GRADUALLY MATURING, SELF-GENERATING UNIQUE NANOTOOLS ADAPTED TO THEIR CURRENT ENVIRONMENT.
TEEP
WAIT A MINUTE...
DID THE BIRD JUST SAY I HAVE A ROBOT GROWING INSIDE ME?
PRUNE AWAY THE TECHNO-BABBLE AND I THINK THAT'S WHAT YOU'RE LEFT WITH.
FOR #### SAKE.
BUT IT SHOULD BE ADAPTIVE, NOT HOSTILE.
SEE HOW ADAPTIVE IT FEELS WHEN MY HEALING FACTOR GETS ALL OVER IT.
YES, WELL, YOU MAY BE MISSING OUT ON WHAT "ADAPTIVE" IMPLIES.
I'VE READ A DICTIONARY. I KNOW WHAT THE DAMN WORD...OH.
THE NANITES ARE ADAPTING TO MY HEALING FACTOR.
HIDING FROM IT PROBABLY.
TEEP
YES?
IN A HOSTILE ENVIRONMENT, NANOTOOL COMPONENTS WILL ASSIMILATE RATHER THAN ENGAGE.

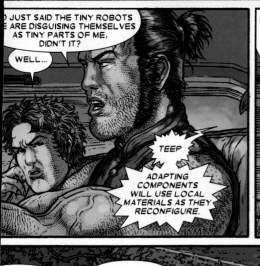

JUST SAID THE TINY ROBOTS
ARE DISGUISING THEMSELVES
AS TINY PARTS OF ME,
DIDN'T IT?

WELL...

TEEP

ADAPTING COMPONENTS WILL USE LOCAL MATERIALS AS THEY RECONFIGURE.

BIRD JUST SAID THE TINY ROBOTS ARE BUILDING MORE TINY ROBOTS FROM SCRATCH USING ME FOR THE INGREDIENTS, DIDN'T IT?

YES, THAT'S WHAT THE BIRD SAID.

BIRD IS STARTING TO GET ON MY NERVES.

YES, WELL, IMAGINE IF THE BIRD HOUSED YOUR LOVER'S NERVOUS SYSTEM AND PERSONALITY. TALK ABOUT IRRITATING.

ET YOUR
ET OFF THE
DASH.

WE SHOULD HAVE JUST BROUGHT THE CUTTER'S SHUTTLE.

YOU ALMOST CRASHED IT TWICE GETTING BACK TO MY WHEELS.

YES, "WHEELS," HOW QUAINT. PERHAPS WE CAN TRAVEL THE LAST LEG OF OUR JOURNEY VIA HORSE AND CARRIAGE.

WHEN DOES MONARK GET HIS HEAD BACK SO I CAN HEAR SOMEONE BESIDES YOU AND THE BIRD?

TEEP

OH, #### ME.

THE STARSTALKER PERIPHERAL HAS BEEN UPDATED. REBOOT HAS COMMENCED.

BUT I'LL STILL BE STUCK WITH ULYSSES. YOU KNOW HE HAS TO BE IN THE ROOM WITH US WHEN WE--

I DO NOT WANT TO HEAR THE END OF THAT SENTENCE.

TEEP

PRUDE.

COLLISION--

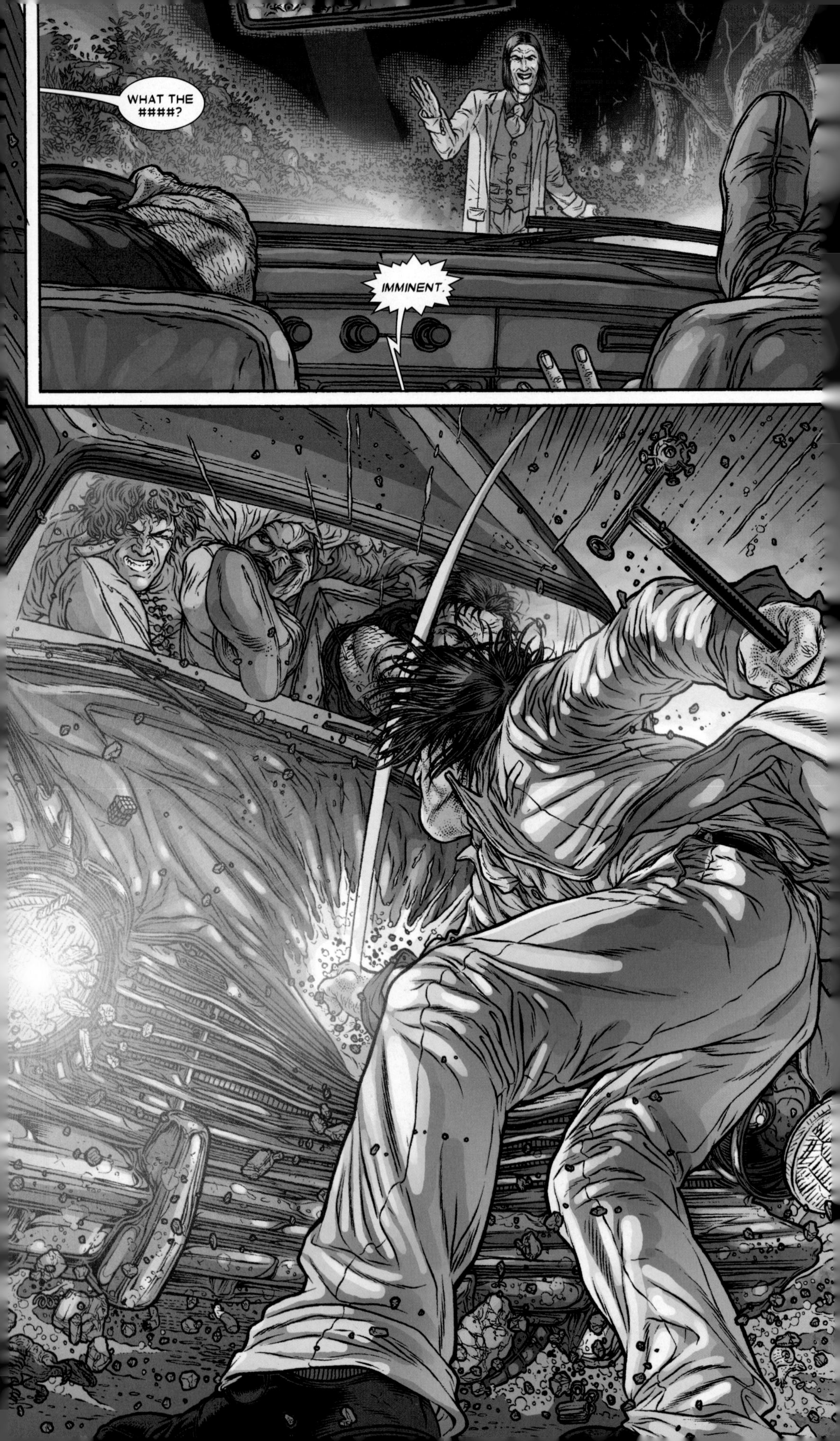
WHAT THE ####?
IMMINENT.

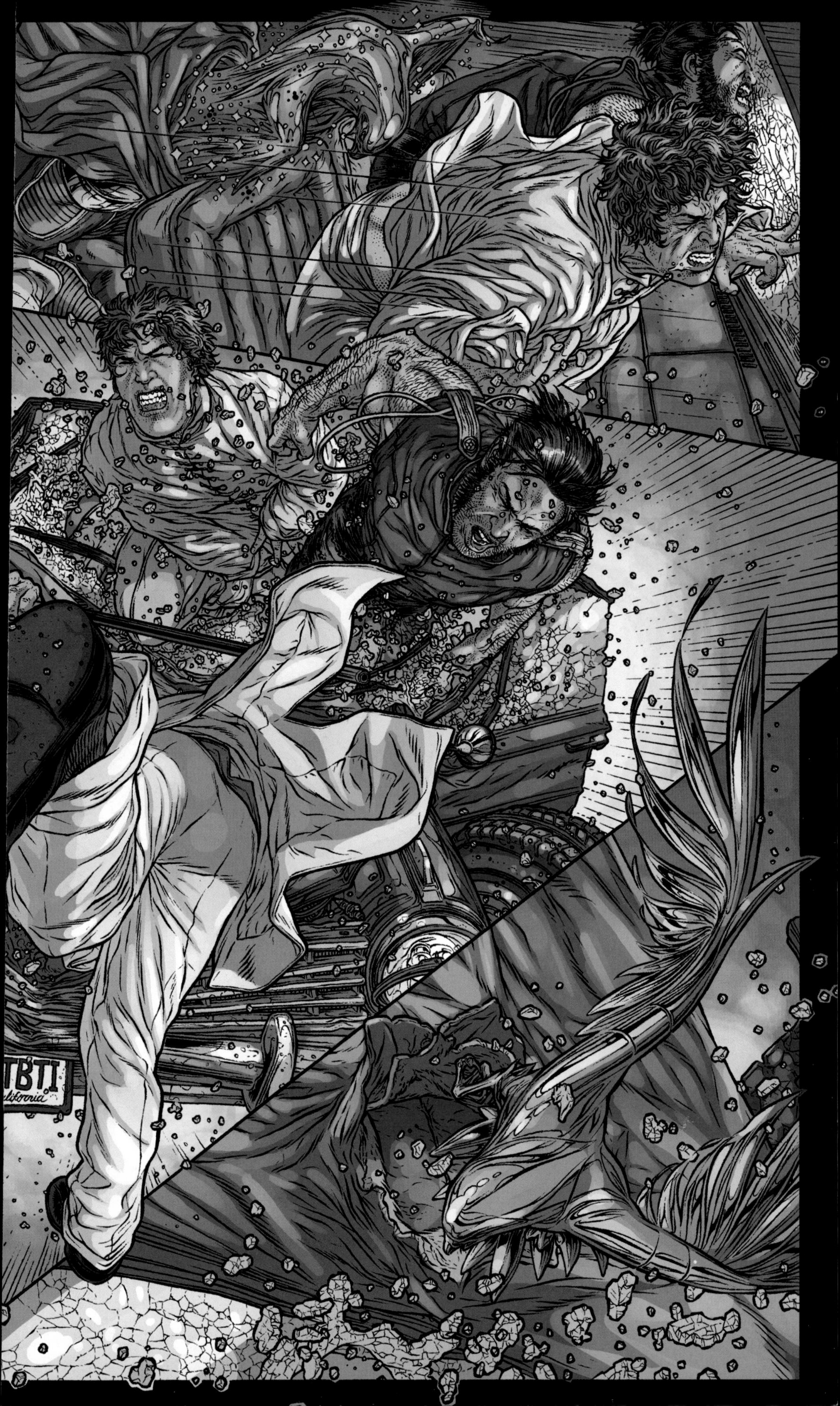
TBTI
alifornia

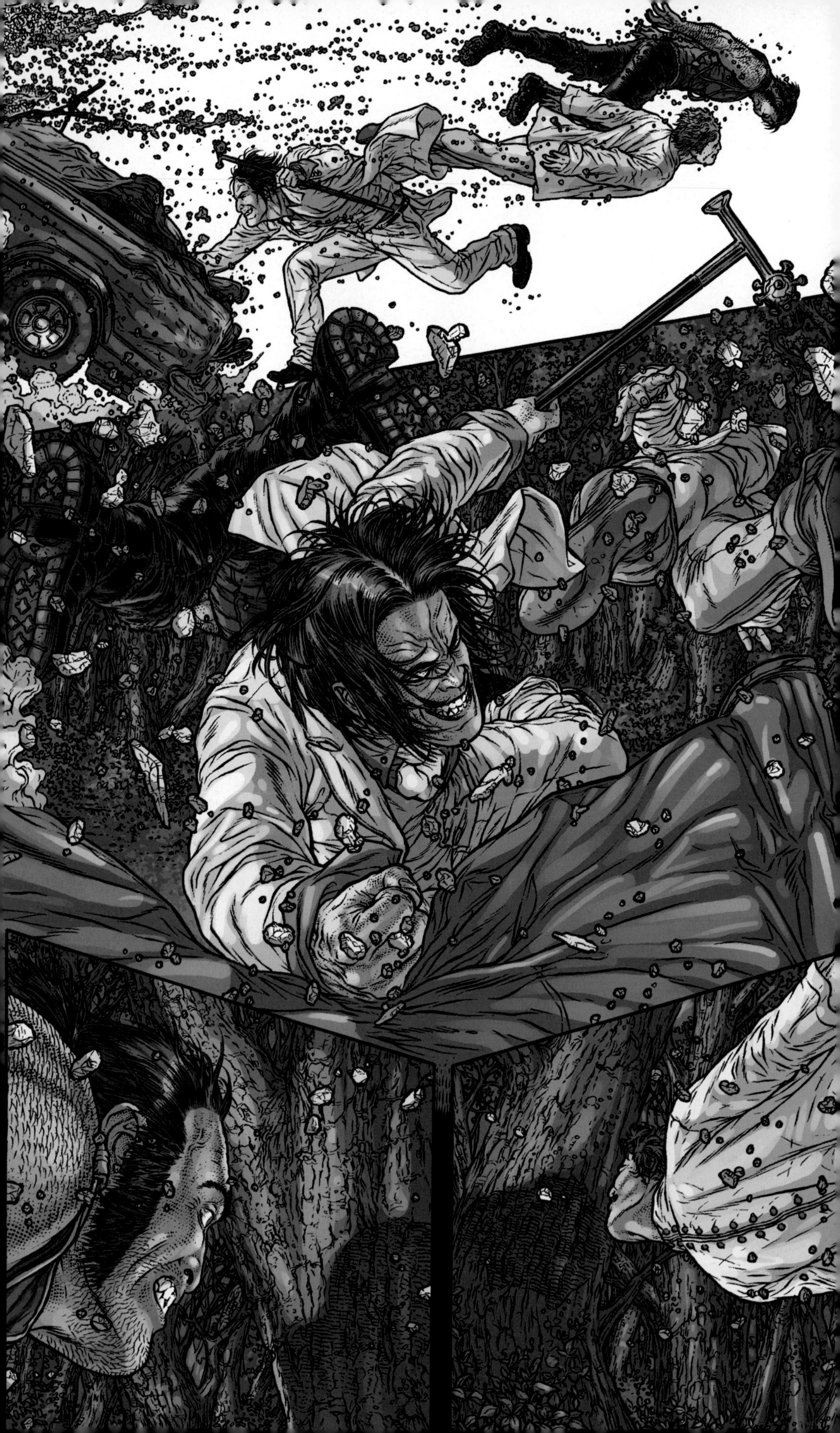

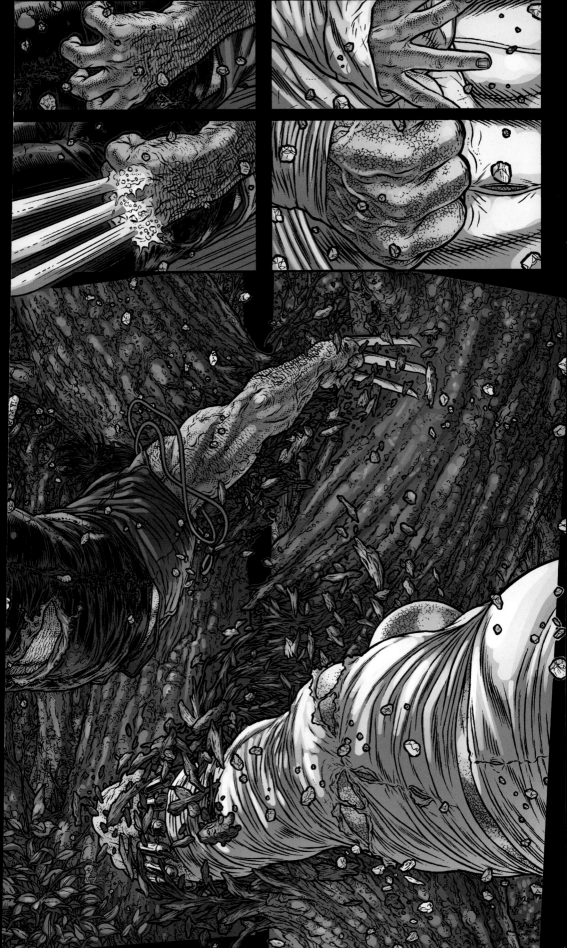

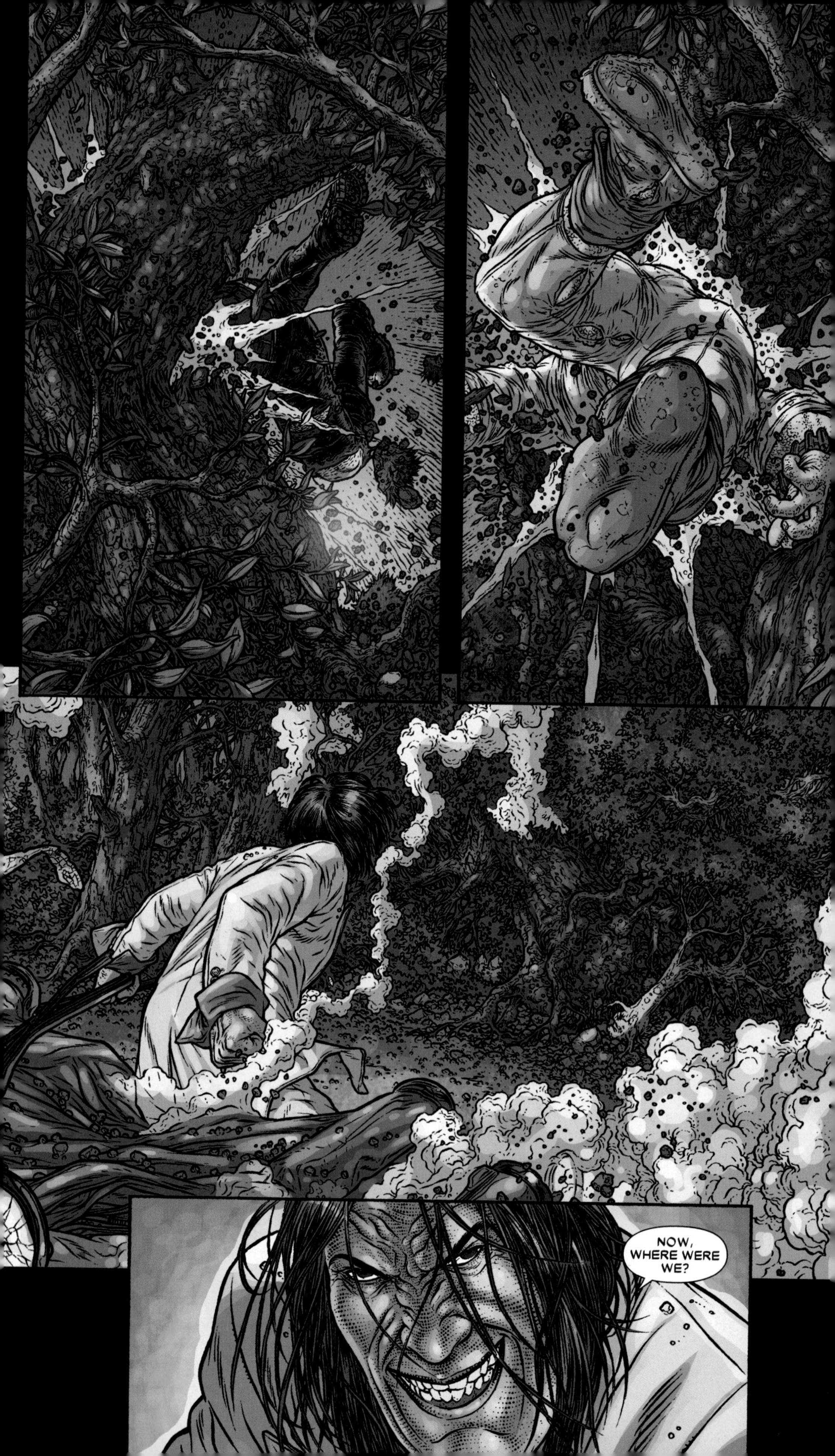
NOW, WHERE WERE WE?

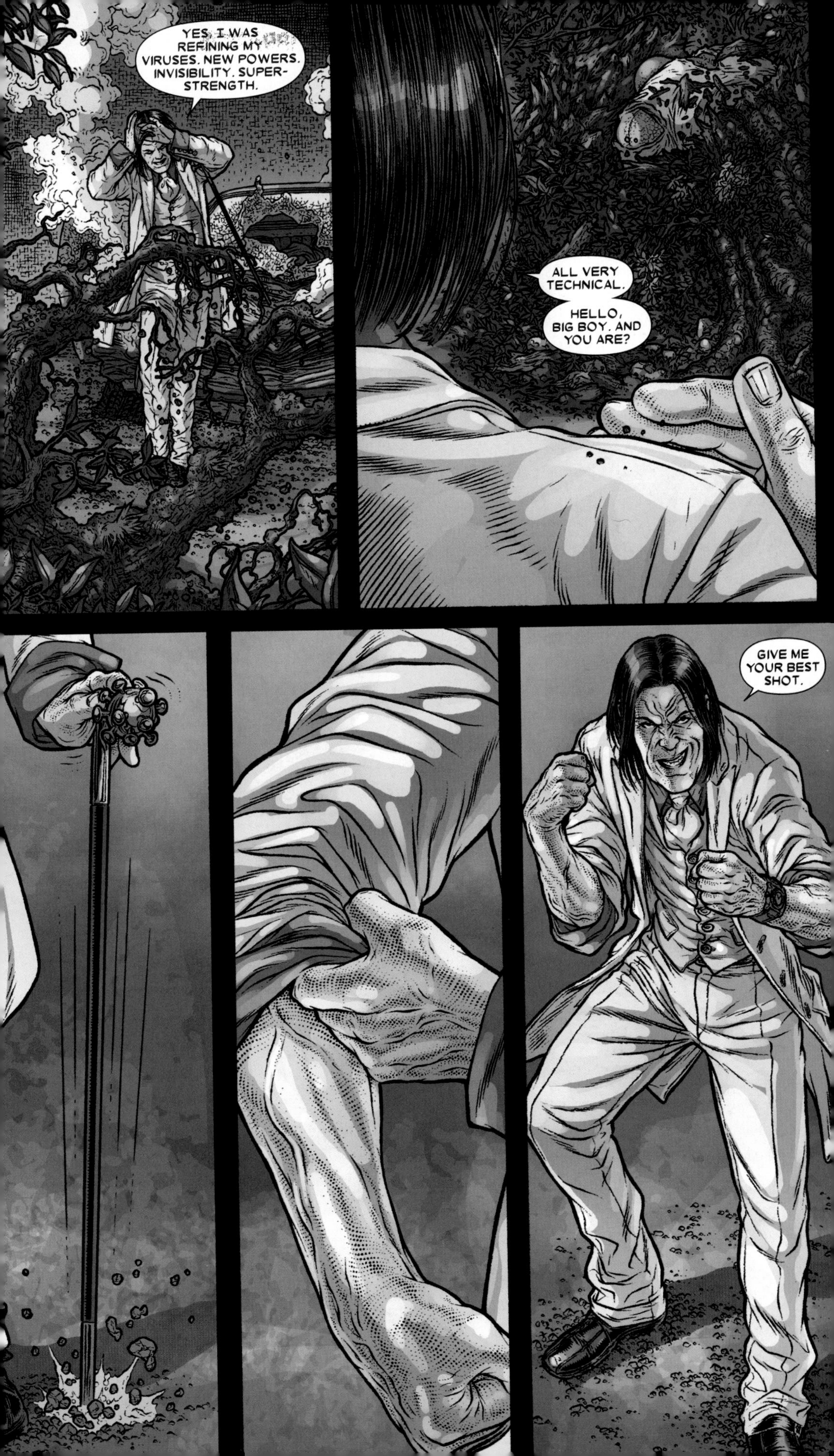
YES, I WAS REFINING MY VIRUSES. NEW POWERS. INVISIBILITY. SUPER-STRENGTH.
ALL VERY TECHNICAL.
HELLO, BIG BOY. AND YOU ARE?
GIVE ME YOUR BEST SHOT.

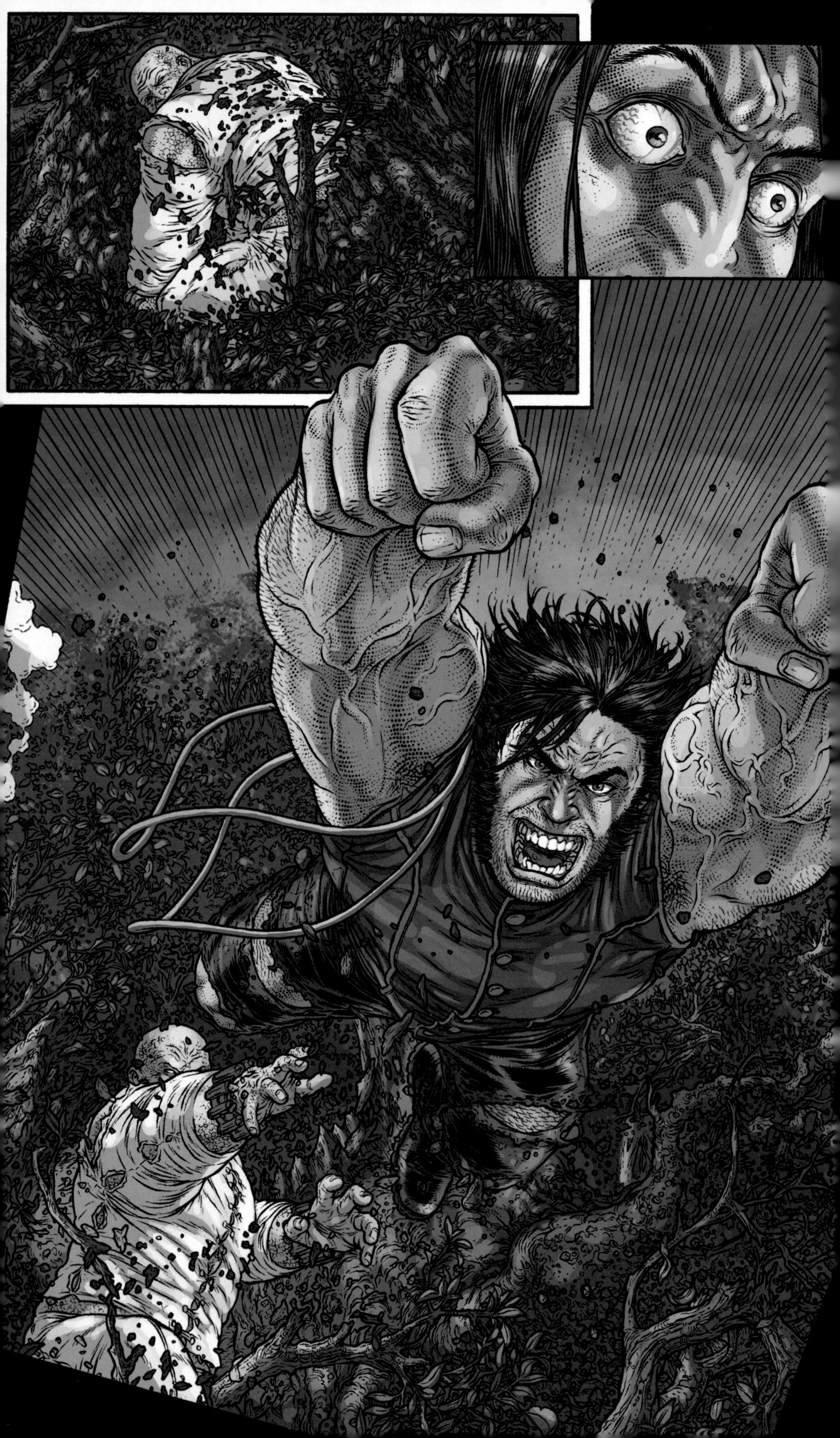

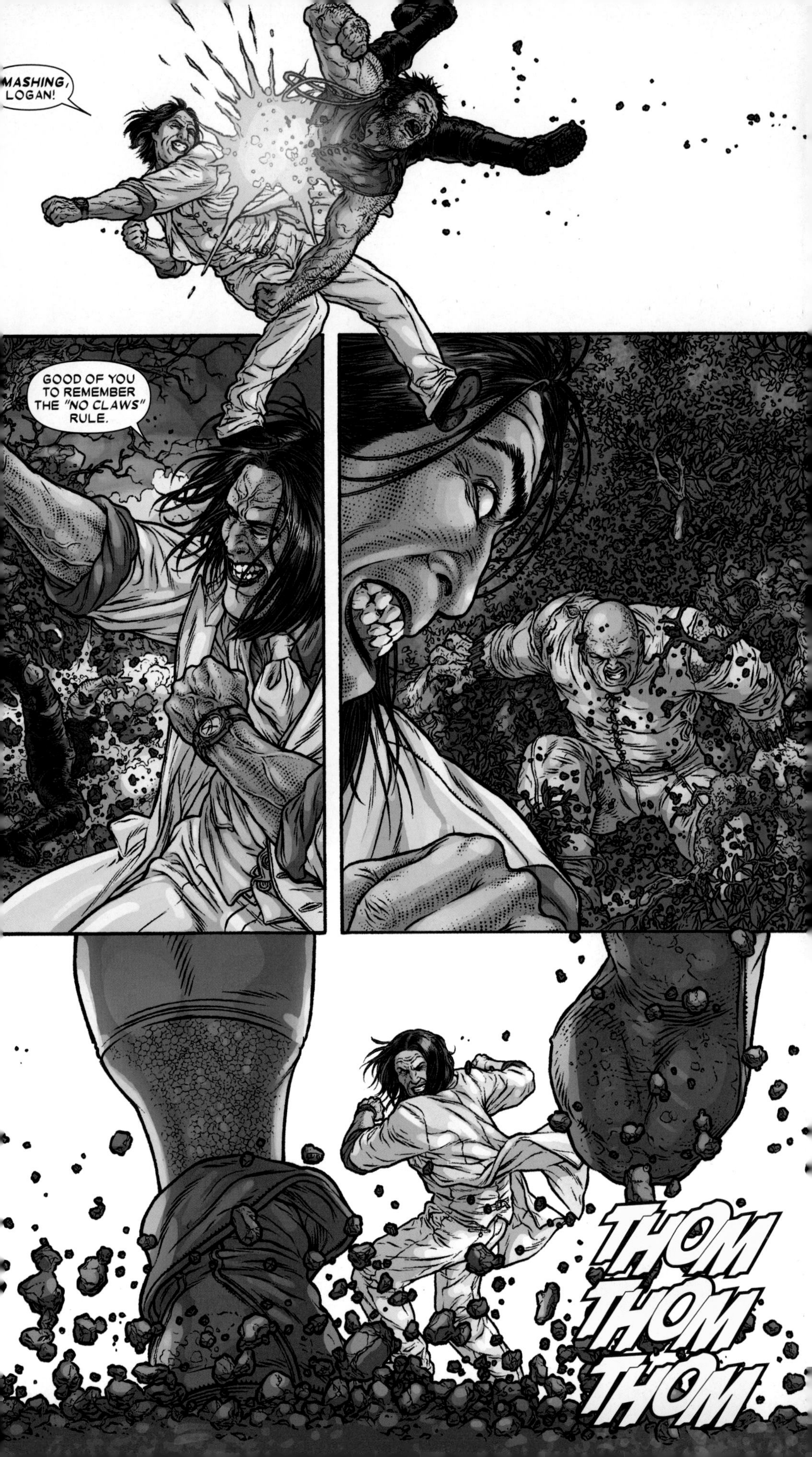
MASHING, LOGAN!
GOOD OF YOU TO REMEMBER THE "NO CLAWS" RULE.
THOM THOM THOM

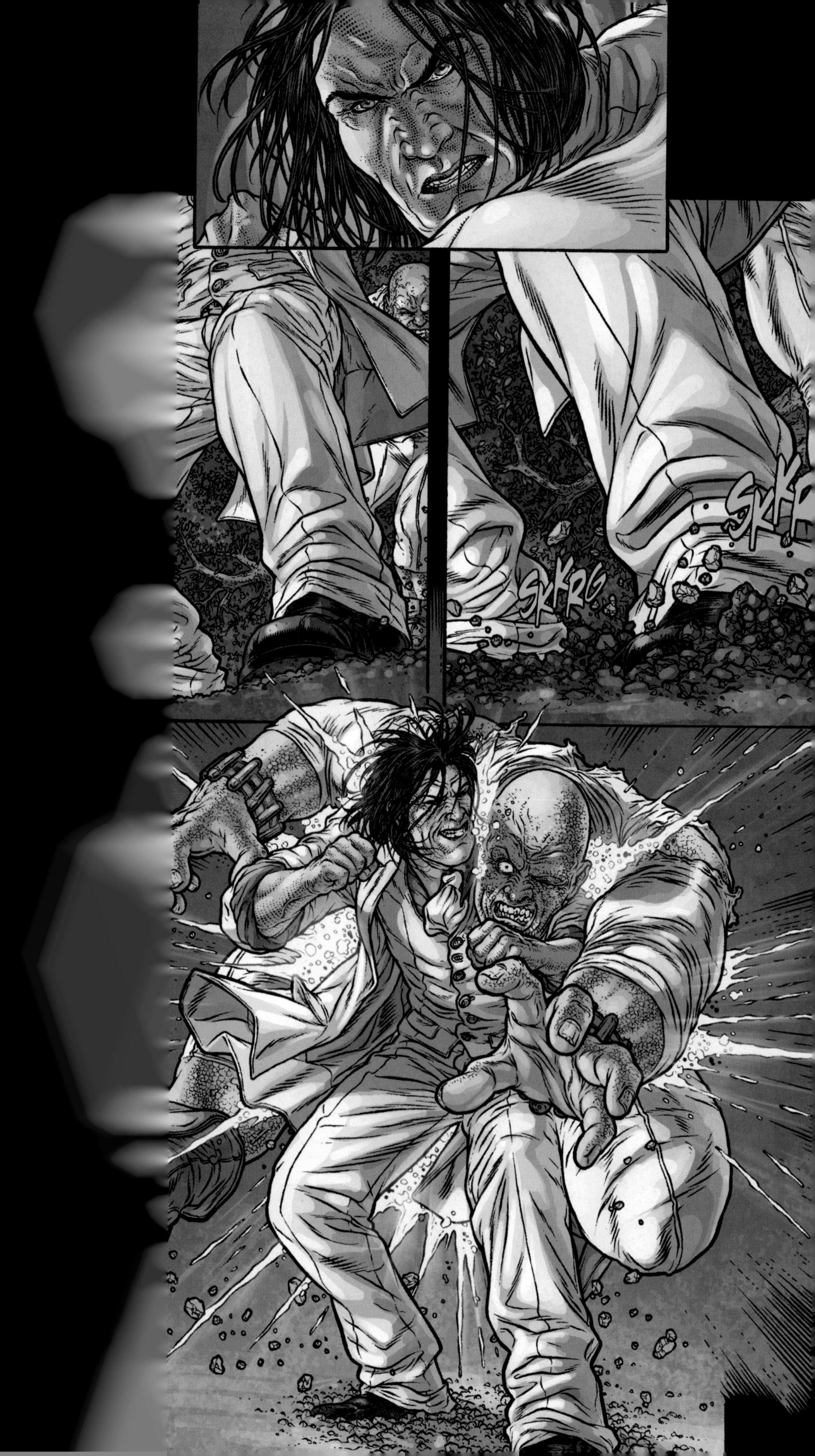
SKRG

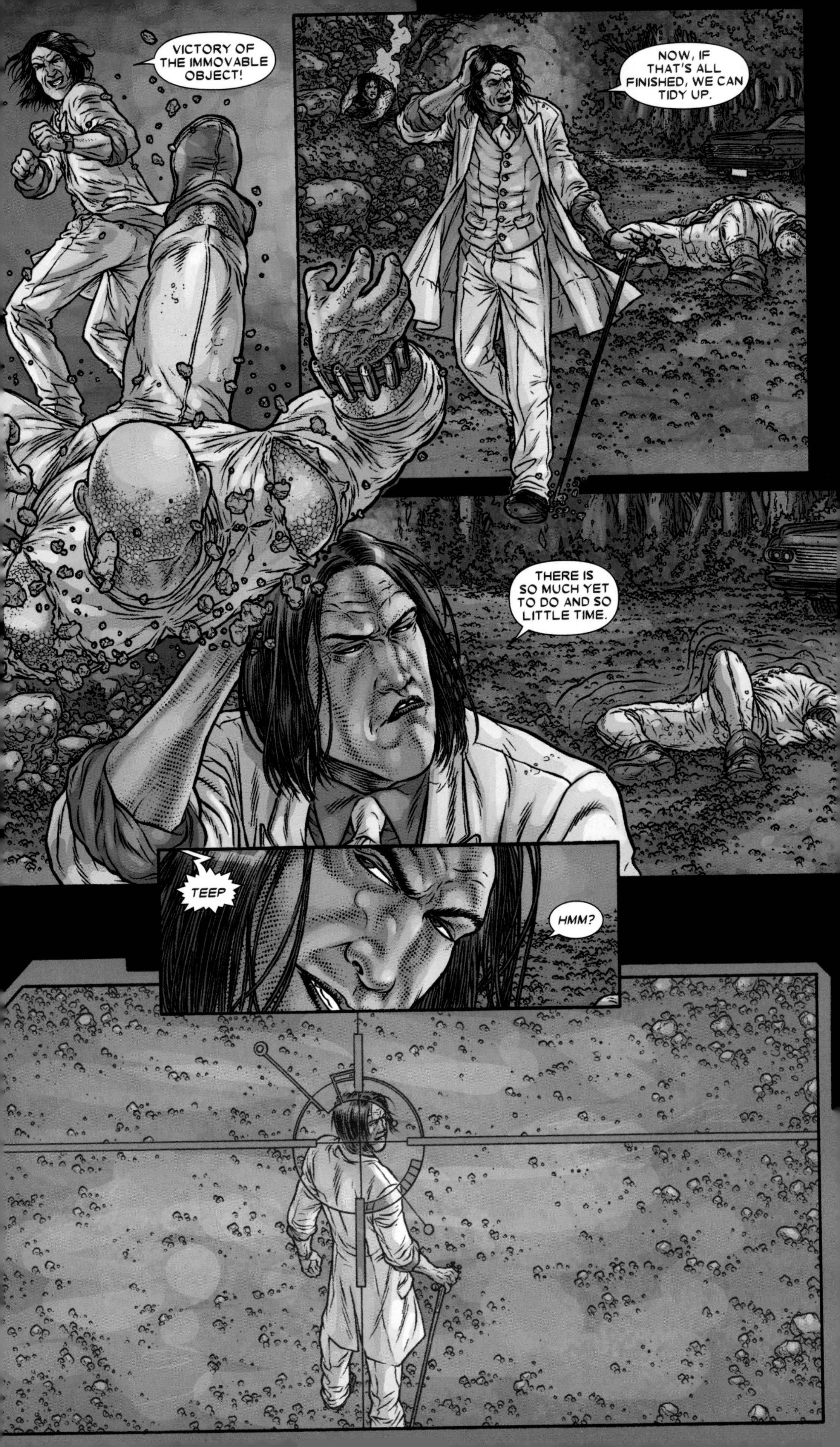
VICTORY OF THE IMMOVABLE OBJECT!
NOW, IF THAT'S ALL FINISHED, WE CAN TIDY UP.
THERE IS SO MUCH YET TO DO AND SO LITTLE TIME.
TEEP
HMM?

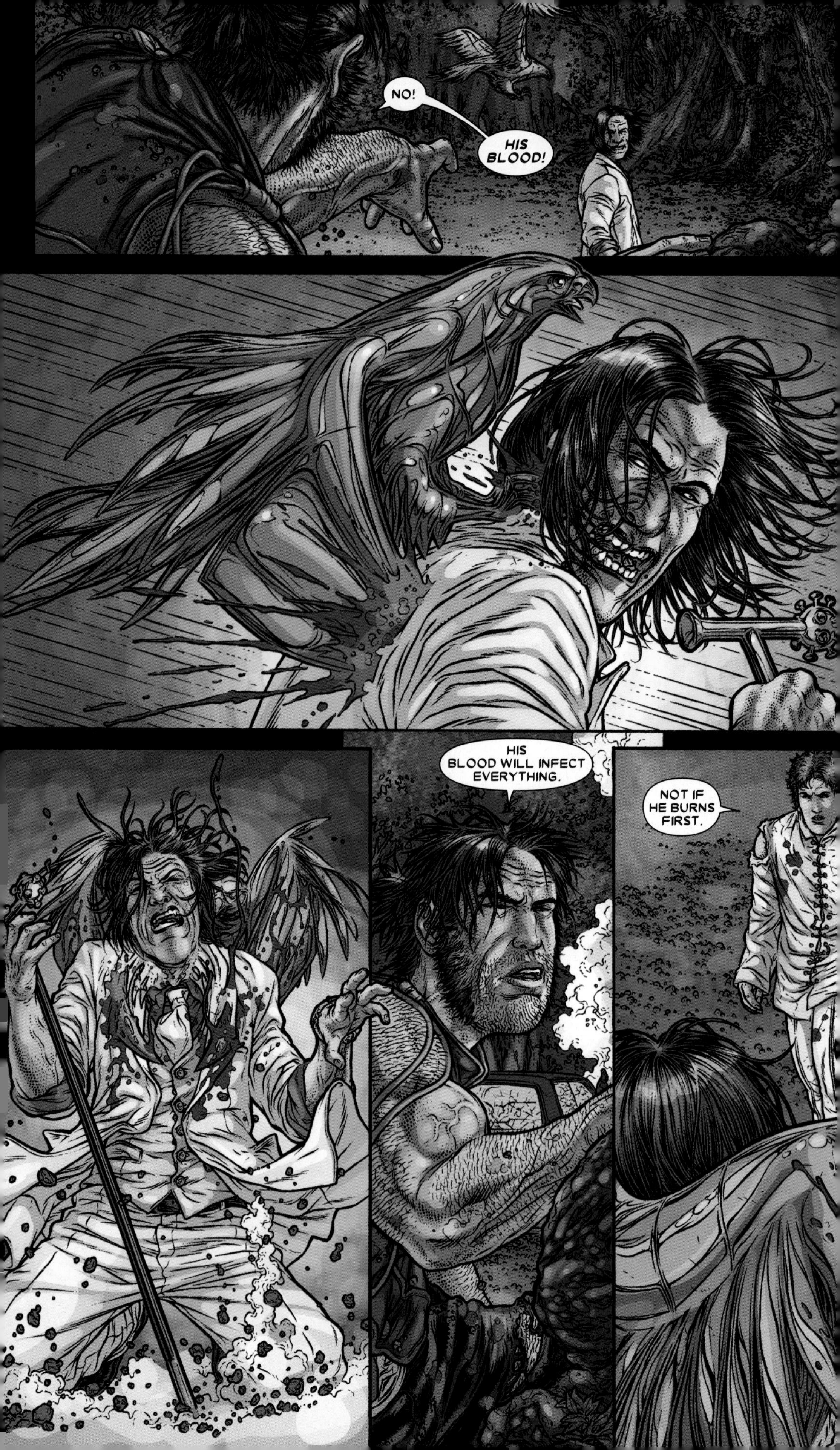
NO!
HIS BLOOD!
HIS BLOOD WILL INFECT EVERYTHING.
NOT IF HE BURNS FIRST.

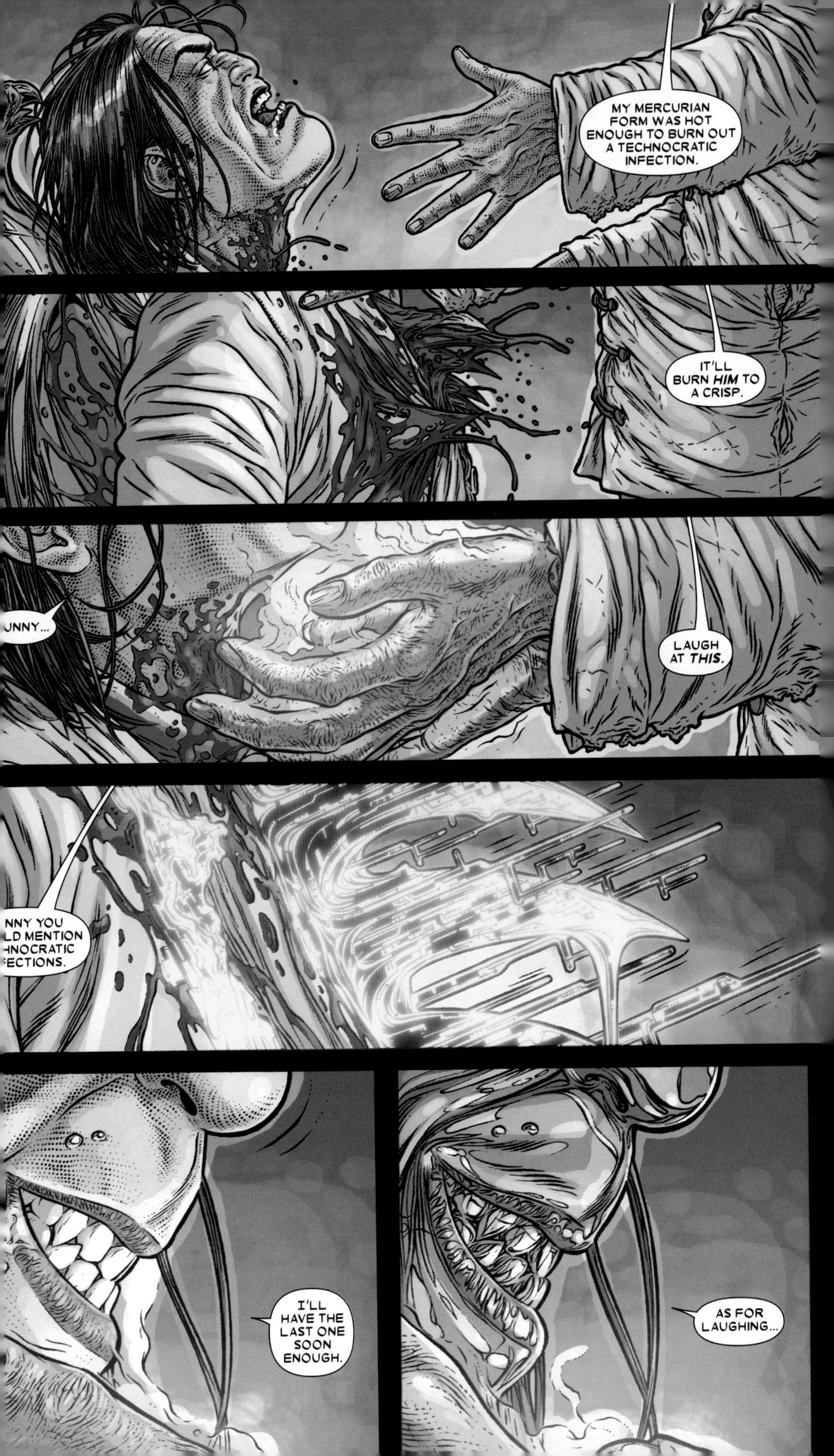
MY MERCURIAN FORM WAS HOT ENOUGH TO BURN OUT A TECHNOCRATIC INFECTION.
IT'LL BURN HIM TO A CRISP.
UNNY...
LAUGH AT THIS.
NNY YOU LD MENTION HNOCRATIC ECTIONS.
I'LL HAVE THE LAST ONE SOON ENOUGH.
AS FOR LAUGHING...

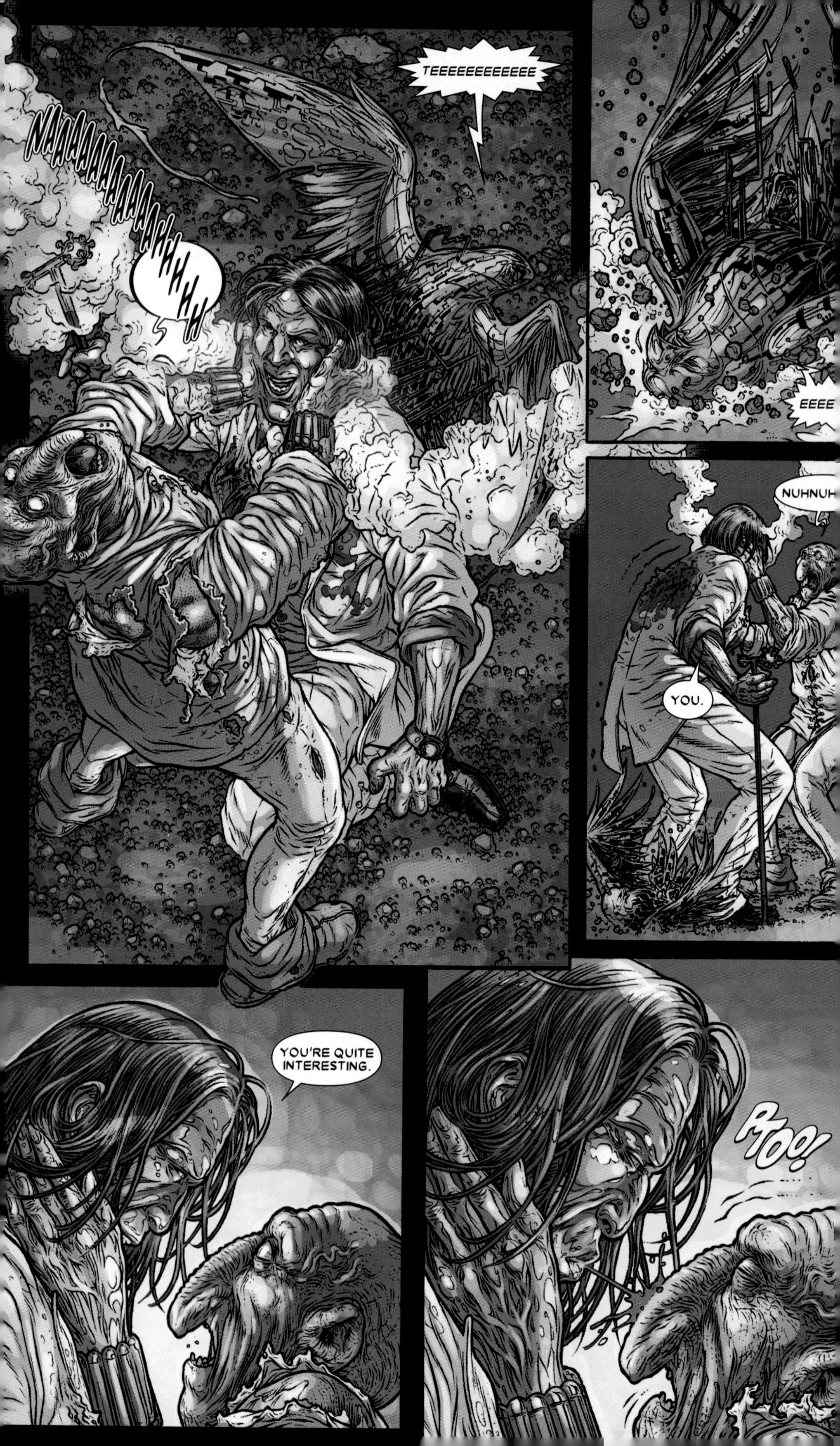
NAAAAAAAAAAAAAAAAAAAAAAAAAAAAAAAAAAAAAAAACKKKKKKH
TEEEEEEEEEEEE
EEEE
NUHNUH
YOU.
YOU'RE QUITE INTERESTING.
PTOO!

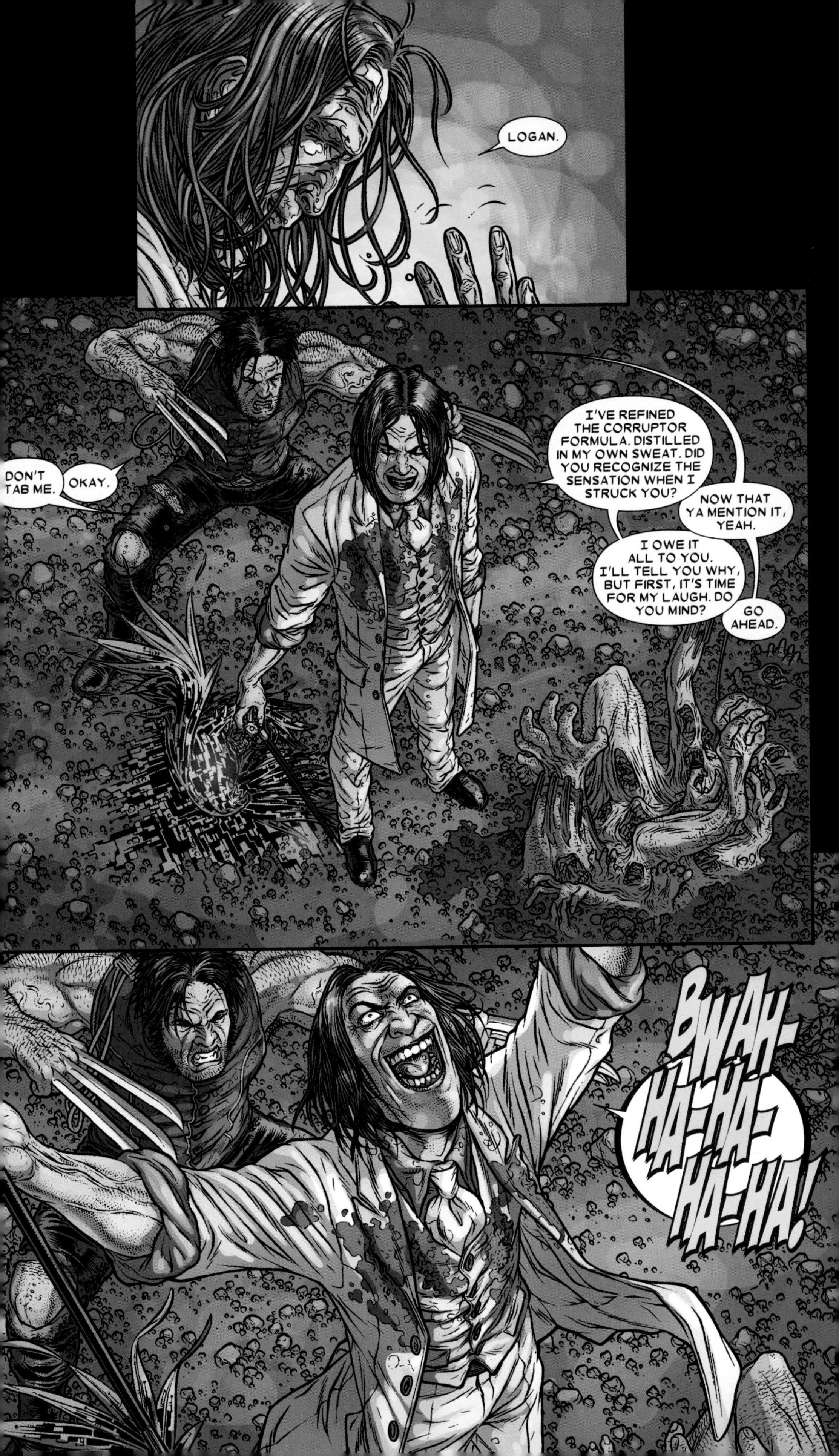
LOGAN.
DON'T TAB ME.
OKAY.
I'VE REFINED THE CORRUPTOR FORMULA. DISTILLED IN MY OWN SWEAT. DID YOU RECOGNIZE THE SENSATION WHEN I STRUCK YOU?
NOW THAT YA MENTION IT, YEAH.
I OWE IT ALL TO YOU. I'LL TELL YOU WHY, BUT FIRST, IT'S TIME FOR MY LAUGH. DO YOU MIND?
GO AHEAD.
BWAH-HA-HA-HA-HA-HA!

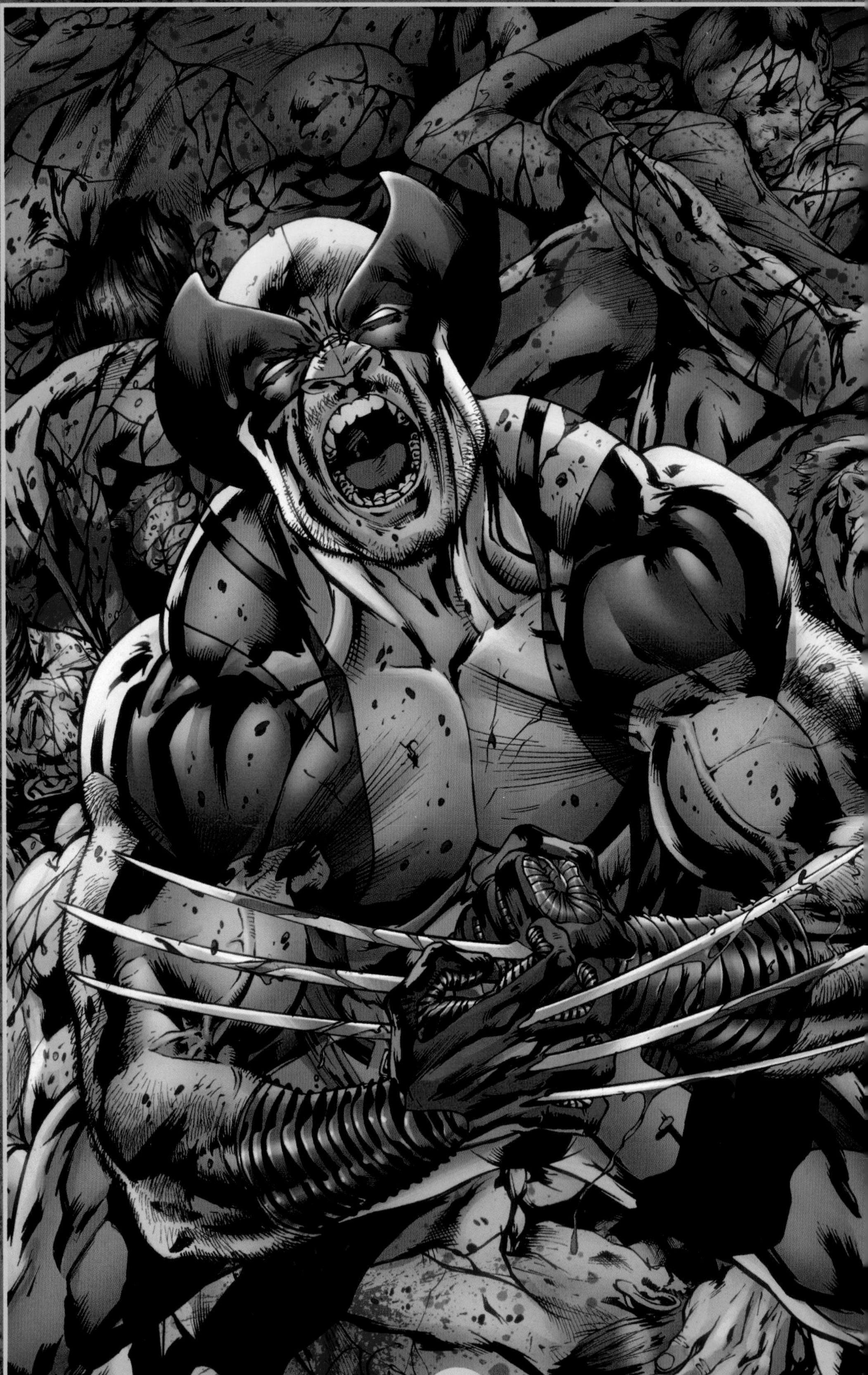
11

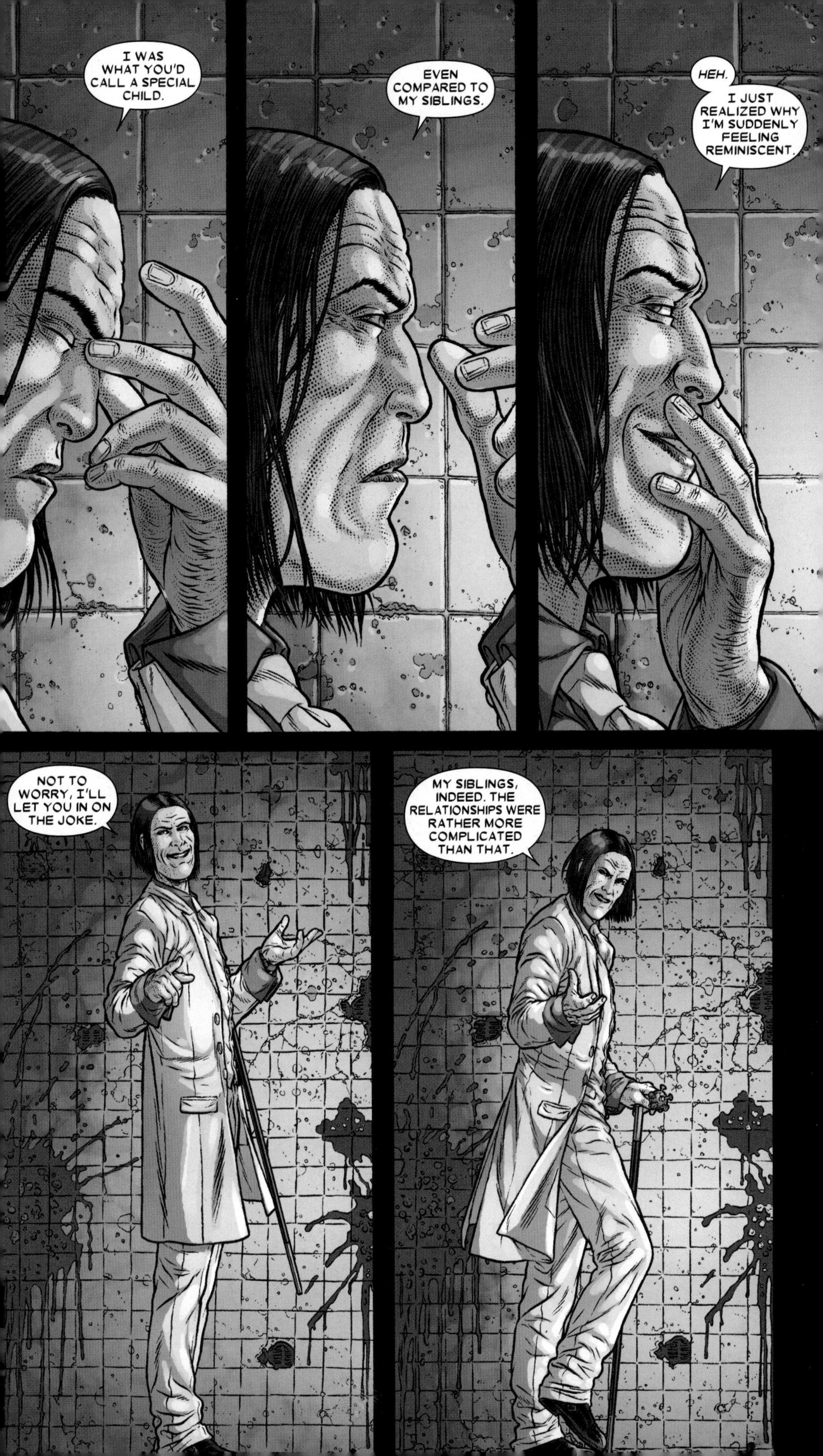
I WAS WHAT YOU'D CALL A SPECIAL CHILD.
EVEN COMPARED TO MY SIBLINGS.
HEH.
I JUST REALIZED WHY I'M SUDDENLY FEELING REMINISCENT.
NOT TO WORRY, I'LL LET YOU IN ON THE JOKE.
MY SIBLINGS, INDEED. THE RELATIONSHIPS WERE RATHER MORE COMPLICATED THAN THAT.

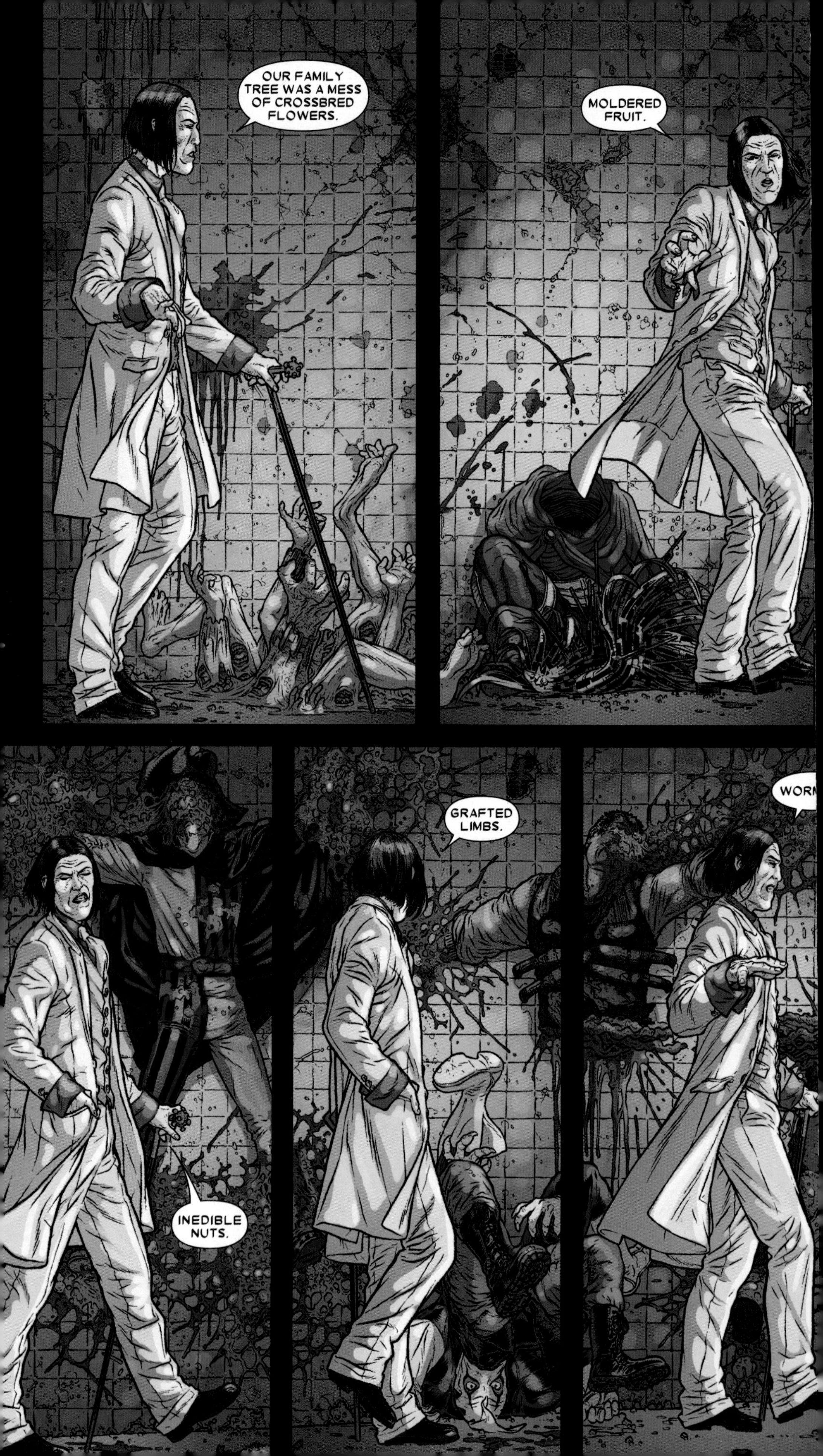
OUR FAMILY TREE WAS A MESS OF CROSSBRED FLOWERS.
MOLDERED FRUIT.
INEDIBLE NUTS.
GRAFTED LIMBS.
WORM

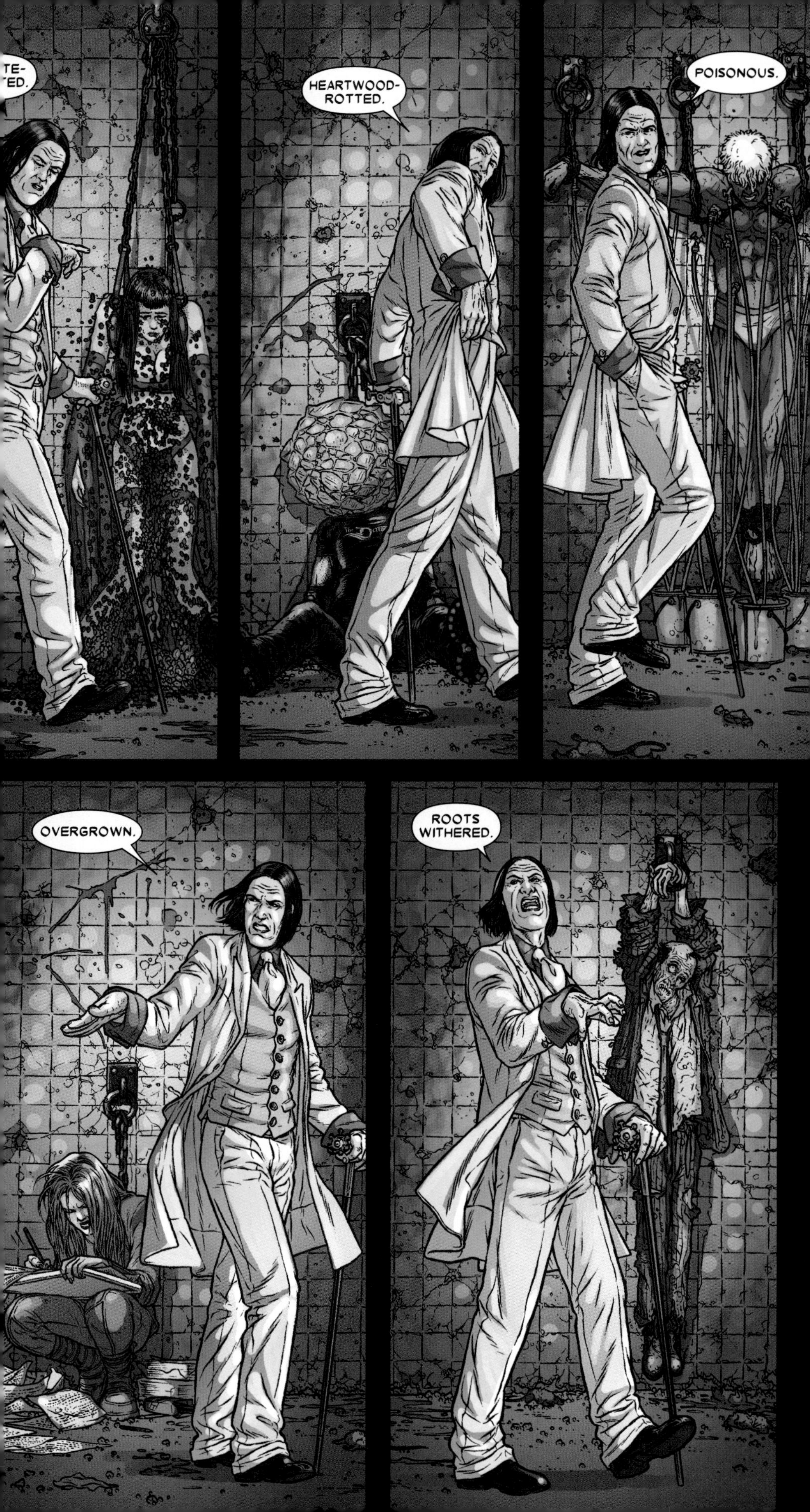
TE- TED.
HEARTWOOD-ROTTED.
POISONOUS.
OVERGROWN.
ROOTS WITHERED.

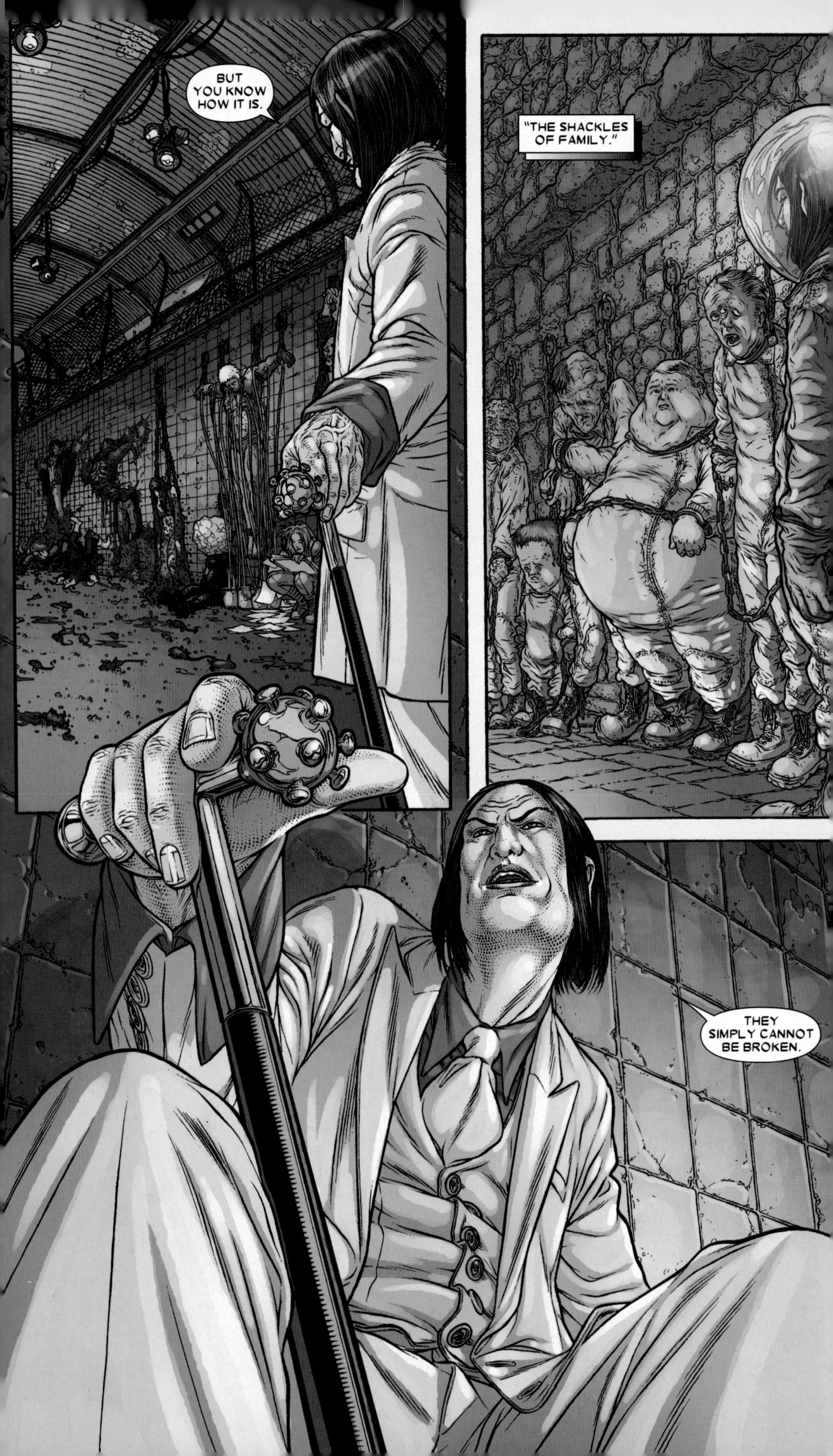
BUT YOU KNOW HOW IT IS.
"THE SHACKLES OF FAMILY."
THEY SIMPLY CANNOT BE BROKEN.

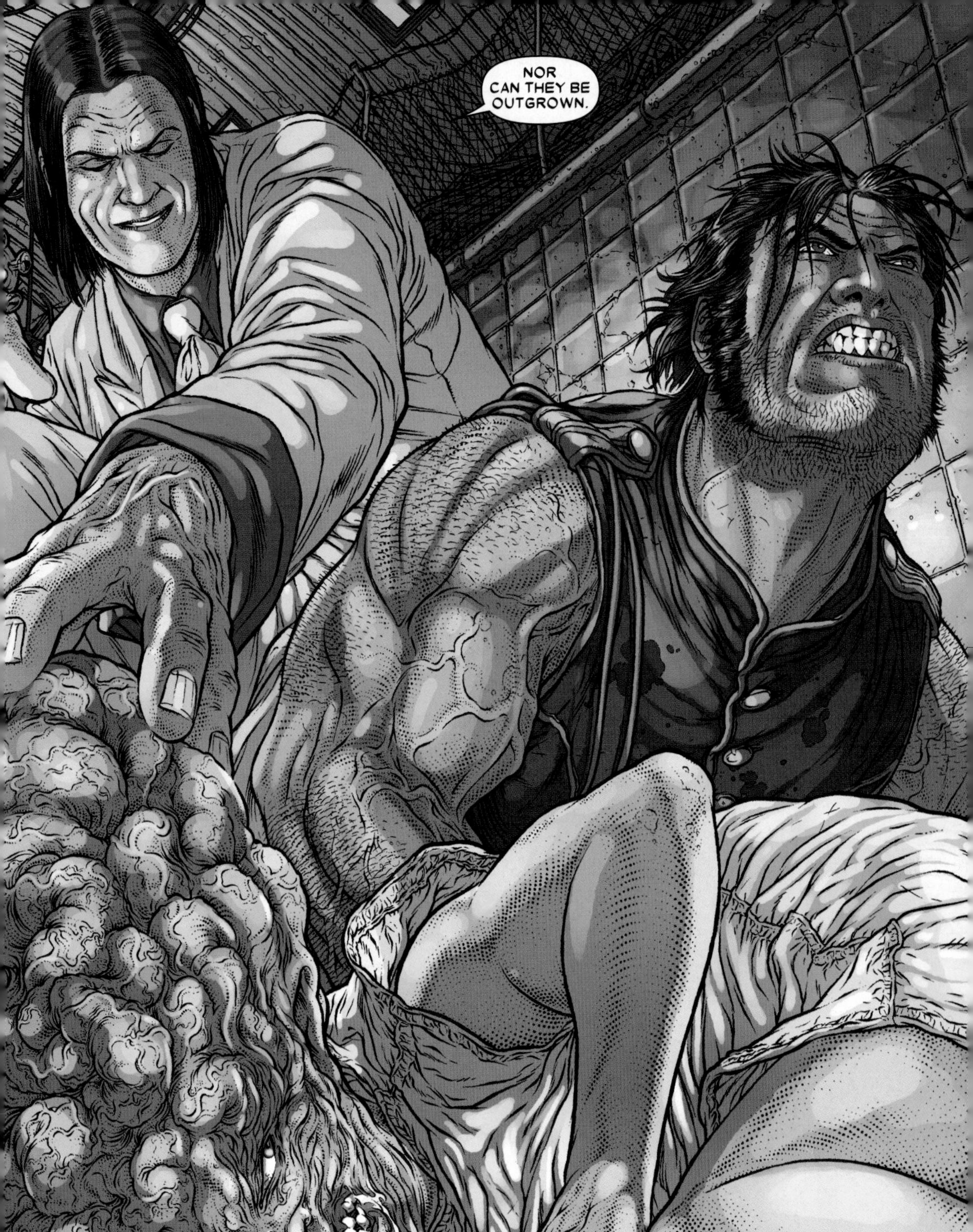
NOR CAN THEY BE OUTGROWN.

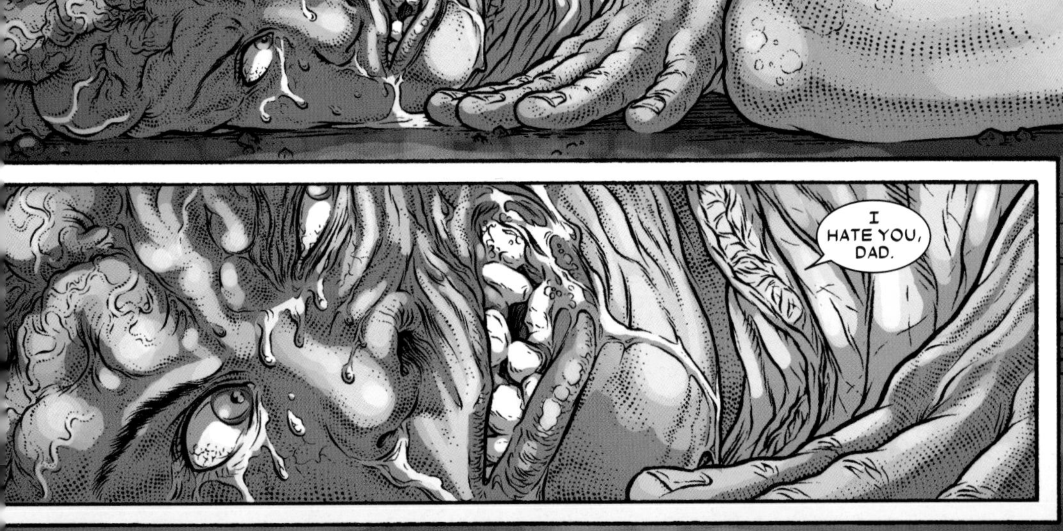
I HATE YOU, DAD.

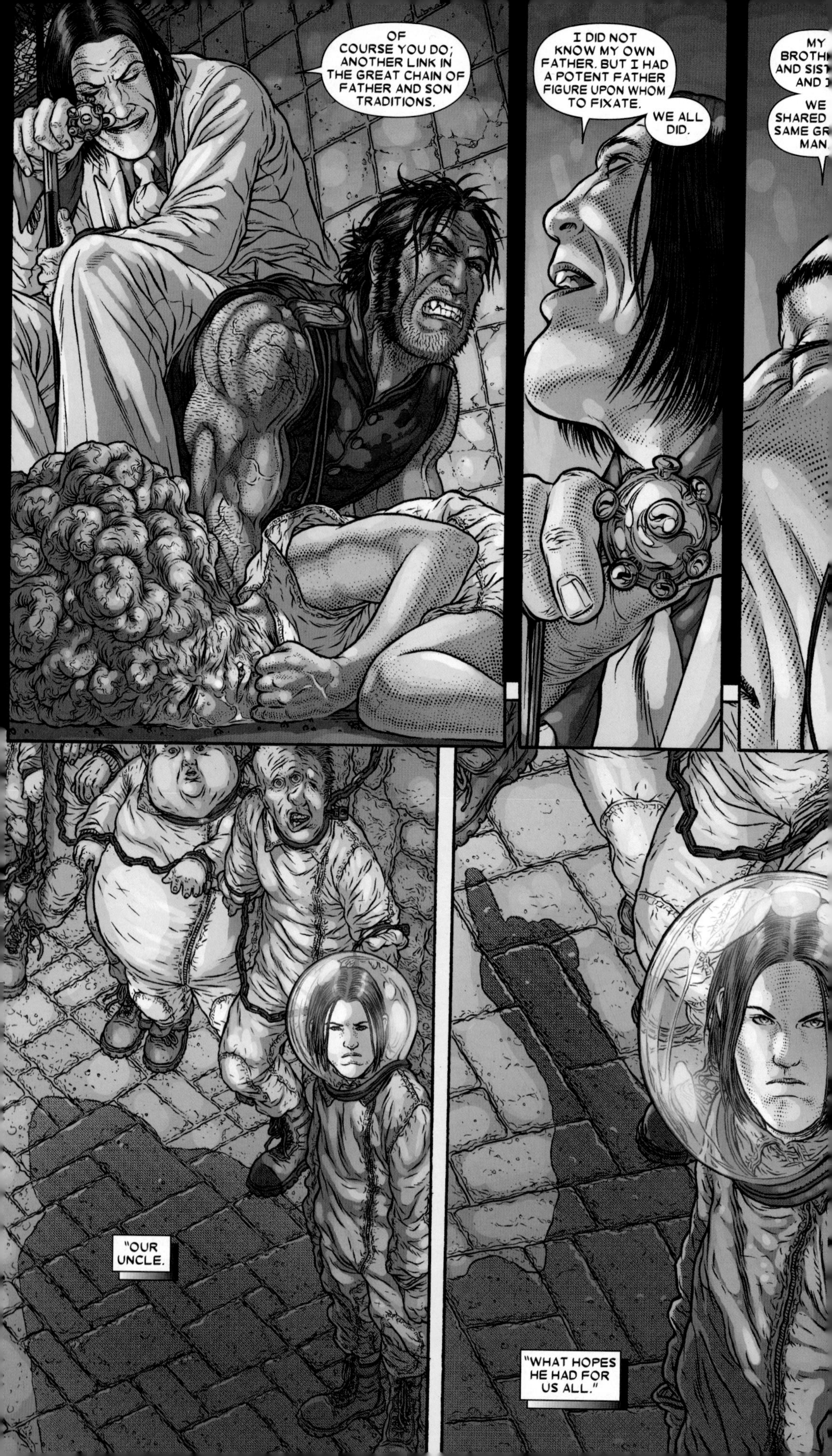
OF COURSE YOU DO; ANOTHER LINK IN THE GREAT CHAIN OF FATHER AND SON TRADITIONS.
I DID NOT KNOW MY OWN FATHER. BUT I HAD A POTENT FATHER FIGURE UPON WHOM TO FIXATE.
WE ALL DID.
MY BROTH AND SIST AND I
WE SHARED SAME GR MAN
"OUR UNCLE.
"WHAT HOPES HE HAD FOR US ALL."

"HOPES
HAT HIGH--

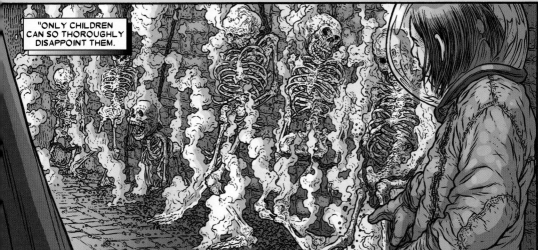

"ONLY CHILDREN CAN SO THOROUGHLY DISAPPOINT THEM.

"AH, THE TINY TRAUMAS OF CHILDHOOD.

E LESSONS
EY TEACH.

"HOW THEY LINGER."

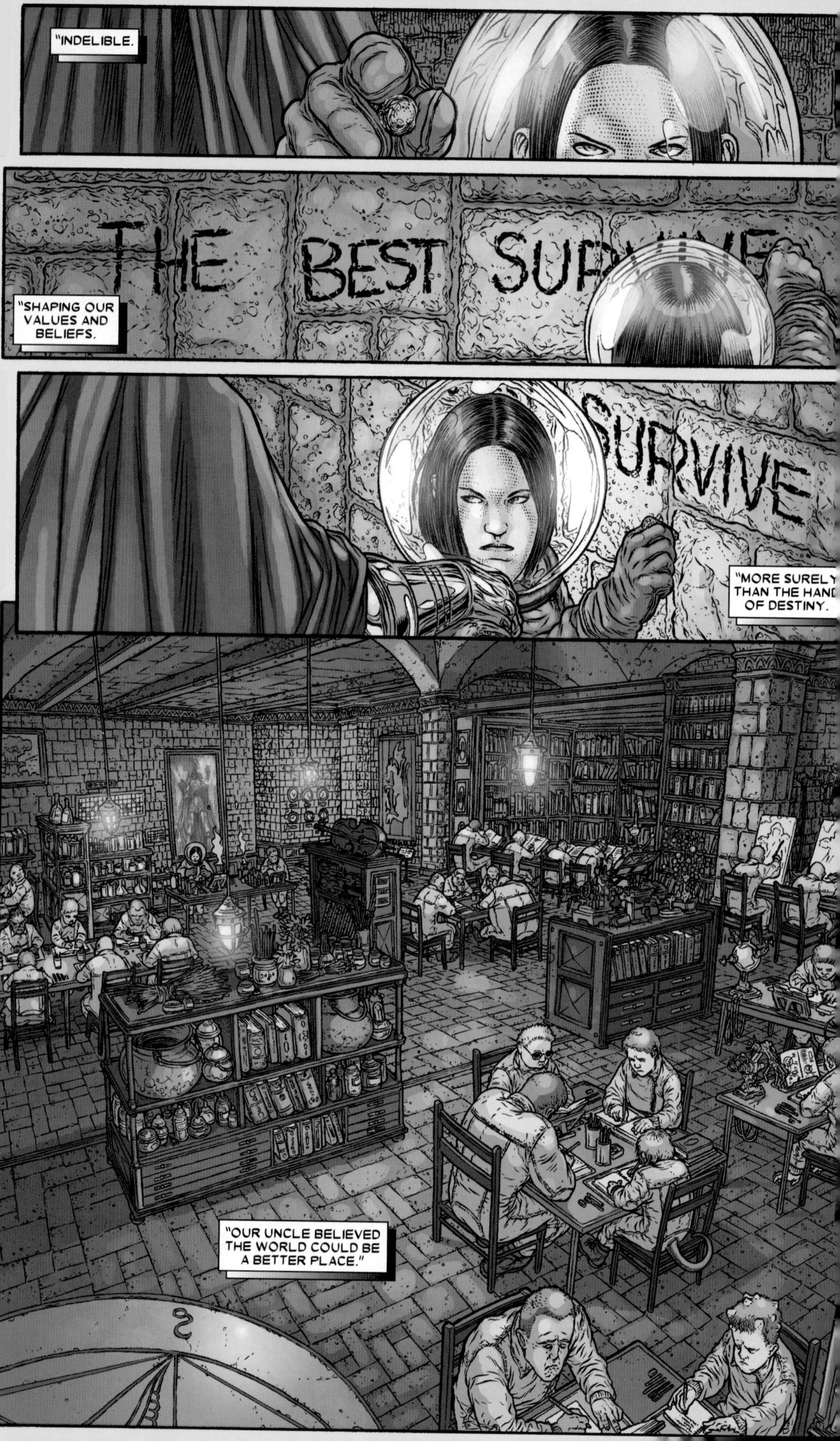
"INDELIBLE.
THE BEST
"SHAPING OUR VALUES AND BELIEFS.
SURVIVE
"MORE SURELY THAN THE HAND OF DESTINY.
"OUR UNCLE BELIEVED THE WORLD COULD BE A BETTER PLACE."

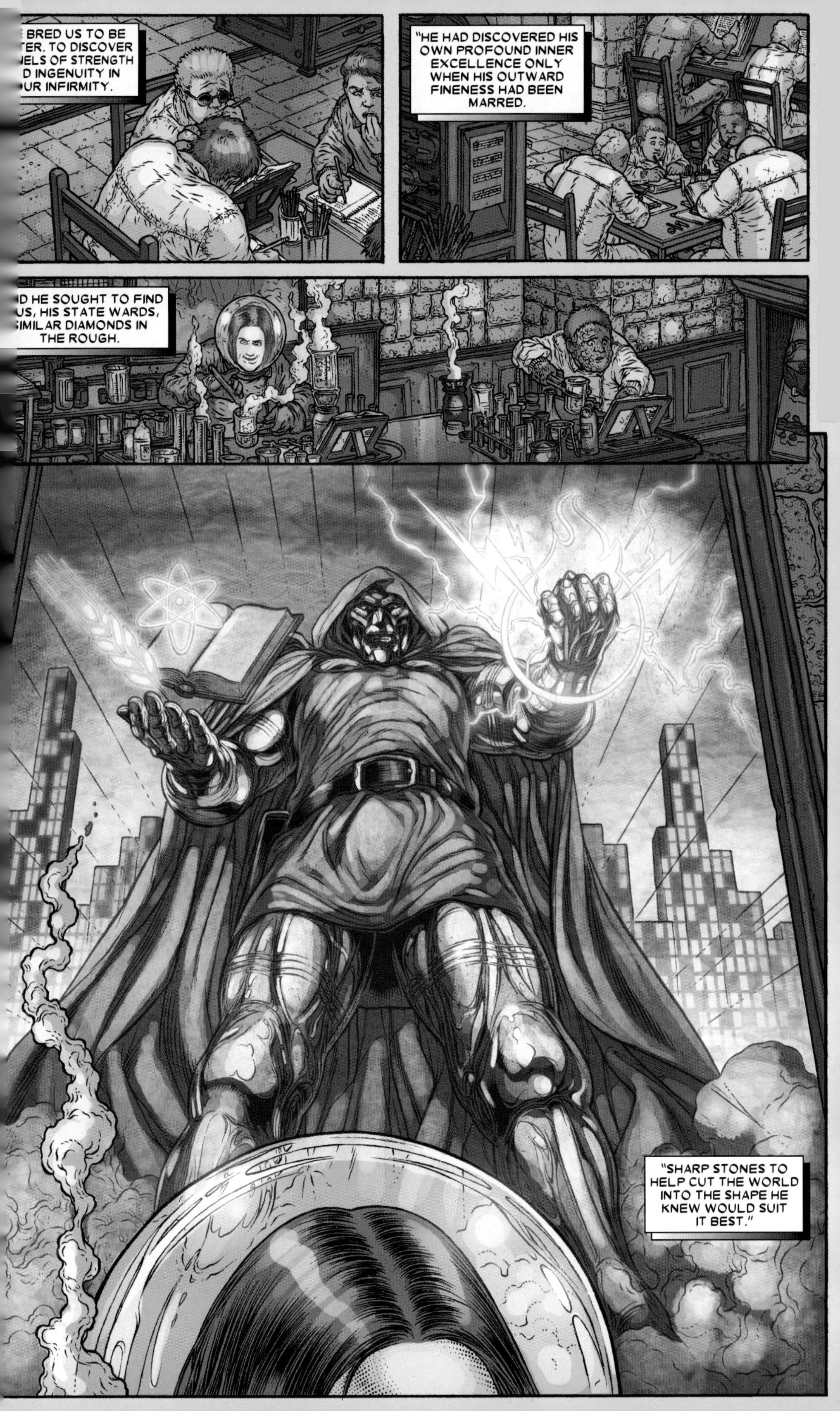
E BRED US TO BE
TER. TO DISCOVER
NELS OF STRENGTH
D INGENUITY IN
UR INFIRMITY.
"HE HAD DISCOVERED HIS OWN PROFOUND INNER EXCELLENCE ONLY WHEN HIS OUTWARD FINENESS HAD BEEN MARRED.
D HE SOUGHT TO FIND
US, HIS STATE WARDS,
SIMILAR DIAMONDS IN
THE ROUGH.
"SHARP STONES TO HELP CUT THE WORLD INTO THE SHAPE HE KNEW WOULD SUIT IT BEST."

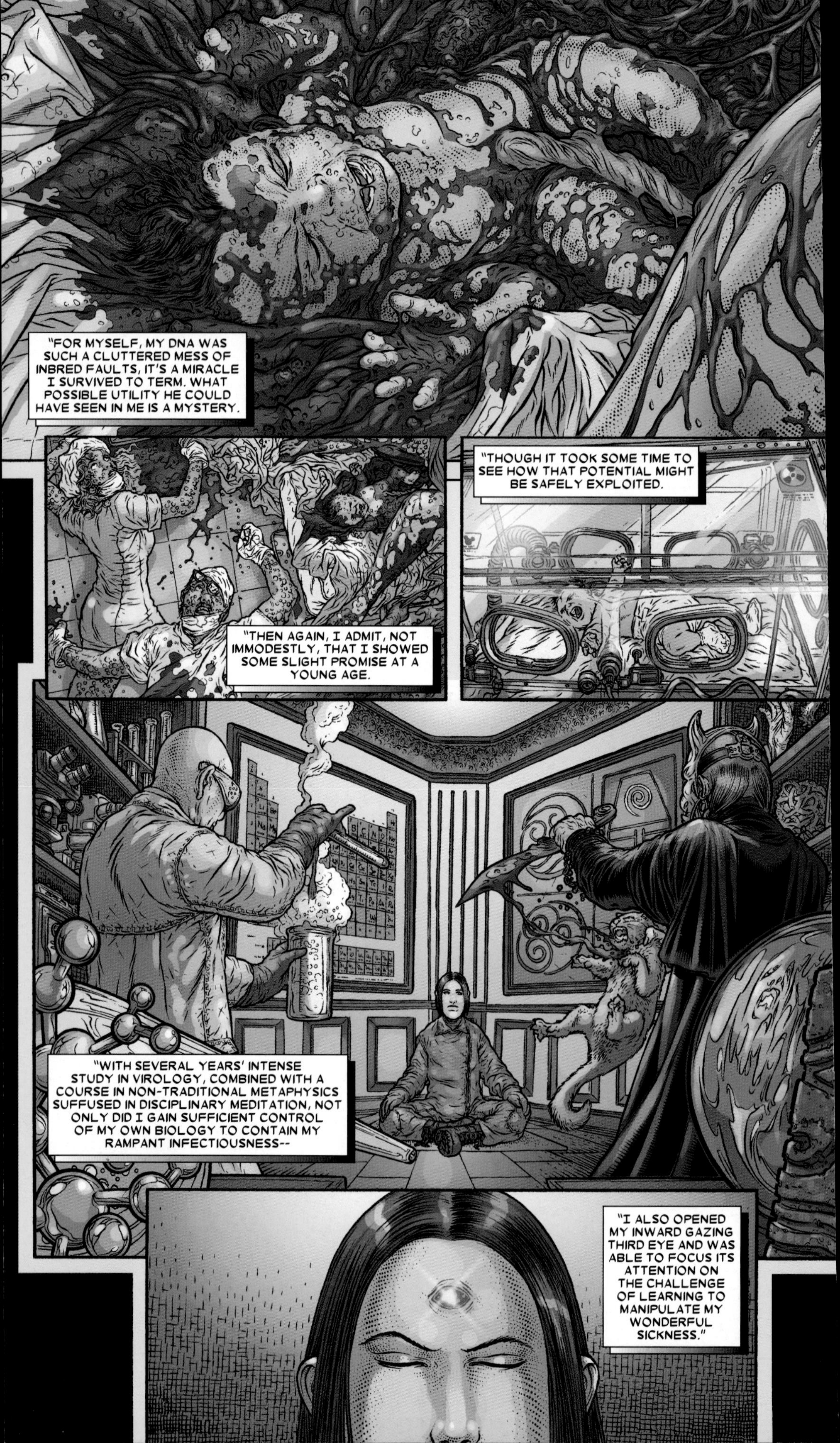
"FOR MYSELF, MY DNA WAS SUCH A CLUTTERED MESS OF INBRED FAULTS, IT'S A MIRACLE I SURVIVED TO TERM. WHAT POSSIBLE UTILITY HE COULD HAVE SEEN IN ME IS A MYSTERY.
"THEN AGAIN, I ADMIT, NOT IMMODESTLY, THAT I SHOWED SOME SLIGHT PROMISE AT A YOUNG AGE.
"THOUGH IT TOOK SOME TIME TO SEE HOW THAT POTENTIAL MIGHT BE SAFELY EXPLOITED.
"WITH SEVERAL YEARS' INTENSE STUDY IN VIROLOGY, COMBINED WITH A COURSE IN NON-TRADITIONAL METAPHYSICS SUFFUSED IN DISCIPLINARY MEDITATION, NOT ONLY DID I GAIN SUFFICIENT CONTROL OF MY OWN BIOLOGY TO CONTAIN MY RAMPANT INFECTIOUSNESS--
"I ALSO OPENED MY INWARD GAZING THIRD EYE AND WAS ABLE TO FOCUS ITS ATTENTION ON THE CHALLENGE OF LEARNING TO MANIPULATE MY WONDERFUL SICKNESS."

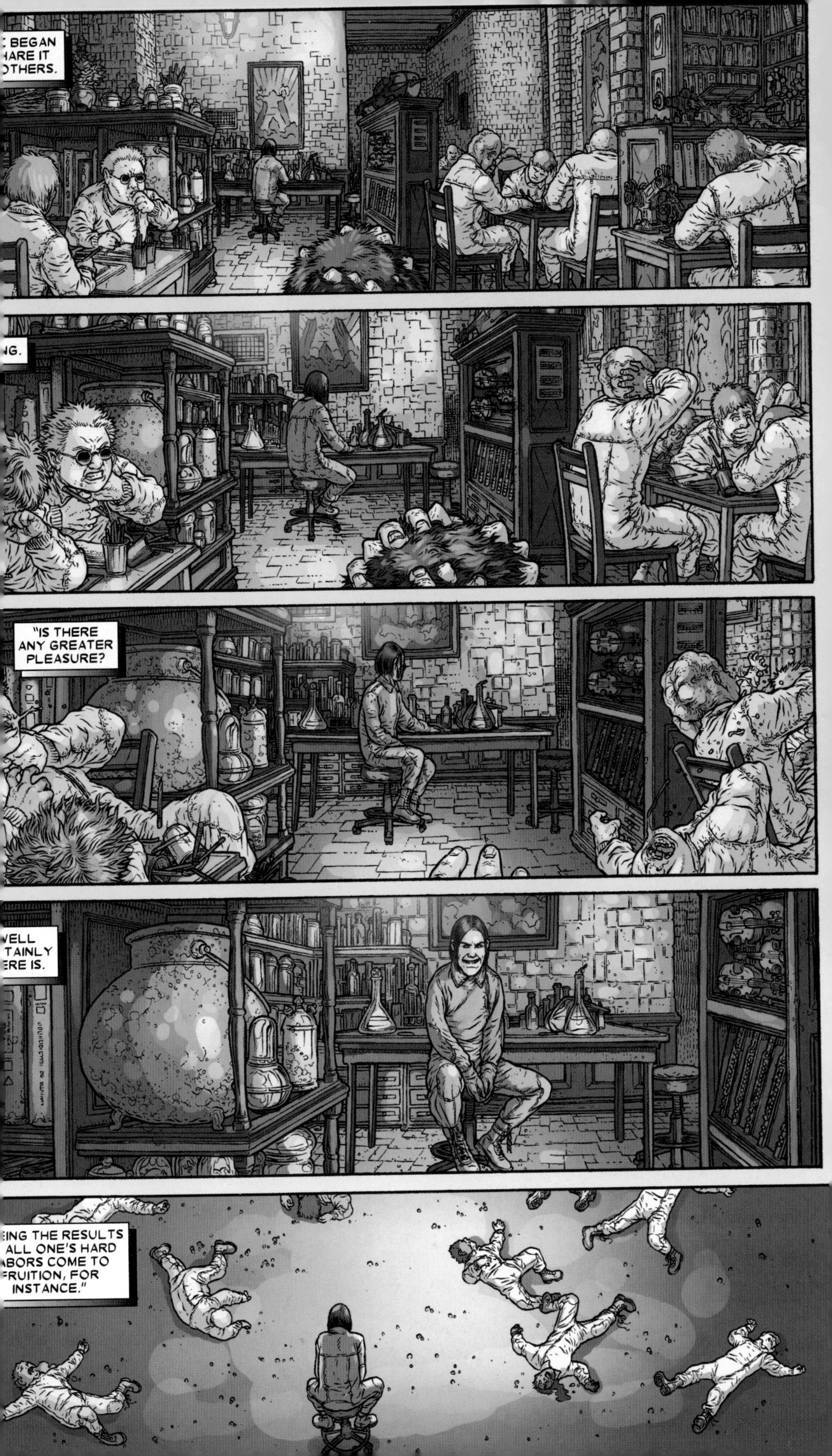

BEGAN
HARE IT
OTHERS.
NG.
"IS THERE ANY GREATER PLEASURE?
WELL
TAINLY
ERE IS.
EING THE RESULTS
ALL ONE'S HARD
ABORS COME TO
FRUITION, FOR
INSTANCE."

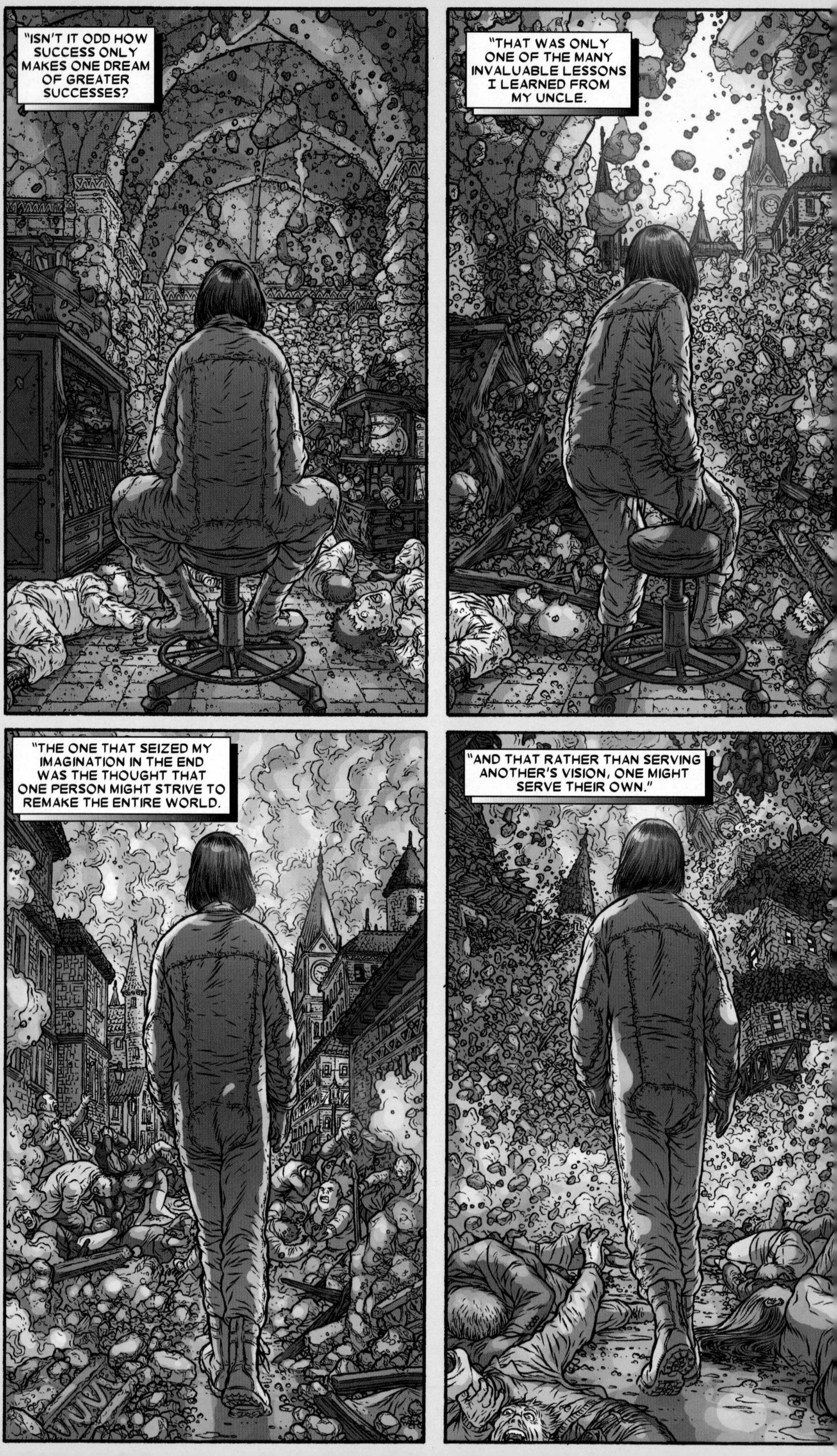
"ISN'T IT ODD HOW SUCCESS ONLY MAKES ONE DREAM OF GREATER SUCCESSES?
"THAT WAS ONLY ONE OF THE MANY INVALUABLE LESSONS I LEARNED FROM MY UNCLE.
"THE ONE THAT SEIZED MY IMAGINATION IN THE END WAS THE THOUGHT THAT ONE PERSON MIGHT STRIVE TO REMAKE THE ENTIRE WORLD.
"AND THAT RATHER THAN SERVING ANOTHER'S VISION, ONE MIGHT SERVE THEIR OWN."

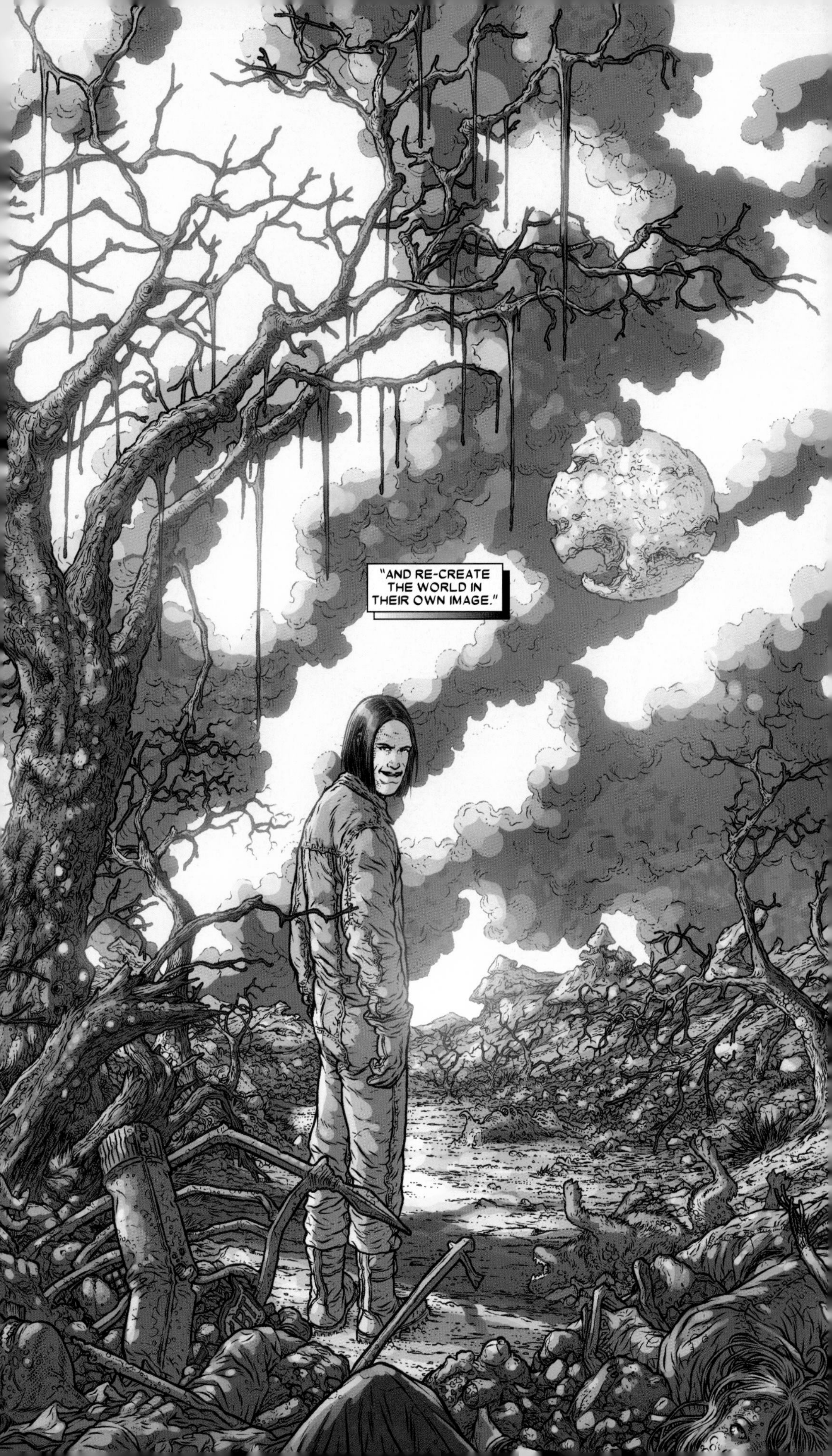
"AND RE-CREATE THE WORLD IN THEIR OWN IMAGE."

INSERT A HORRIBLY DANGEROUS BETRAYAL OF MY UNCLE, A MORE THAN FORTUITOUS DISAPPEARANCE BY SAME, MANY YEARS OF RESEARCH AND PLANNING, AND THAT JUST ABOUT BRINGS US UP TO THE PRESENT.

THINGS WORKING OUT ALMOST EXACTLY AS I ALWAYS PLANNED.

HAVING RECRUITED A TEAM OF EMINENT SELF-HEALERS, I INFECTED EACH WITH A NUMBER OF CUSTOM-DESIGNED VIRUSES.

HARVESTING THE ANTIBODIES EACH DEVELOPED TO FIGHT OFF THE INFECTIONS. THEN REINFECTING THEM WITH MORE ROBUST VERSIONS OF THE ORIGINAL VIRUSES. AND SO ON.

"EACH OF THEM WITH UNIQUE HEALING FACTORS.

"BIOLOGICAL AND CHEMICAL.

"OR SIMPL BIZARRE UNDERST

"SUPERNATURAL AND METAPHYSICAL.

ALLOWING ME TO DISTILL A VIRUS THAT WILL KILL ANYTHING ON EARTH, HEAVEN OR HELL.

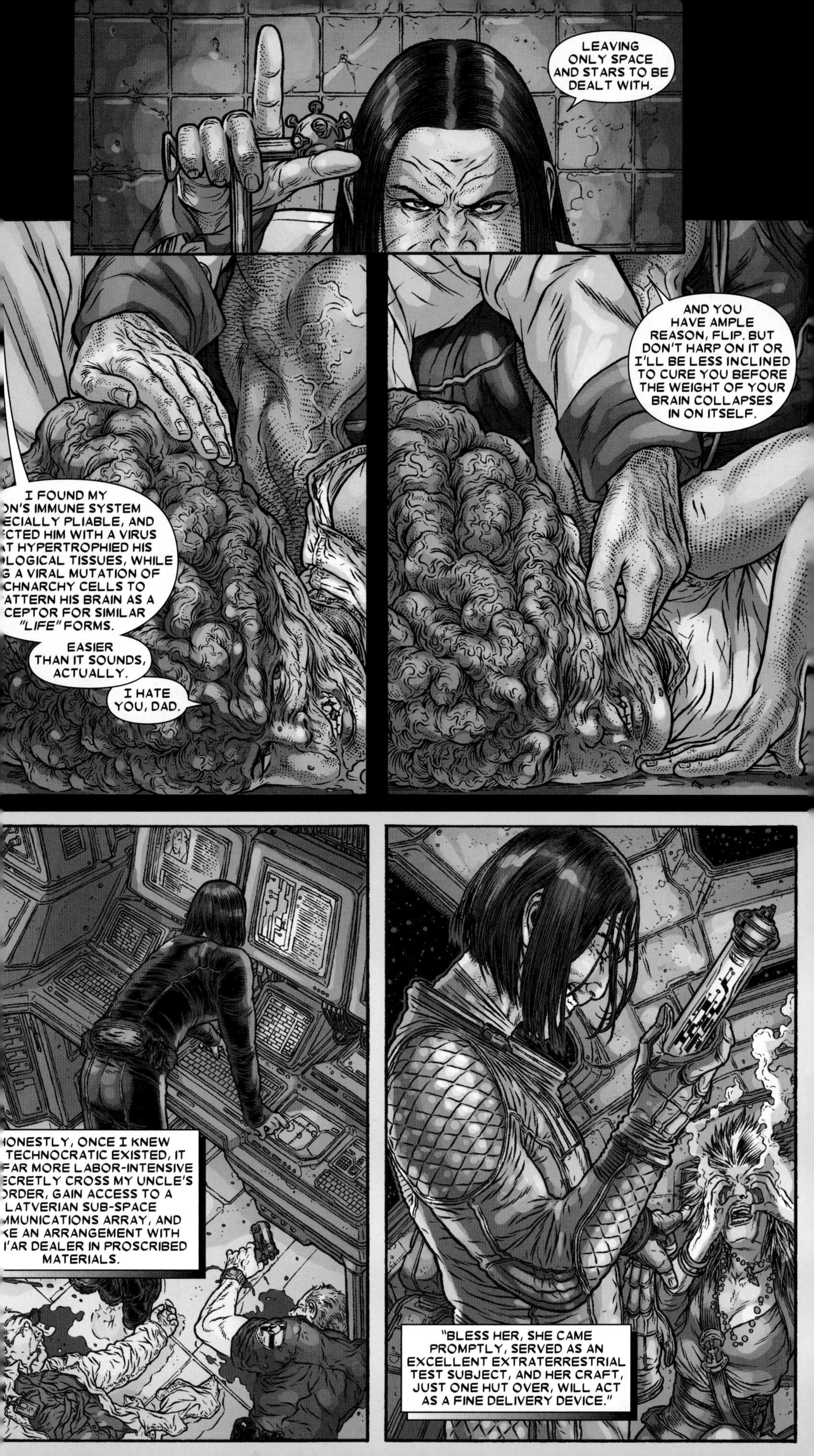
LEAVING ONLY SPACE AND STARS TO BE DEALT WITH.
I FOUND MY ON'S IMMUNE SYSTEM ECIALLY PLIABLE, AND ECTED HIM WITH A VIRUS AT HYPERTROPHIED HIS OLOGICAL TISSUES, WHILE G A VIRAL MUTATION OF CHNARCHY CELLS TO ATTERN HIS BRAIN AS A CEPTOR FOR SIMILAR "LIFE" FORMS.
EASIER THAN IT SOUNDS, ACTUALLY.
I HATE YOU, DAD.
AND YOU HAVE AMPLE REASON, FLIP. BUT DON'T HARP ON IT OR I'LL BE LESS INCLINED TO CURE YOU BEFORE THE WEIGHT OF YOUR BRAIN COLLAPSES IN ON ITSELF.
HONESTLY, ONCE I KNEW TECHNOCRATIC EXISTED, IT FAR MORE LABOR-INTENSIVE ECRETLY CROSS MY UNCLE'S ORDER, GAIN ACCESS TO A LATVERIAN SUB-SPACE MMUNICATIONS ARRAY, AND KE AN ARRANGEMENT WITH I'AR DEALER IN PROSCRIBED MATERIALS.
"BLESS HER, SHE CAME PROMPTLY, SERVED AS AN EXCELLENT EXTRATERRESTRIAL TEST SUBJECT, AND HER CRAFT, JUST ONE HUT OVER, WILL ACT AS A FINE DELIVERY DEVICE."

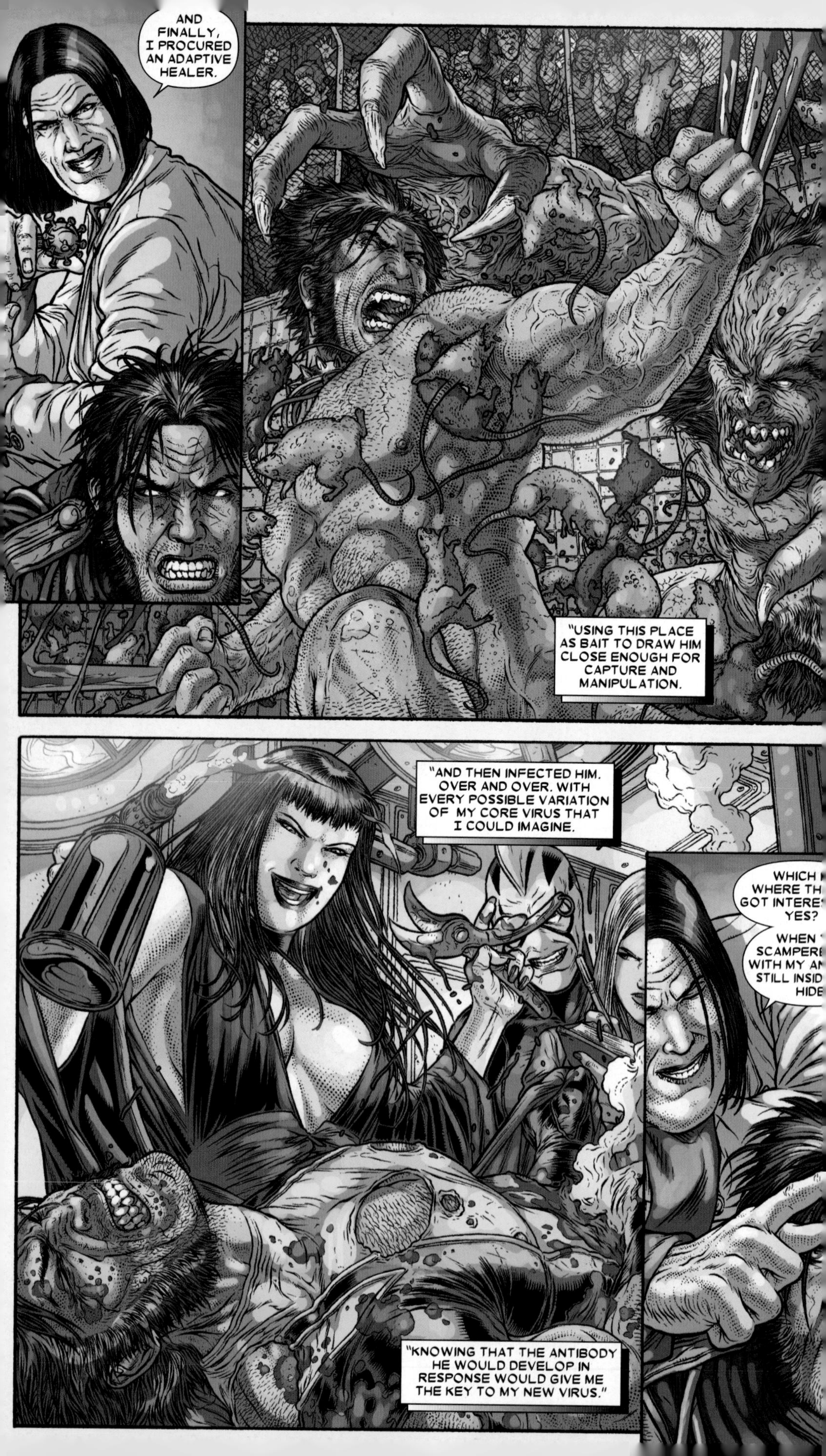

AND FINALLY, I PROCURED AN ADAPTIVE HEALER.
"USING THIS PLACE AS BAIT TO DRAW HIM CLOSE ENOUGH FOR CAPTURE AND MANIPULATION.
"AND THEN INFECTED HIM. OVER AND OVER. WITH EVERY POSSIBLE VARIATION OF MY CORE VIRUS THAT I COULD IMAGINE.
"KNOWING THAT THE ANTIBODY HE WOULD DEVELOP IN RESPONSE WOULD GIVE ME THE KEY TO MY NEW VIRUS."
WHICH WHERE TH GOT INTERES YES?
WHEN SCAMPERE WITH MY A STILL INSID HIDE

"DID YOU KNOW, EVEN AS I BECAME CAPABLE OF INFECTING VIRTUALLY ANYONE, WITH VIRUSES AS COMPLEX AS MY KNOWLEDGE AND SELF-DISCIPLINE WOULD ALLOW ME TO CONSTRUCT, I COULD NOT INFECT MYSELF.

UNTIL YOU [SAI]D THE MAGIC WORDS:

BREW A NEW VIRUS. SOMETHING THAT EATS ALL THE BAD STUFF IN YOUR DNA. HEAL YOURSELF.

"CLEAR ENOUGH A COMMAND.

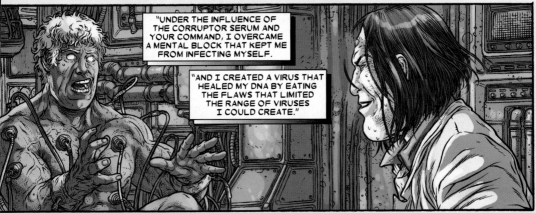

"UNDER THE INFLUENCE OF THE CORRUPTOR SERUM AND YOUR COMMAND, I OVERCAME A MENTAL BLOCK THAT KEPT ME FROM INFECTING MYSELF.

"AND I CREATED A VIRUS THAT HEALED MY DNA BY EATING THE FLAWS THAT LIMITED THE RANGE OF VIRUSES I COULD CREATE."

AFTER WHICH, TAKING MY MINIONS BACK IN HAND WAS SIMPLE ENOUGH.

AS WAS SEEDING DEAR DRIVER REESE WITH AN INFECTION THAT WOULD ONLY FULLY ACTIVATE WITH YOUR DNA IN CLOSE PROXIMITY.

WHICH CONNECTS HER TO ME. AND I ASSUMED YOU'D FOLLOW THE TRAIL TO COME HERE.

AND HERE YOU ARE.

GOOD FOR YOU.

OH, LOOK!

YEP. AND I ALREADY KNOW HOW I'M GONNA KILL YOU AND EVERYTHING.

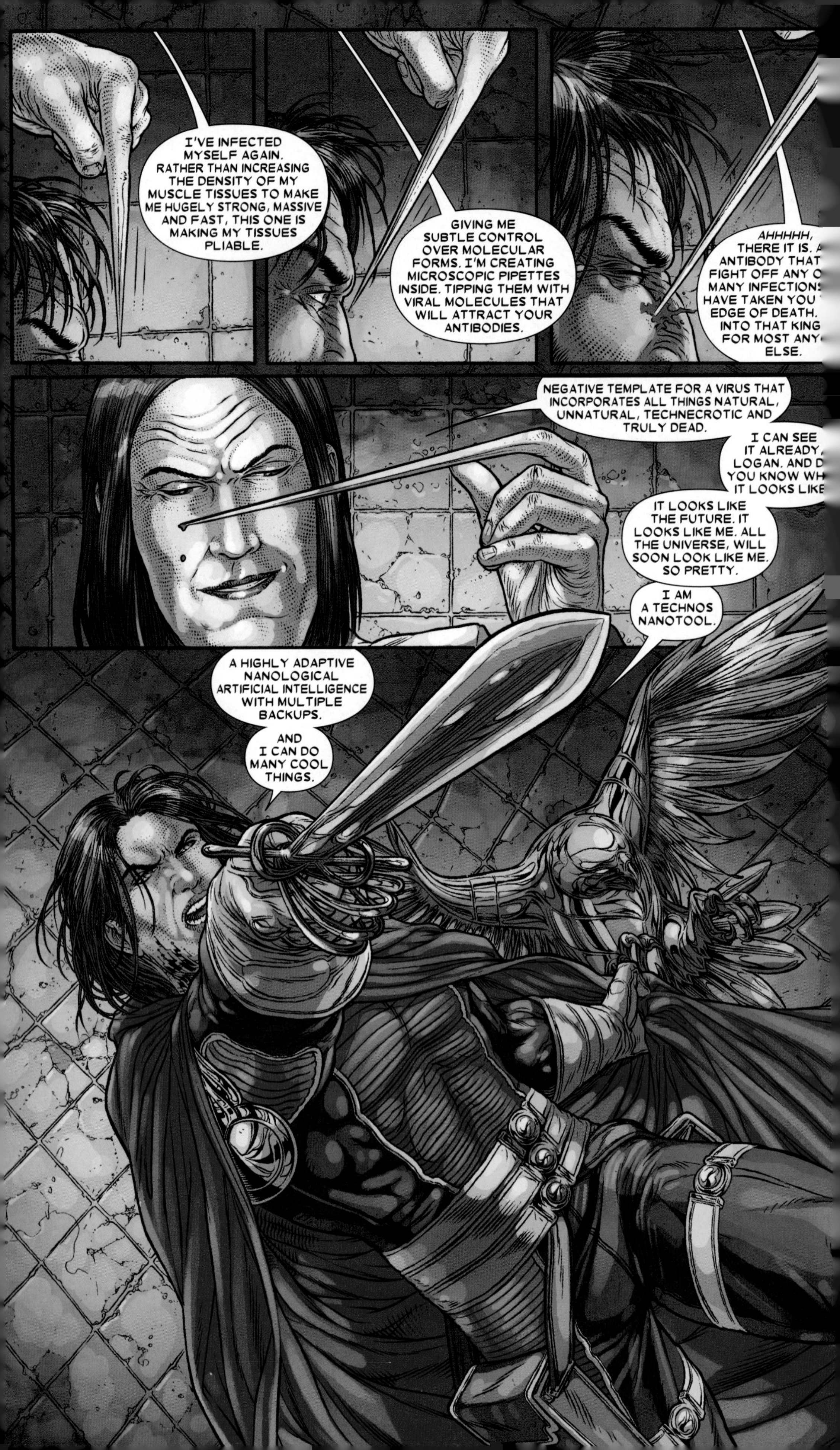
I'VE INFECTED MYSELF AGAIN. RATHER THAN INCREASING THE DENSITY OF MY MUSCLE TISSUES TO MAKE ME HUGELY STRONG, MASSIVE AND FAST, THIS ONE IS MAKING MY TISSUES PLIABLE.
GIVING ME SUBTLE CONTROL OVER MOLECULAR FORMS. I'M CREATING MICROSCOPIC PIPETTES INSIDE. TIPPING THEM WITH VIRAL MOLECULES THAT WILL ATTRACT YOUR ANTIBODIES.
AHHHHH, THERE IT IS. A ANTIBODY THAT FIGHT OFF ANY O MANY INFECTIONS HAVE TAKEN YOU EDGE OF DEATH. INTO THAT KING FOR MOST ANY ELSE.
NEGATIVE TEMPLATE FOR A VIRUS THAT INCORPORATES ALL THINGS NATURAL, UNNATURAL, TECHNECROTIC AND TRULY DEAD.
I CAN SEE IT ALREADY, LOGAN. AND D YOU KNOW WH IT LOOKS LIKE
IT LOOKS LIKE THE FUTURE. IT LOOKS LIKE ME. ALL THE UNIVERSE, WILL SOON LOOK LIKE ME. SO PRETTY.
I AM A TECHNOS NANOTOOL.
A HIGHLY ADAPTIVE NANOLOGICAL ARTIFICIAL INTELLIGENCE WITH MULTIPLE BACKUPS.
AND I CAN DO MANY COOL THINGS.

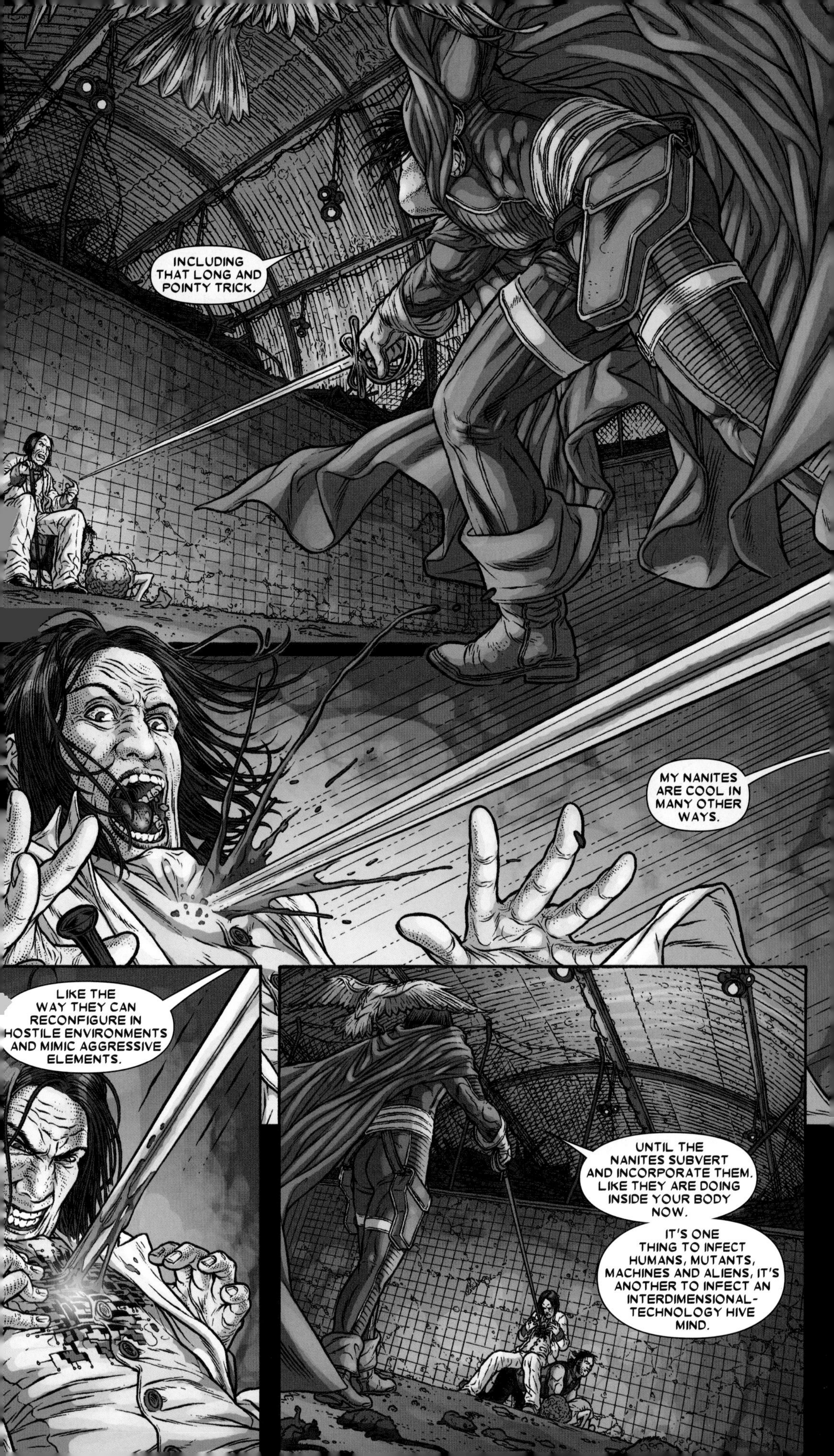
INCLUDING THAT LONG AND POINTY TRICK.
MY NANITES ARE COOL IN MANY OTHER WAYS.
LIKE THE WAY THEY CAN RECONFIGURE IN HOSTILE ENVIRONMENTS AND MIMIC AGGRESSIVE ELEMENTS.
UNTIL THE NANITES SUBVERT AND INCORPORATE THEM. LIKE THEY ARE DOING INSIDE YOUR BODY NOW.
IT'S ONE THING TO INFECT HUMANS, MUTANTS, MACHINES AND ALIENS, IT'S ANOTHER TO INFECT AN INTERDIMENSIONAL-TECHNOLOGY HIVE MIND.

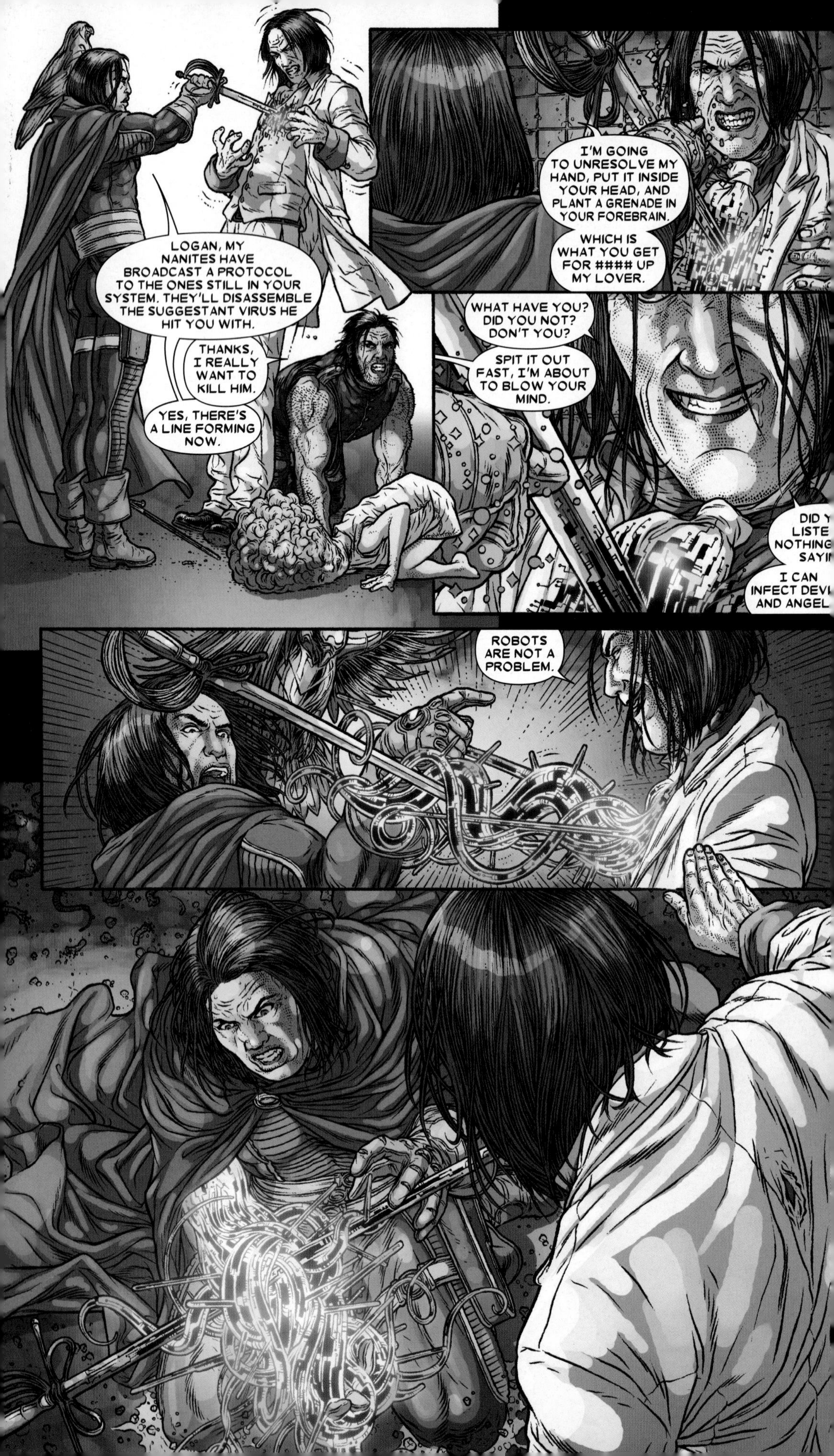
LOGAN, MY NANITES HAVE BROADCAST A PROTOCOL TO THE ONES STILL IN YOUR SYSTEM. THEY'LL DISASSEMBLE THE SUGGESTANT VIRUS HE HIT YOU WITH.
THANKS, I REALLY WANT TO KILL HIM.
YES, THERE'S A LINE FORMING NOW.
I'M GOING TO UNRESOLVE MY HAND, PUT IT INSIDE YOUR HEAD, AND PLANT A GRENADE IN YOUR FOREBRAIN.
WHICH IS WHAT YOU GET FOR #### UP MY LOVER.
WHAT HAVE YOU? DID YOU NOT? DON'T YOU?
SPIT IT OUT FAST, I'M ABOUT TO BLOW YOUR MIND.
ROBOTS ARE NOT A PROBLEM.

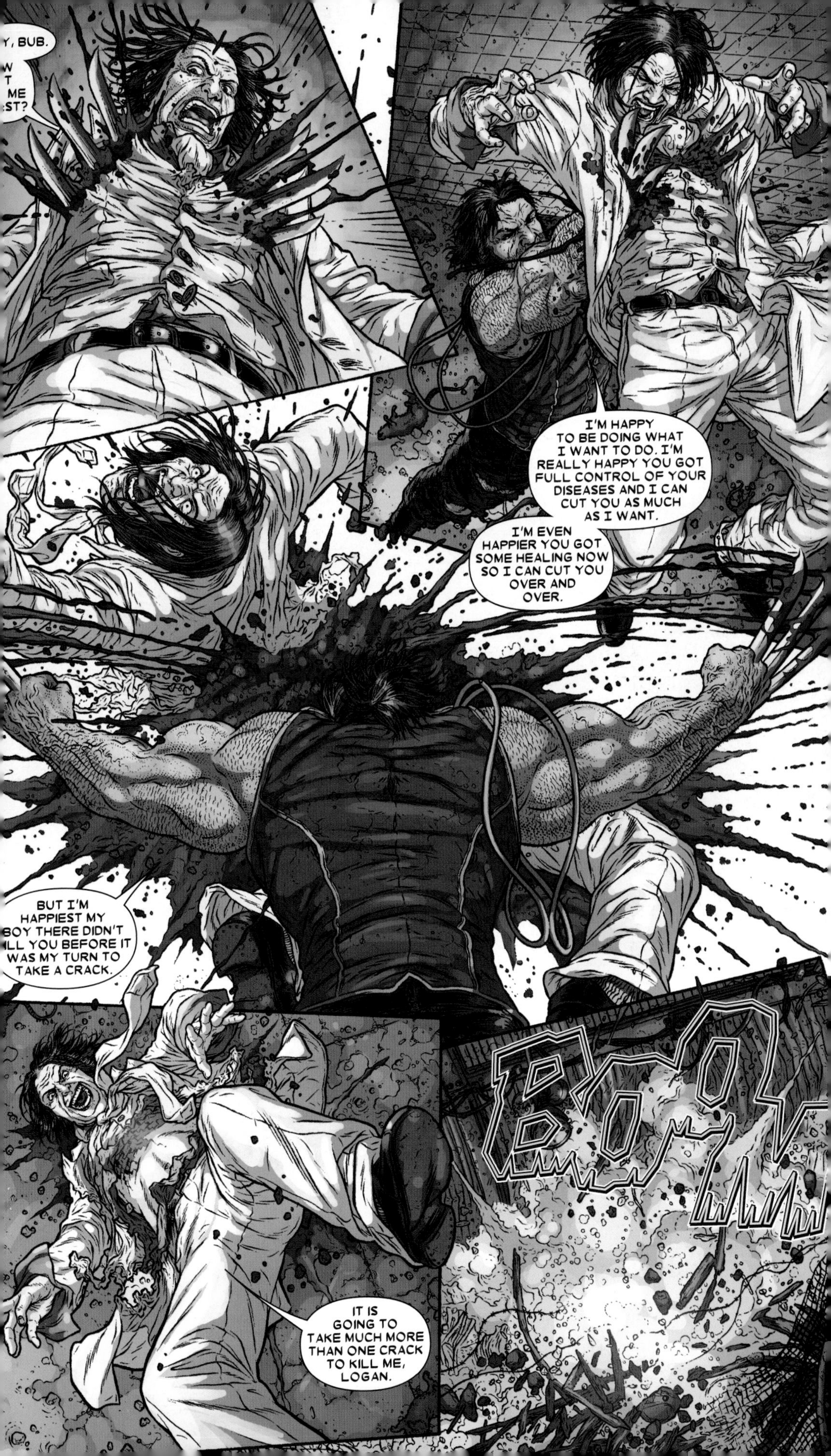

I'M HAPPY TO BE DOING WHAT I WANT TO DO. I'M REALLY HAPPY YOU GOT FULL CONTROL OF YOUR DISEASES AND I CAN CUT YOU AS MUCH AS I WANT.
I'M EVEN HAPPIER YOU GOT SOME HEALING NOW SO I CAN CUT YOU OVER AND OVER.
BUT I'M HAPPIEST MY BOY THERE DIDN'T ILL YOU BEFORE IT WAS MY TURN TO TAKE A CRACK.
IT IS GOING TO TAKE MUCH MORE THAN ONE CRACK TO KILL ME, LOGAN.

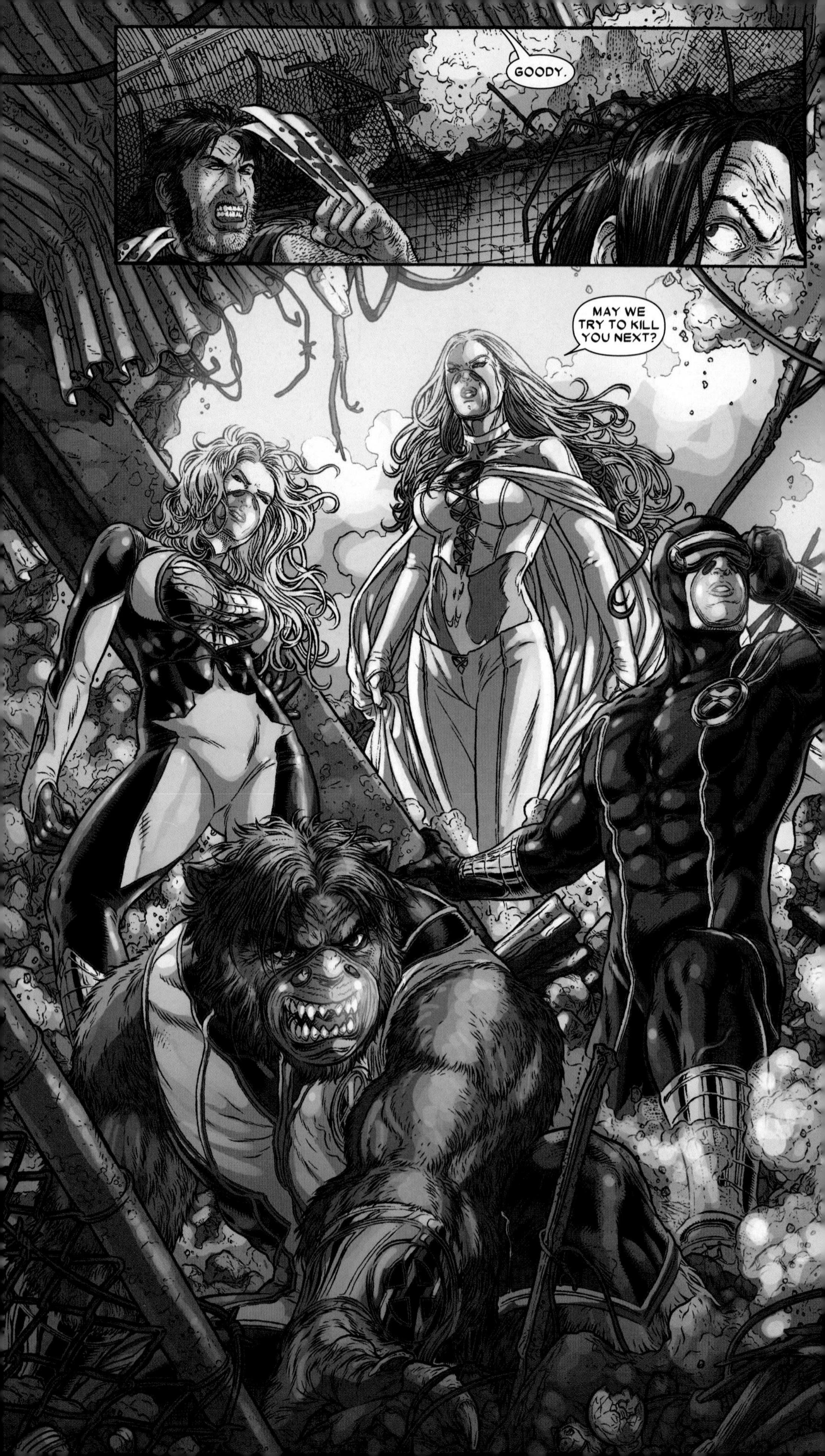
GOODY.
MAY WE TRY TO KILL YOU NEXT?

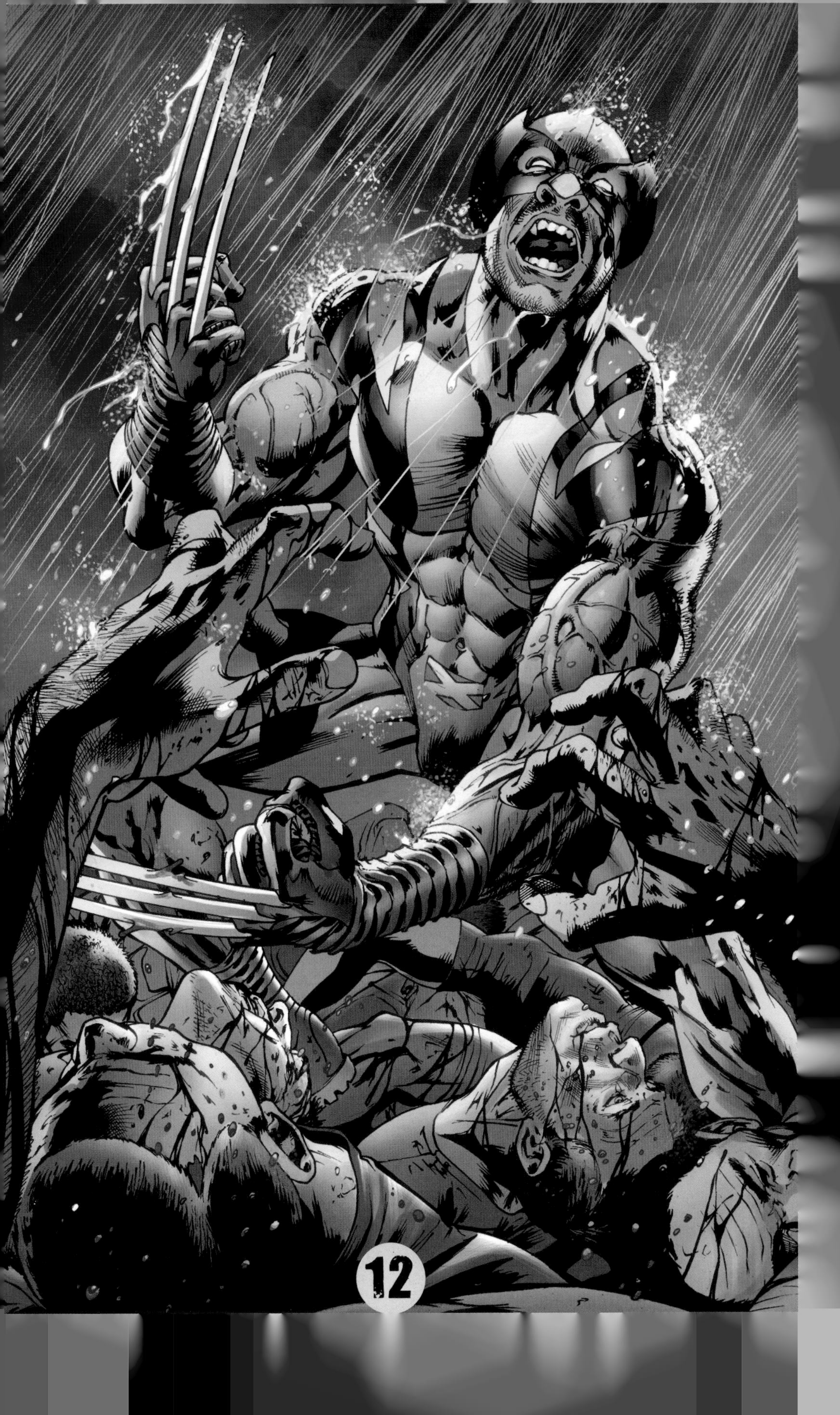

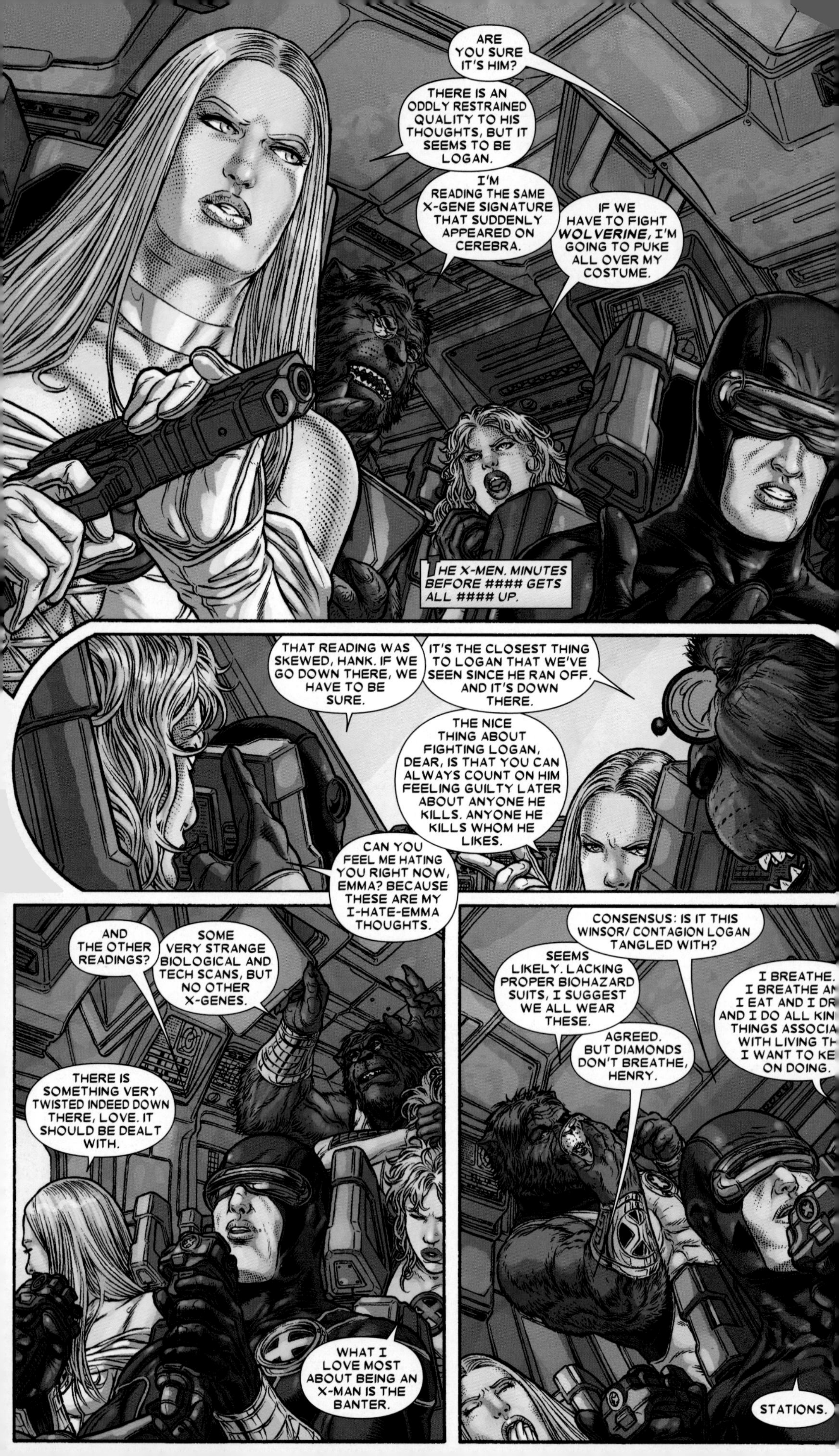

ARE YOU SURE IT'S HIM?
THERE IS AN ODDLY RESTRAINED QUALITY TO HIS THOUGHTS, BUT IT SEEMS TO BE LOGAN.
I'M READING THE SAME X-GENE SIGNATURE THAT SUDDENLY APPEARED ON CEREBRA.
IF WE HAVE TO FIGHT *WOLVERINE*, I'M GOING TO PUKE ALL OVER MY COSTUME.
THE X-MEN. MINUTES BEFORE #### GETS ALL #### UP.
THAT READING WAS SKEWED, HANK. IF WE GO DOWN THERE, WE HAVE TO BE SURE.
IT'S THE CLOSEST THING TO LOGAN THAT WE'VE SEEN SINCE HE RAN OFF. AND IT'S DOWN THERE.
THE NICE THING ABOUT FIGHTING LOGAN, DEAR, IS THAT YOU CAN ALWAYS COUNT ON HIM FEELING GUILTY LATER ABOUT ANYONE HE KILLS. ANYONE HE KILLS WHOM HE LIKES.
CAN YOU FEEL ME HATING YOU RIGHT NOW, EMMA? BECAUSE THESE ARE MY I-HATE-EMMA THOUGHTS.
AND THE OTHER READINGS?
SOME VERY STRANGE BIOLOGICAL AND TECH SCANS, BUT NO OTHER X-GENES.
THERE IS SOMETHING VERY TWISTED INDEED DOWN THERE, LOVE. IT SHOULD BE DEALT WITH.
WHAT I LOVE MOST ABOUT BEING AN X-MAN IS THE BANTER.
CONSENSUS: IS IT THIS WINSOR/ CONTAGION LOGAN TANGLED WITH?
SEEMS LIKELY. LACKING PROPER BIOHAZARD SUITS, I SUGGEST WE ALL WEAR THESE.
AGREED. BUT DIAMONDS DON'T BREATHE, HENRY.
I BREATHE. I BREATHE A I EAT AND I DR AND I DO ALL KIN THINGS ASSOCIA WITH LIVING T I WANT TO KE ON DOING.
STATIONS.

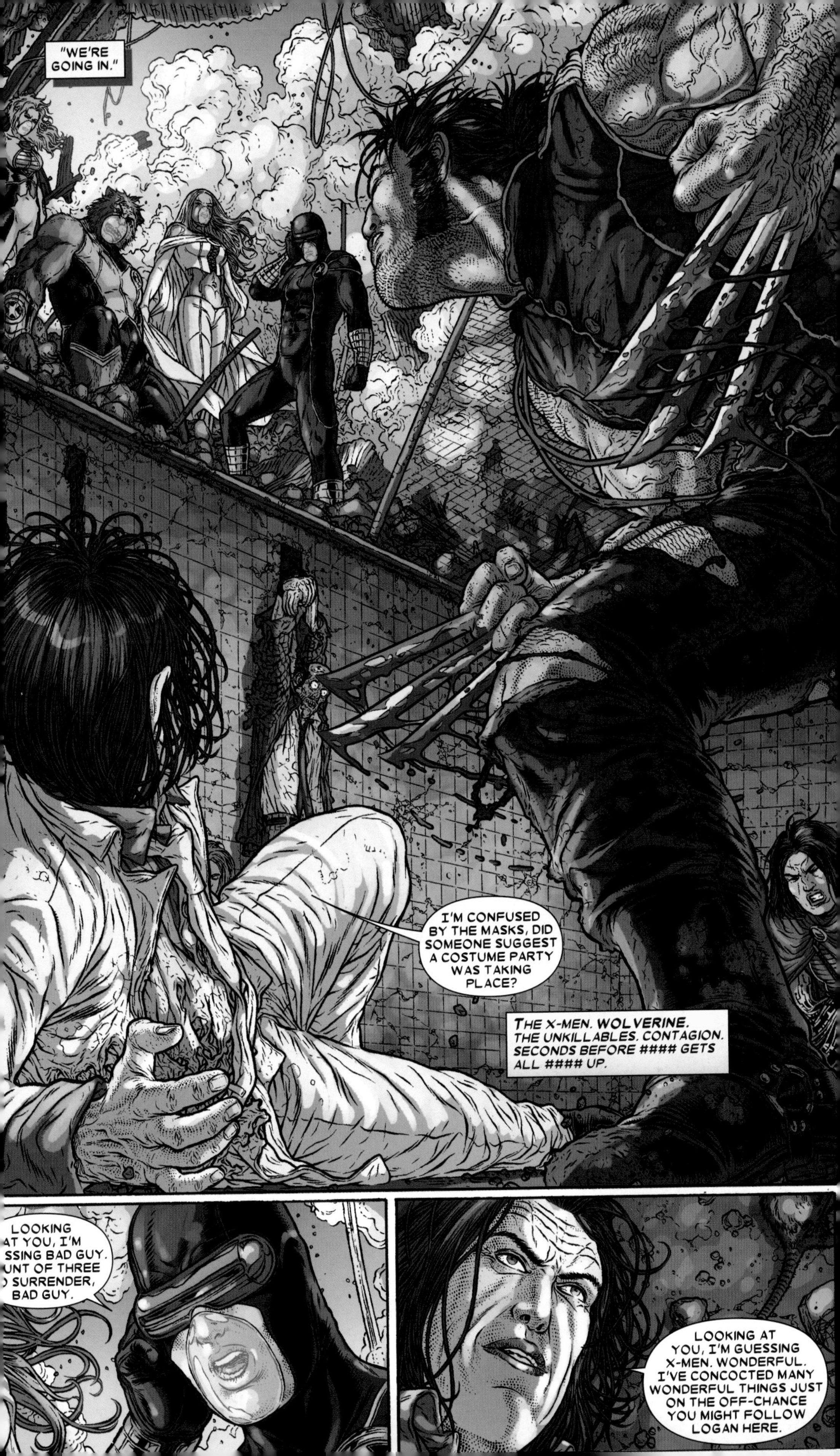
"WE'RE GOING IN."
I'M CONFUSED BY THE MASKS, DID SOMEONE SUGGEST A COSTUME PARTY WAS TAKING PLACE?
THE X-MEN. WOLVERINE. THE UNKILLABLES. CONTAGION. SECONDS BEFORE #### GETS ALL #### UP.
LOOKING AT YOU, I'M SSING BAD GUY. UNT OF THREE SURRENDER, BAD GUY.
LOOKING AT YOU, I'M GUESSING X-MEN. WONDERFUL. I'VE CONCOCTED MANY WONDERFUL THINGS JUST ON THE OFF-CHANCE YOU MIGHT FOLLOW LOGAN HERE.

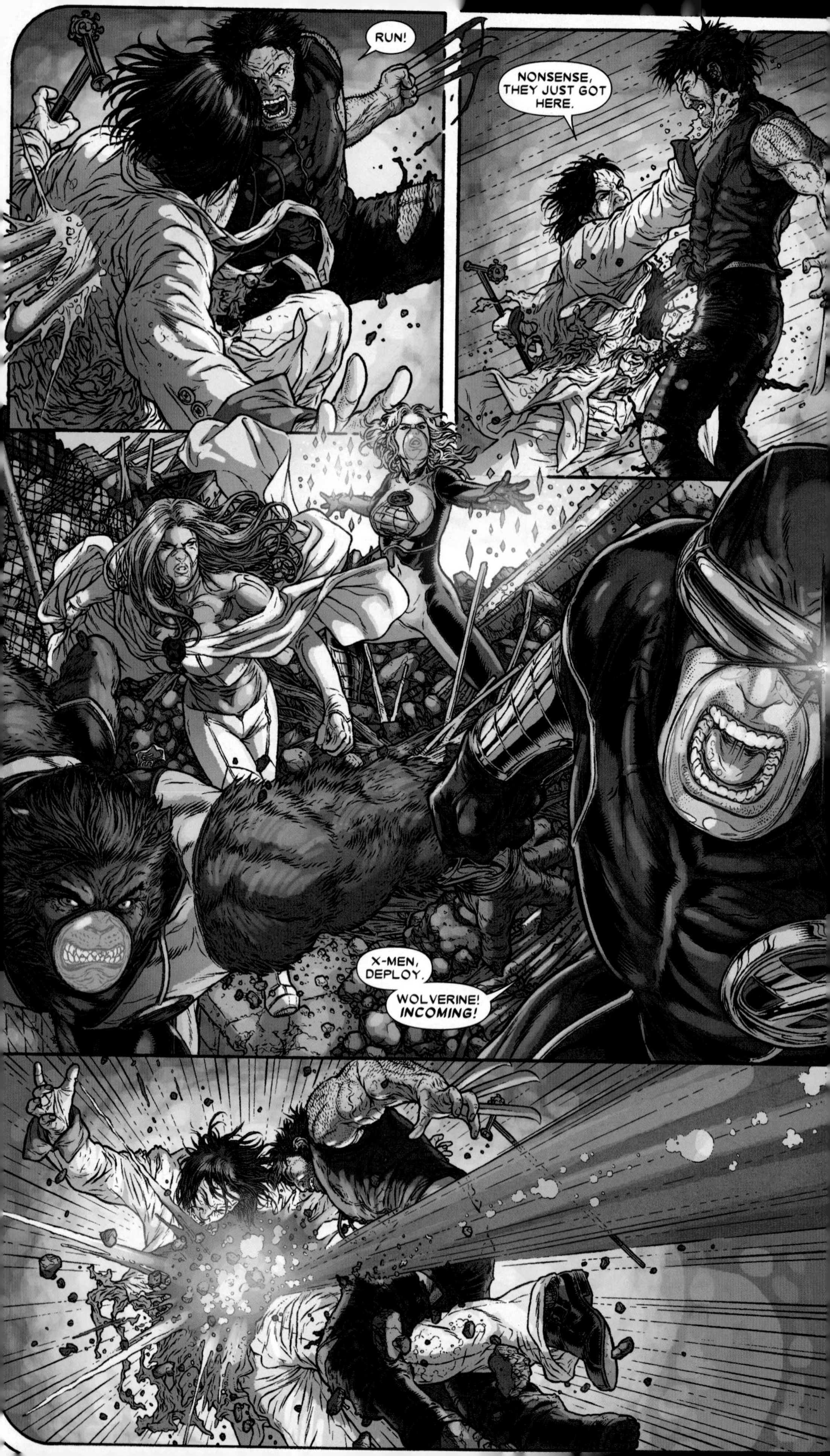
RUN!
NONSENSE, THEY JUST GOT HERE.
X-MEN, DEPLOY.
WOLVERINE! INCOMING!

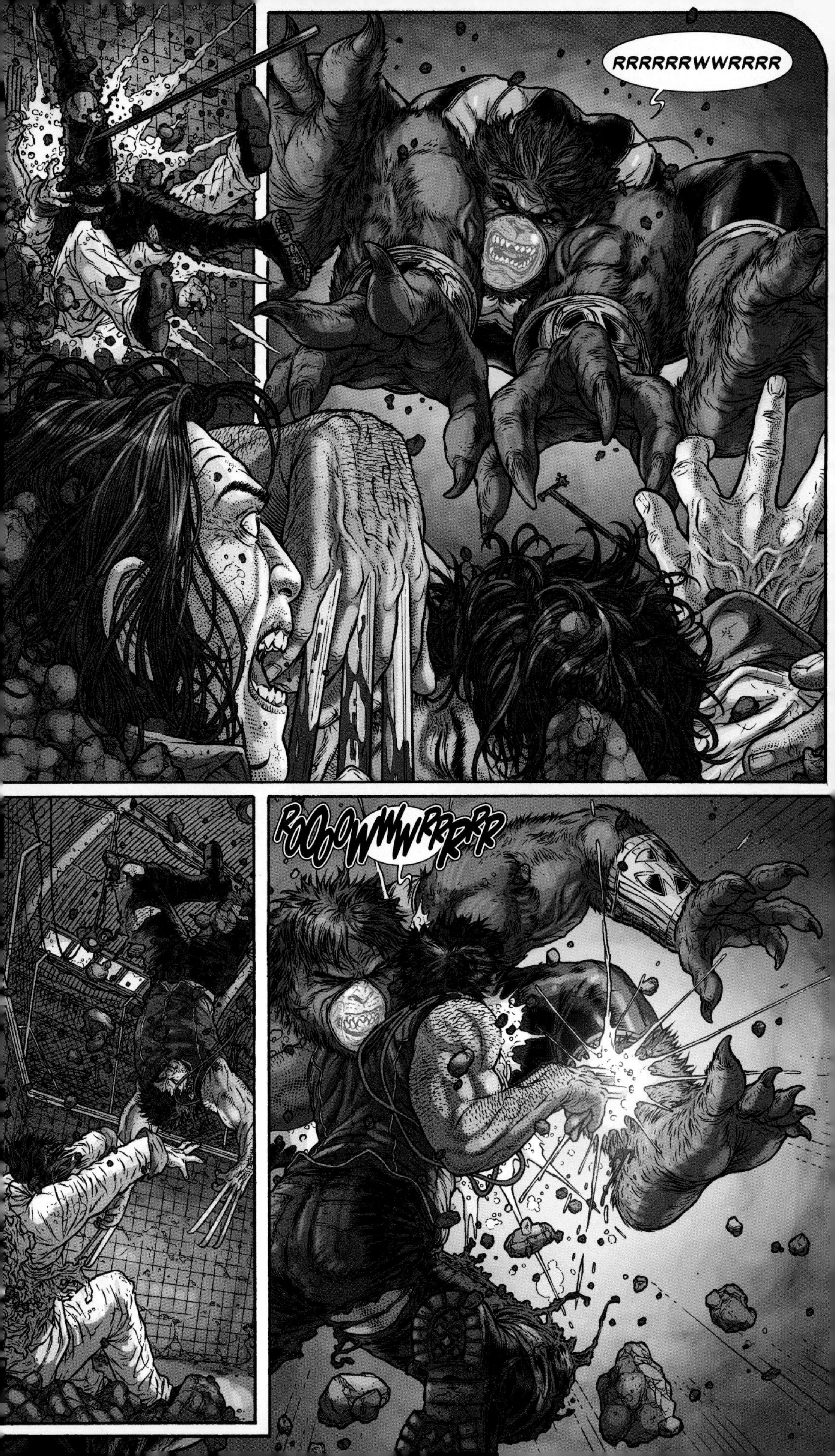
RRRRRRWWRRRR
ROOOOWWWRRRRR

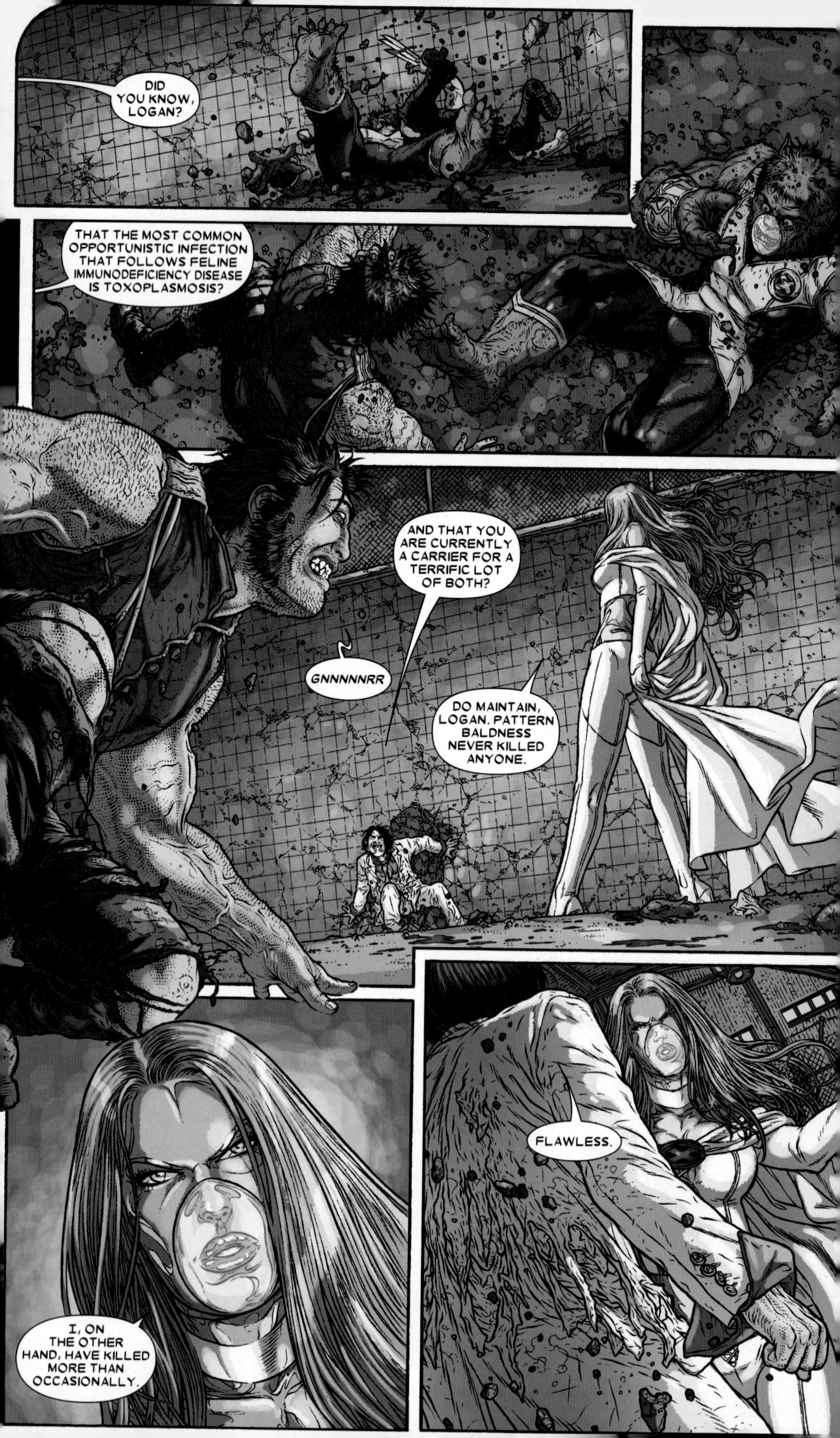
DID YOU KNOW, LOGAN?
THAT THE MOST COMMON OPPORTUNISTIC INFECTION THAT FOLLOWS FELINE IMMUNODEFICIENCY DISEASE IS TOXOPLASMOSIS?
AND THAT YOU ARE CURRENTLY A CARRIER FOR A TERRIFIC LOT OF BOTH?
GNNNNNRR
DO MAINTAIN, LOGAN. PATTERN BALDNESS NEVER KILLED ANYONE.
I, ON THE OTHER HAND, HAVE KILLED MORE THAN OCCASIONALLY.
FLAWLESS.

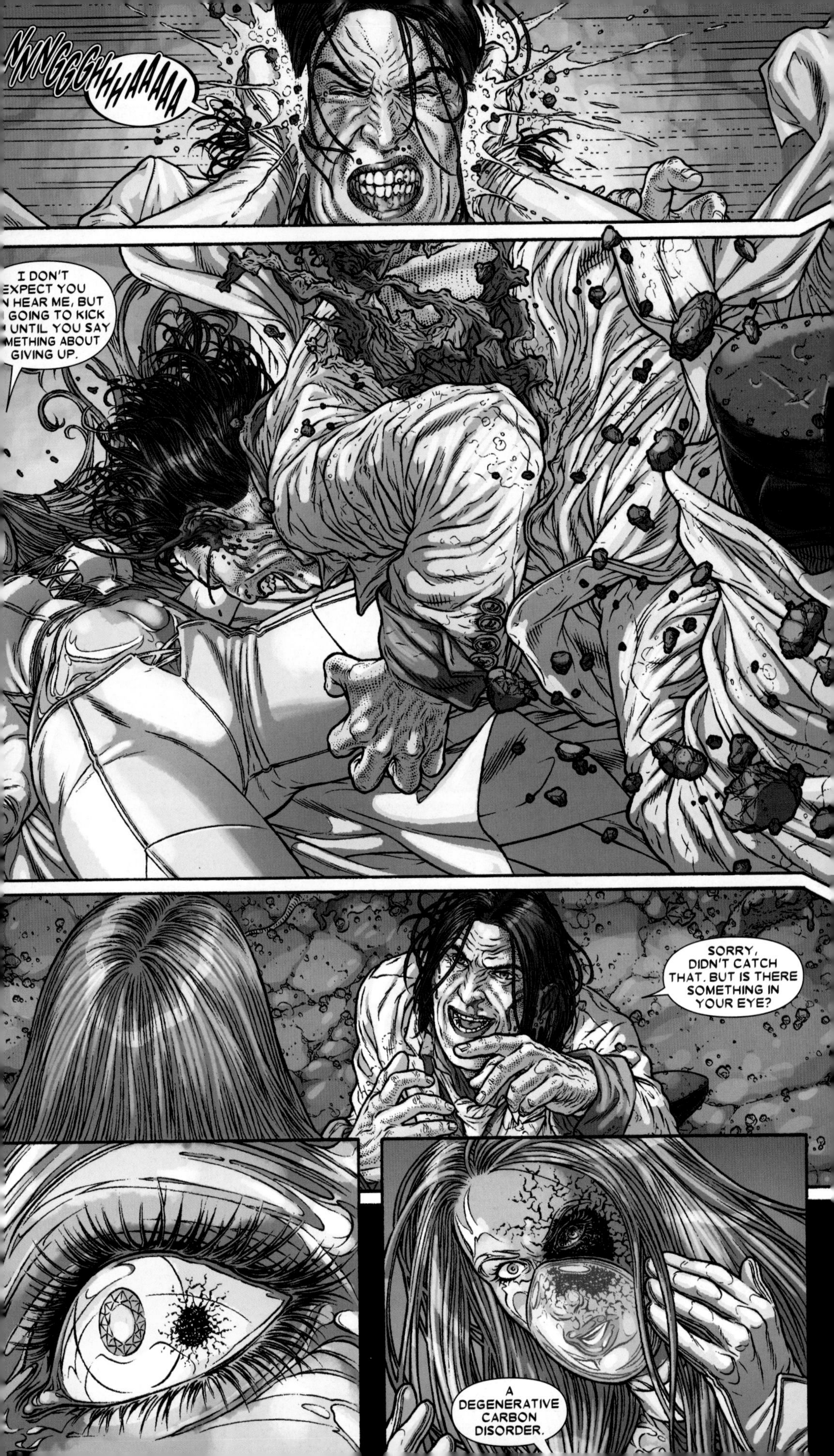
NNNGGGHHHAAAAA
I DON'T EXPECT YOU N HEAR ME, BUT GOING TO KICK UNTIL YOU SAY METHING ABOUT GIVING UP.
SORRY, DIDN'T CATCH THAT. BUT IS THERE SOMETHING IN YOUR EYE?
A DEGENERATIVE CARBON DISORDER.

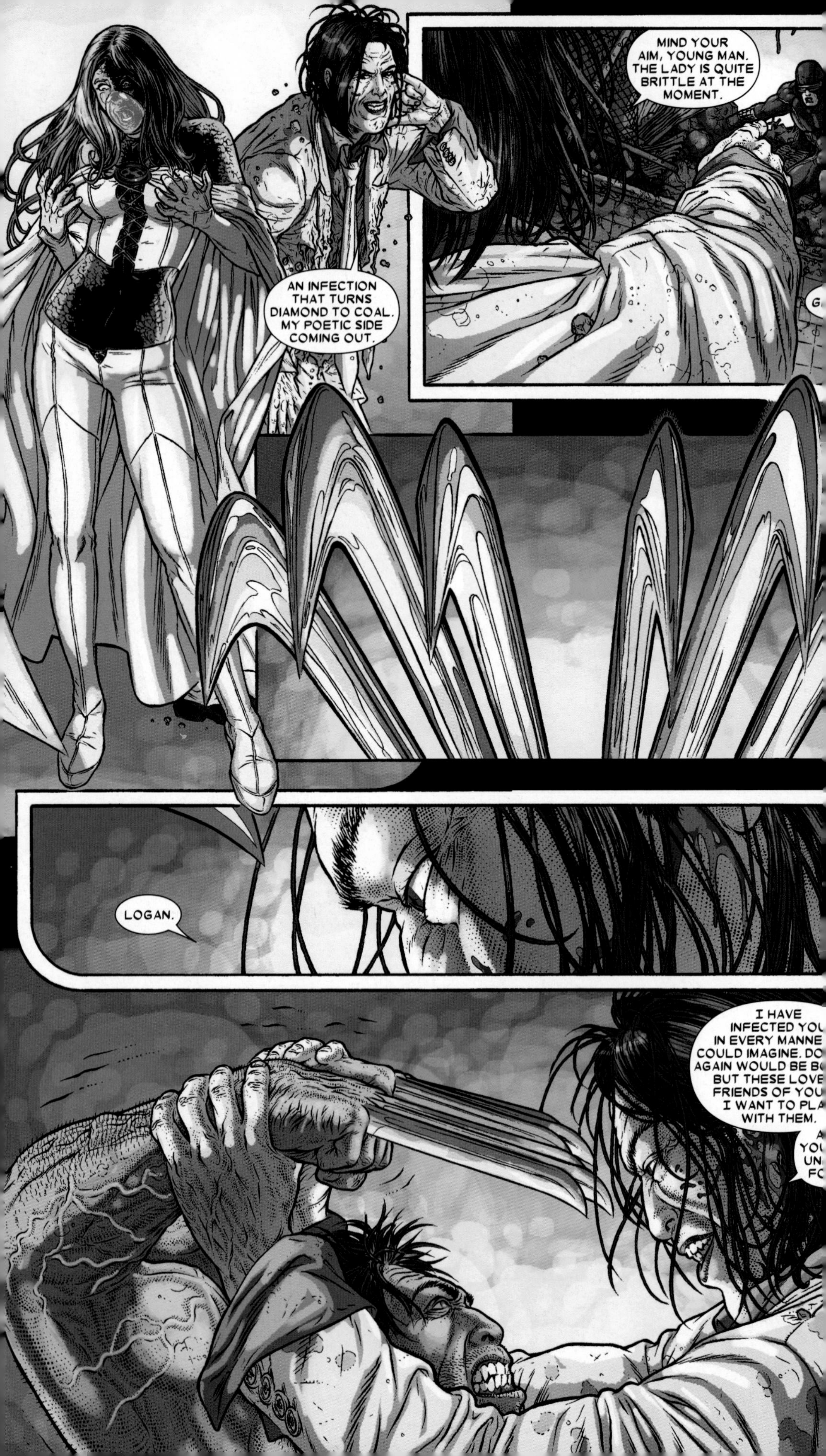

AN INFECTION THAT TURNS DIAMOND TO COAL. MY POETIC SIDE COMING OUT.
MIND YOUR AIM, YOUNG MAN. THE LADY IS QUITE BRITTLE AT THE MOMENT.
LOGAN.
I HAVE INFECTED YOU IN EVERY MANNE COULD IMAGINE. DO AGAIN WOULD BE BO BUT THESE LOVE FRIENDS OF YOU I WANT TO PLA WITH THEM.

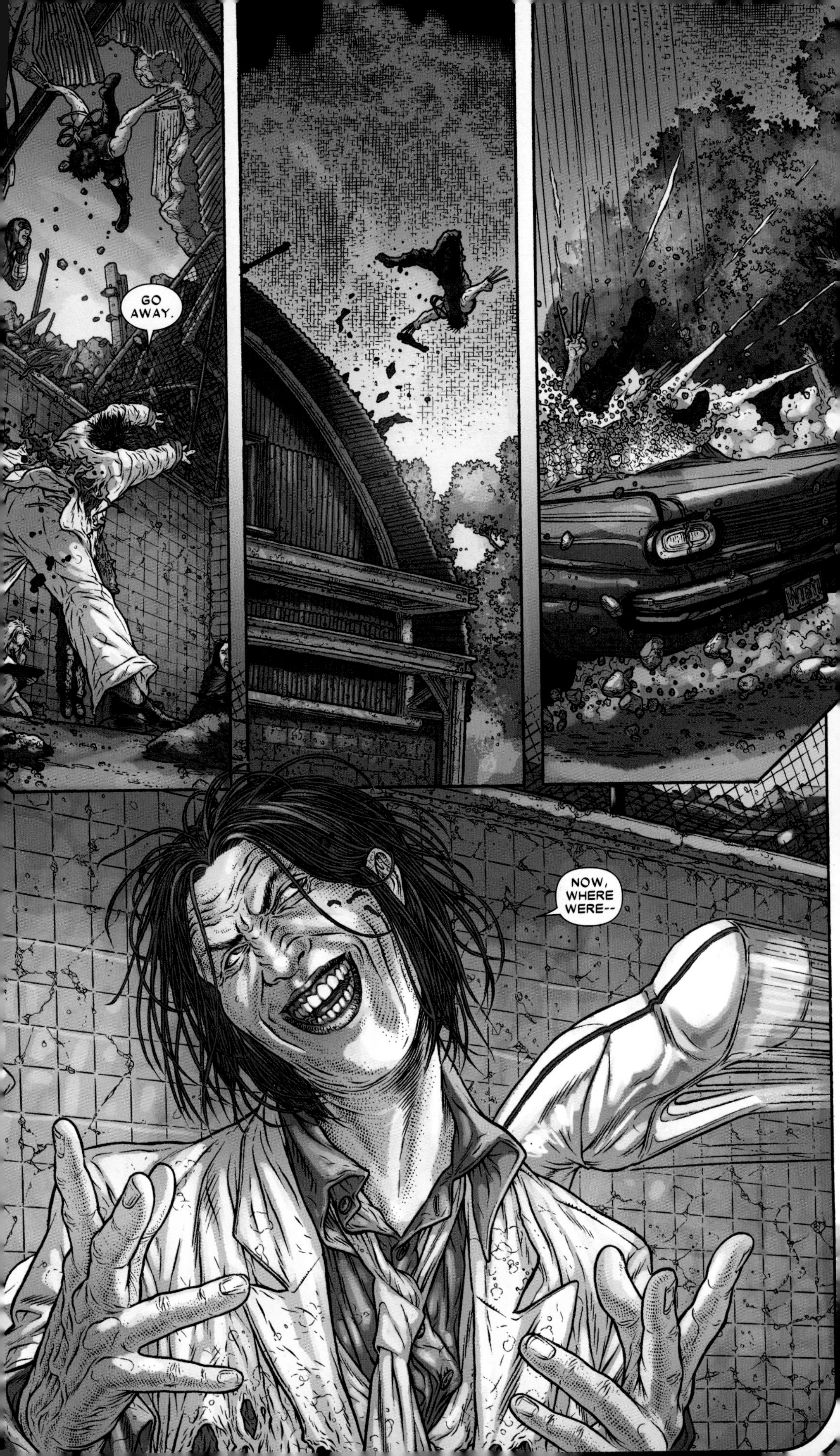
GO AWAY.
NOW, WHERE WERE--

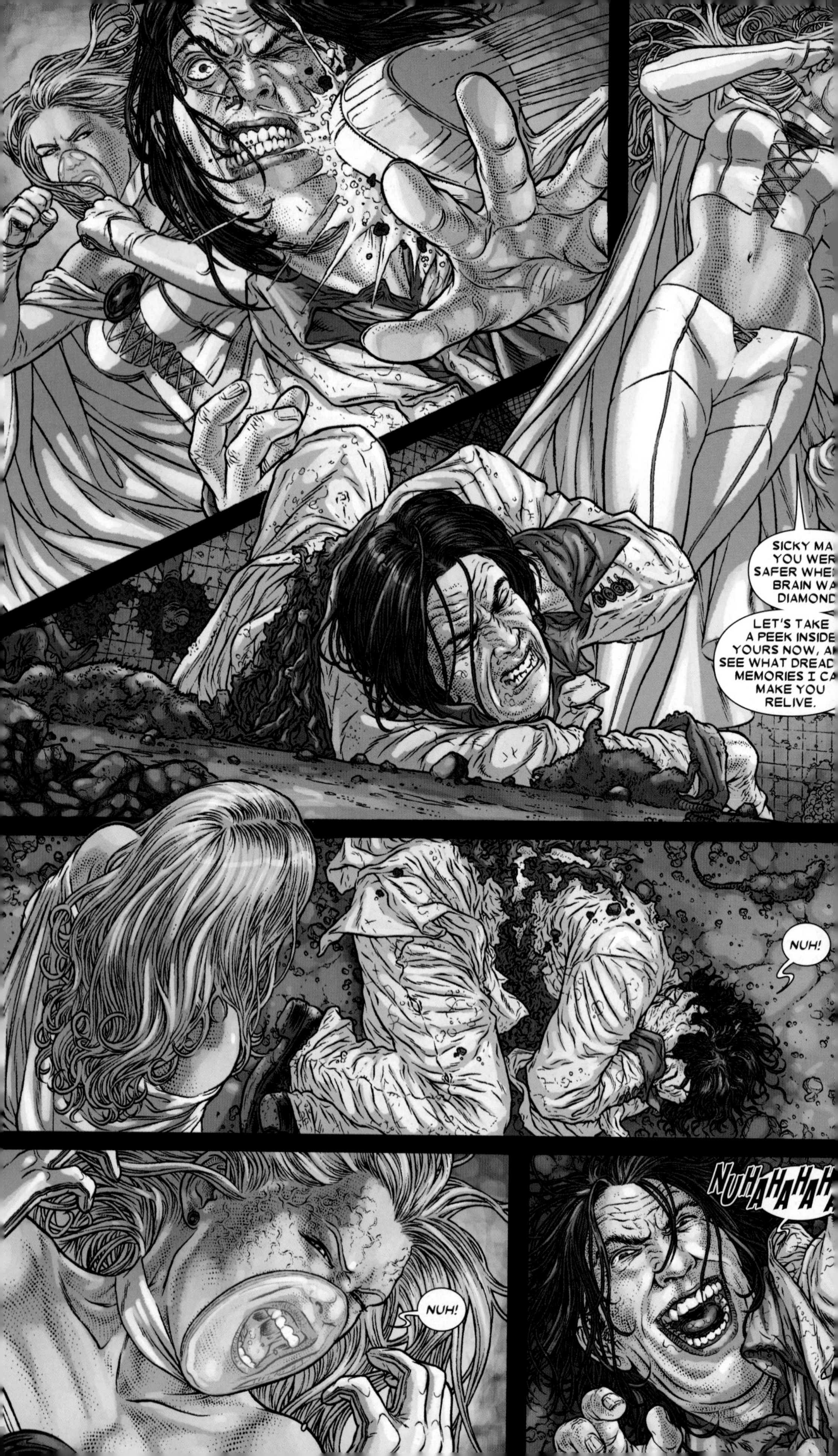
SICKY MA
YOU WER
SAFER WHE
BRAIN WA
DIAMOND
LET'S TAKE A PEEK INSIDE YOURS NOW, A
SEE WHAT DREAD MEMORIES I CA
MAKE YOU RELIVE.
NUH!
NUH!
NUHAHAHAH

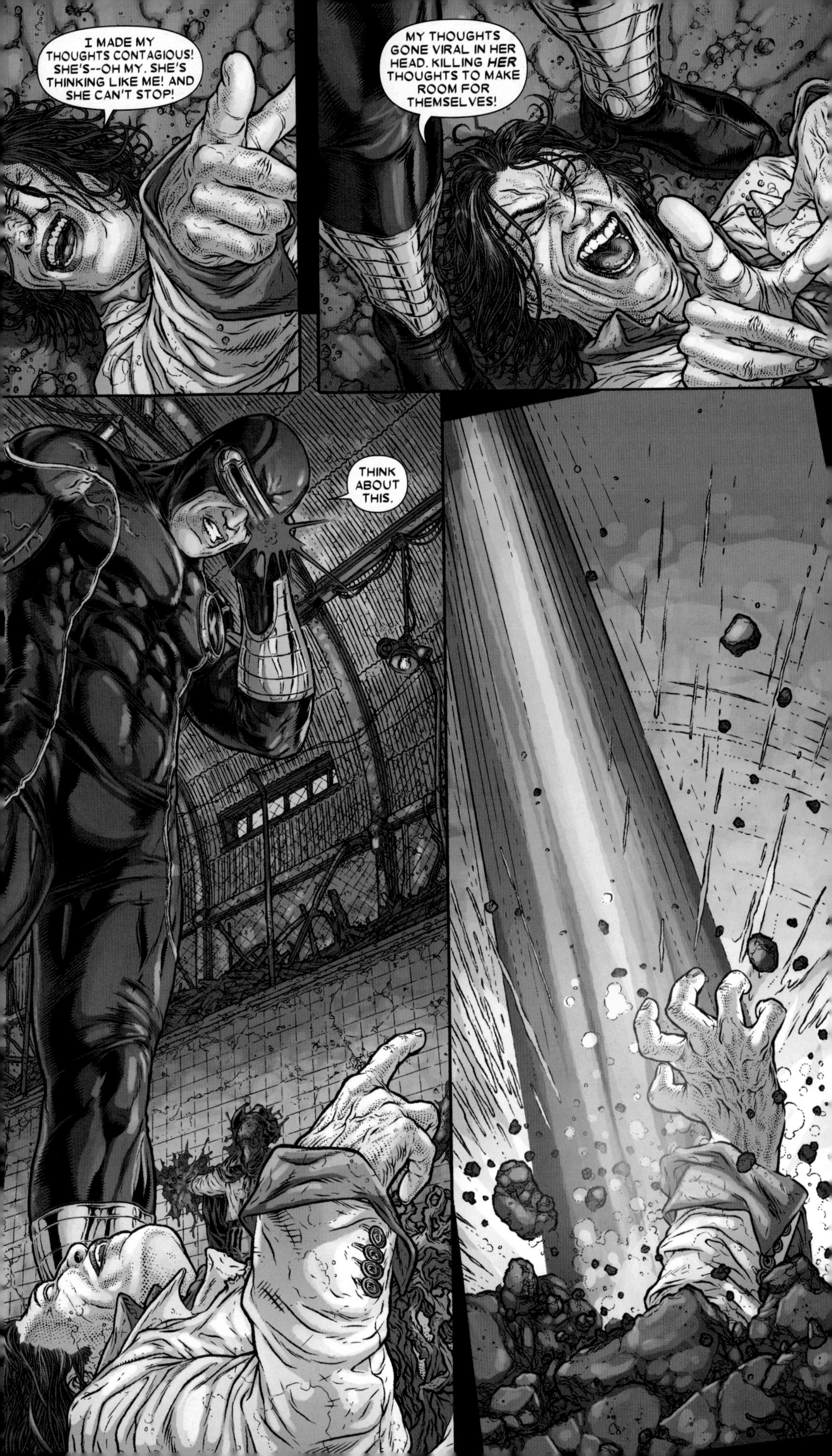
I MADE MY THOUGHTS CONTAGIOUS! SHE'S--OH MY. SHE'S THINKING LIKE ME! AND SHE CAN'T STOP!
MY THOUGHTS GONE VIRAL IN HER HEAD. KILLING HER THOUGHTS TO MAKE ROOM FOR THEMSELVES!
THINK ABOUT THIS.

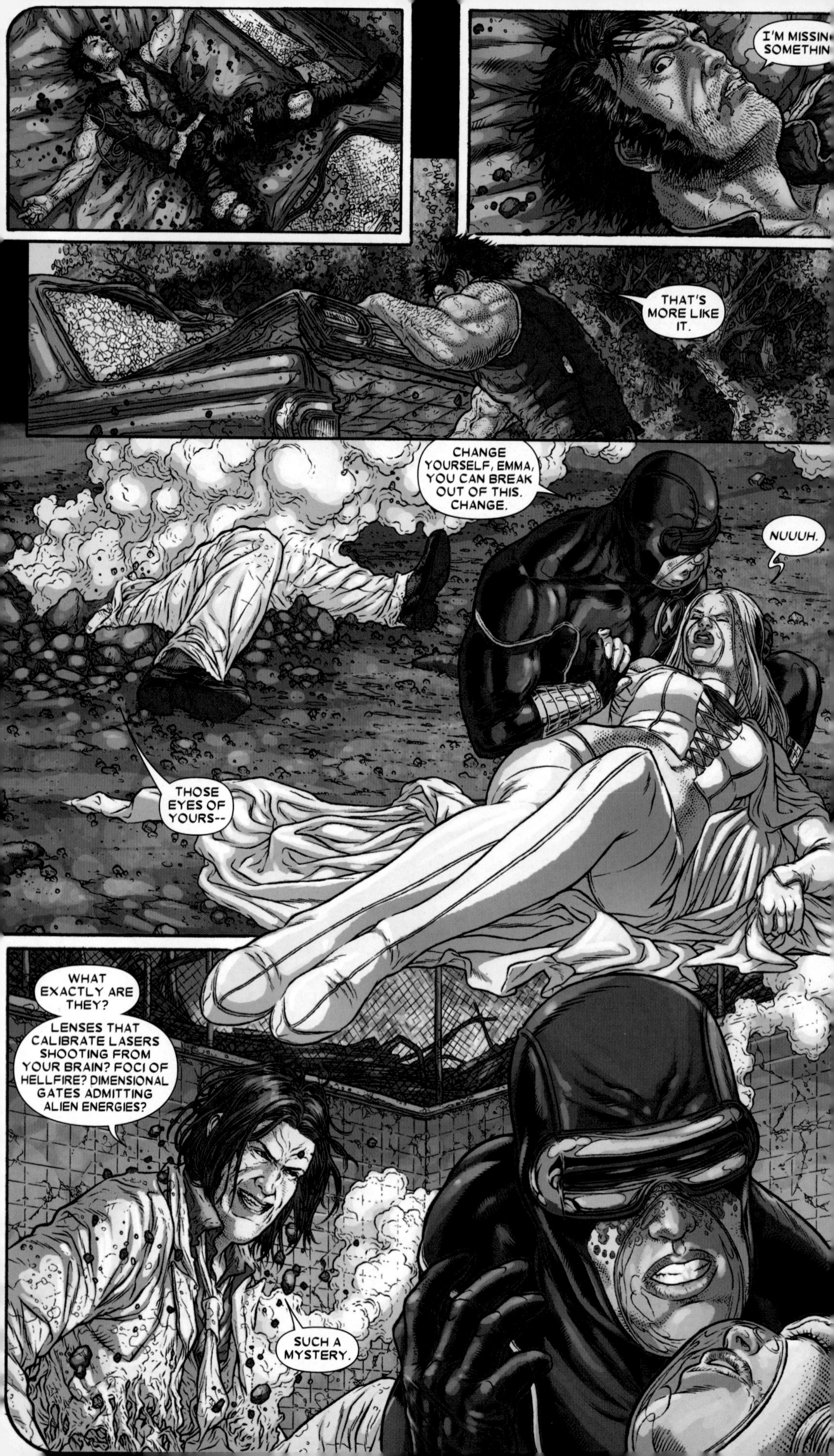
I'M MISSIN SOMETHIN
THAT'S MORE LIKE IT.
CHANGE YOURSELF, EMMA, YOU CAN BREAK OUT OF THIS. CHANGE.
NUUUH.
THOSE EYES OF YOURS--
WHAT EXACTLY ARE THEY?
LENSES THAT CALIBRATE LASERS SHOOTING FROM YOUR BRAIN? FOCI OF HELLFIRE? DIMENSIONAL GATES ADMITTING ALIEN ENERGIES?
SUCH A MYSTERY.

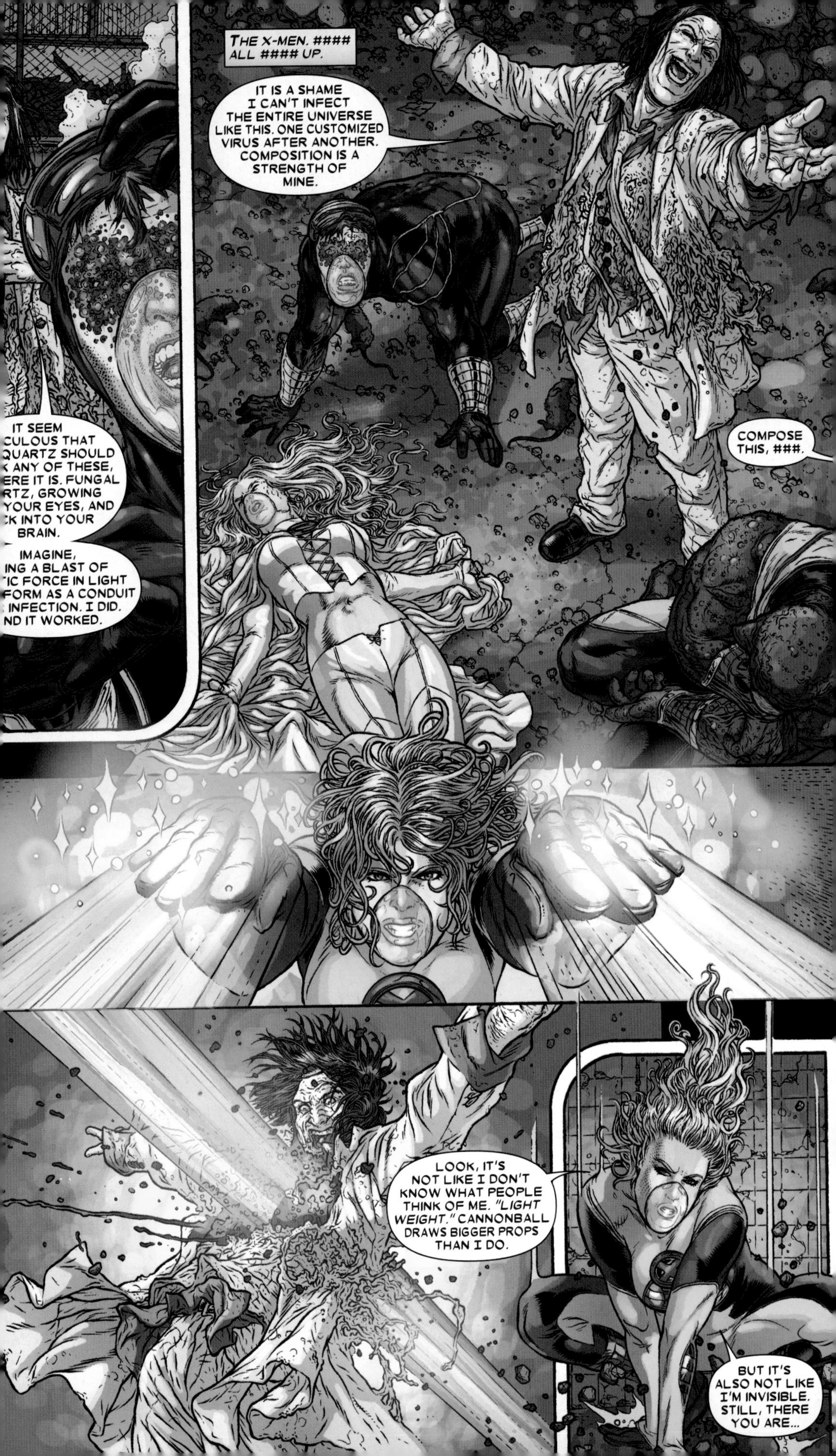

IT SEEM CULOUS THAT QUARTZ SHOULD ANY OF THESE, ERE IT IS. FUNGAL RTZ, GROWING YOUR EYES, AND K INTO YOUR BRAIN.
IMAGINE, ING A BLAST OF TIC FORCE IN LIGHT FORM AS A CONDUIT INFECTION. I DID. ND IT WORKED.
THE X-MEN. #### ALL #### UP.
IT IS A SHAME I CAN'T INFECT THE ENTIRE UNIVERSE LIKE THIS. ONE CUSTOMIZED VIRUS AFTER ANOTHER. COMPOSITION IS A STRENGTH OF MINE.
COMPOSE THIS, ###.
LOOK, IT'S NOT LIKE I DON'T KNOW WHAT PEOPLE THINK OF ME. "LIGHT WEIGHT." CANNONBALL DRAWS BIGGER PROPS THAN I DO.
BUT IT'S ALSO NOT LIKE I'M INVISIBLE. STILL, THERE YOU ARE...

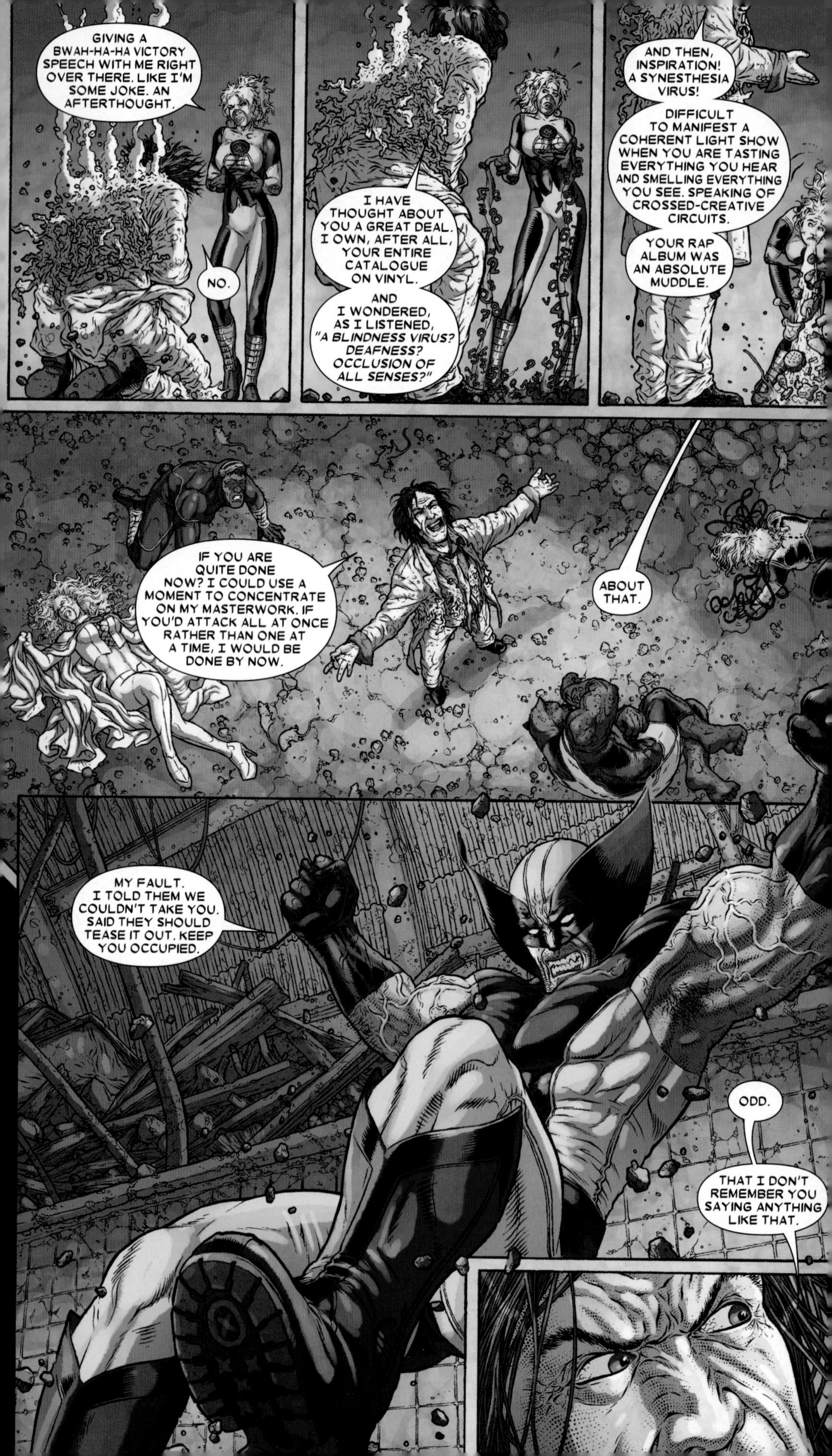
GIVING A BWAH-HA-HA VICTORY SPEECH WITH ME RIGHT OVER THERE. LIKE I'M SOME JOKE. AN AFTERTHOUGHT.
NO.
I HAVE THOUGHT ABOUT YOU A GREAT DEAL. I OWN, AFTER ALL, YOUR ENTIRE CATALOGUE ON VINYL.
AND I WONDERED, AS I LISTENED, "A BLINDNESS VIRUS? DEAFNESS? OCCLUSION OF ALL SENSES?"
AND THEN, INSPIRATION! A SYNESTHESIA VIRUS!
DIFFICULT TO MANIFEST A COHERENT LIGHT SHOW WHEN YOU ARE TASTING EVERYTHING YOU HEAR AND SMELLING EVERYTHING YOU SEE. SPEAKING OF CROSSED-CREATIVE CIRCUITS.
YOUR RAP ALBUM WAS AN ABSOLUTE MUDDLE.
IF YOU ARE QUITE DONE NOW? I COULD USE A MOMENT TO CONCENTRATE ON MY MASTERWORK. IF YOU'D ATTACK ALL AT ONCE RATHER THAN ONE AT A TIME, I WOULD BE DONE BY NOW.
ABOUT THAT.
MY FAULT. I TOLD THEM WE COULDN'T TAKE YOU. SAID THEY SHOULD TEASE IT OUT. KEEP YOU OCCUPIED.
ODD.
THAT I DON'T REMEMBER YOU SAYING ANYTHING LIKE THAT.

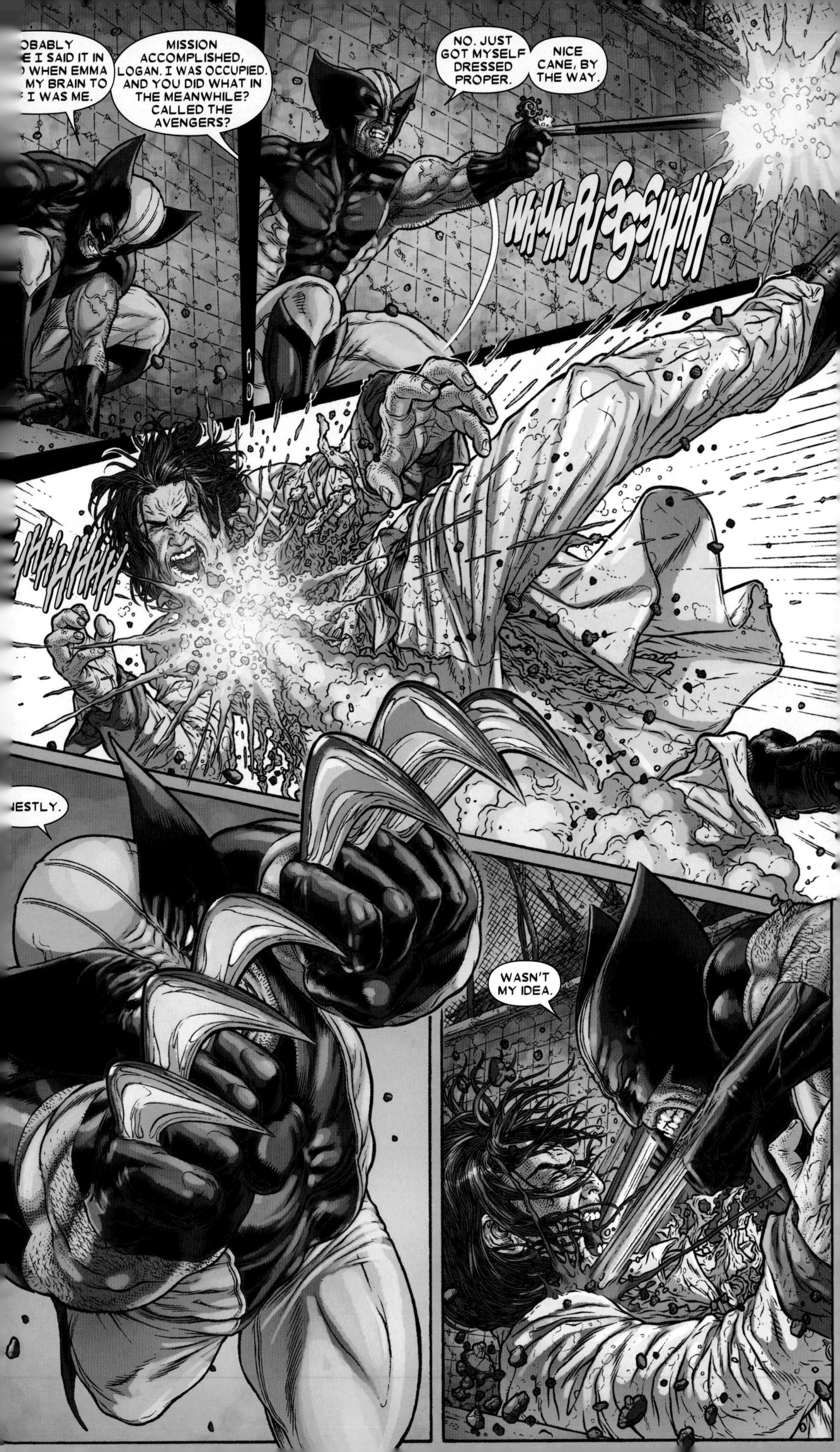
OBABLY
E I SAID IT IN
D WHEN EMMA
MY BRAIN TO
F I WAS ME.
MISSION ACCOMPLISHED, LOGAN. I WAS OCCUPIED. AND YOU DID WHAT IN THE MEANWHILE? CALLED THE AVENGERS?
NO. JUST GOT MYSELF DRESSED PROPER.
NICE CANE, BY THE WAY.
WHUMPH SSSHHHH
HHHHHH
NESTLY.
WASN'T MY IDEA.

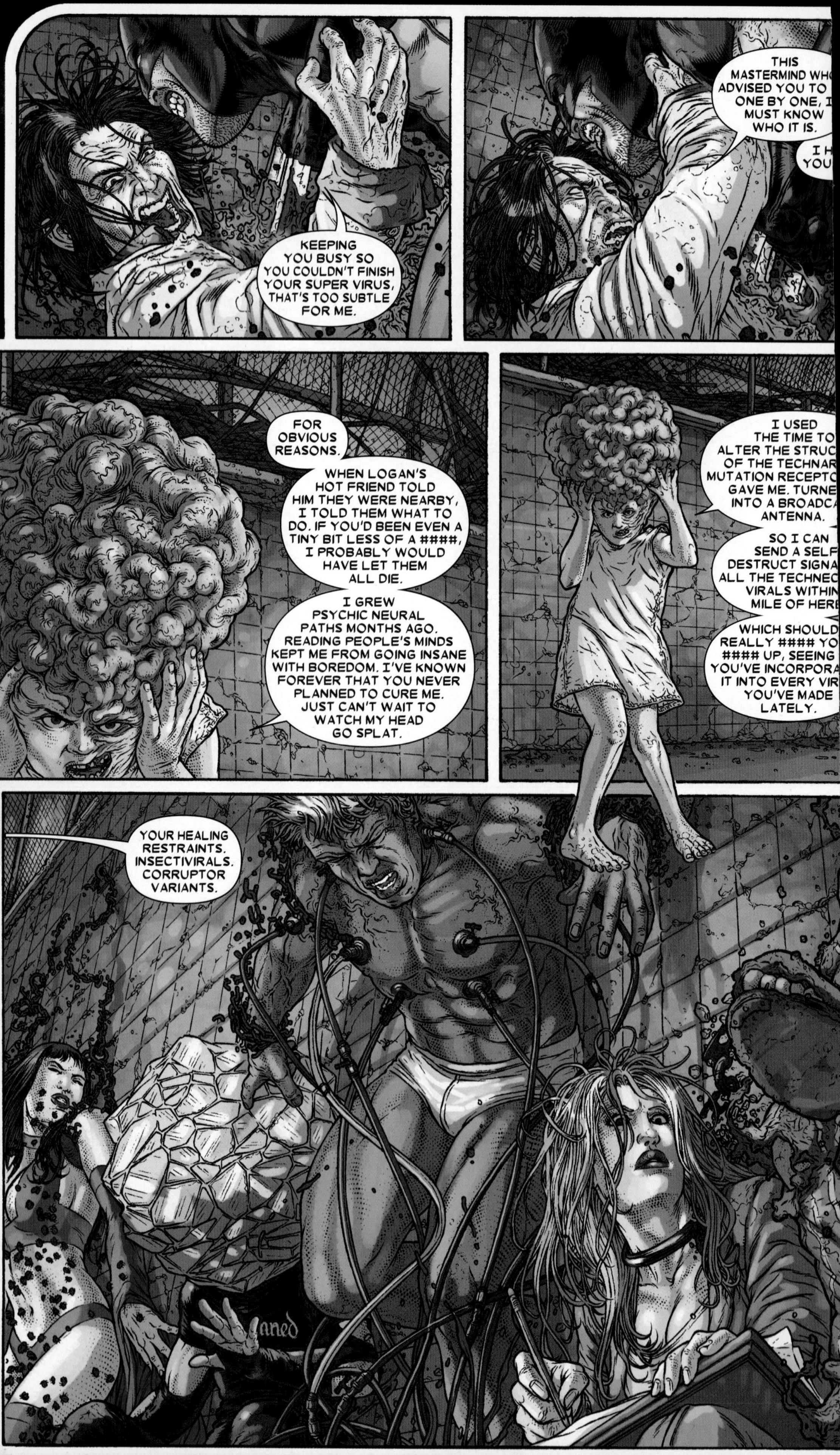
KEEPING YOU BUSY SO YOU COULDN'T FINISH YOUR SUPER VIRUS, THAT'S TOO SUBTLE FOR ME.
THIS MASTERMIND WHO ADVISED YOU TO ONE BY ONE, I MUST KNOW WHO IT IS.
FOR OBVIOUS REASONS.
WHEN LOGAN'S HOT FRIEND TOLD HIM THEY WERE NEARBY, I TOLD THEM WHAT TO DO. IF YOU'D BEEN EVEN A TINY BIT LESS OF A ####, I PROBABLY WOULD HAVE LET THEM ALL DIE.
I GREW PSYCHIC NEURAL PATHS MONTHS AGO. READING PEOPLE'S MINDS KEPT ME FROM GOING INSANE WITH BOREDOM. I'VE KNOWN FOREVER THAT YOU NEVER PLANNED TO CURE ME. JUST CAN'T WAIT TO WATCH MY HEAD GO SPLAT.
I USED THE TIME TO ALTER THE STRUC OF THE TECHNAR MUTATION RECEPTO GAVE ME. TURNE INTO A BROADCA ANTENNA.
SO I CAN SEND A SELF DESTRUCT SIGNA ALL THE TECHNEC VIRALS WITHIN MILE OF HERE
WHICH SHOULD REALLY #### YO #### UP, SEEING YOU'VE INCORPORA IT INTO EVERY VIR YOU'VE MADE LATELY.
YOUR HEALING RESTRAINTS. INSECTIVIRALS. CORRUPTOR VARIANTS.

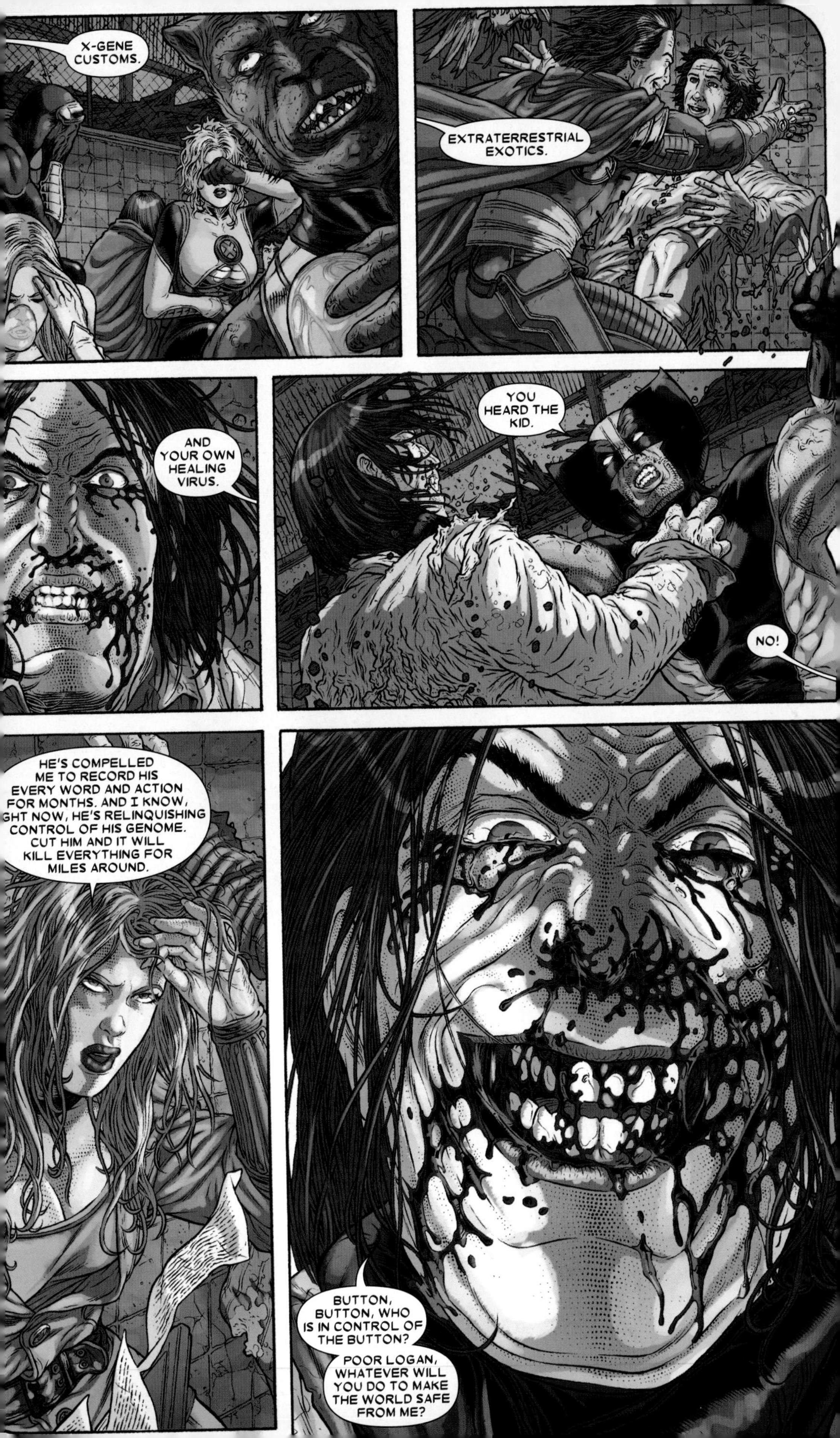
X-GENE CUSTOMS.
EXTRATERRESTRIAL EXOTICS.
AND YOUR OWN HEALING VIRUS.
YOU HEARD THE KID.
NO!
HE'S COMPELLED ME TO RECORD HIS EVERY WORD AND ACTION FOR MONTHS. AND I KNOW, GHT NOW, HE'S RELINQUISHING CONTROL OF HIS GENOME. CUT HIM AND IT WILL KILL EVERYTHING FOR MILES AROUND.
BUTTON, BUTTON, WHO IS IN CONTROL OF THE BUTTON?
POOR LOGAN, WHATEVER WILL YOU DO TO MAKE THE WORLD SAFE FROM ME?

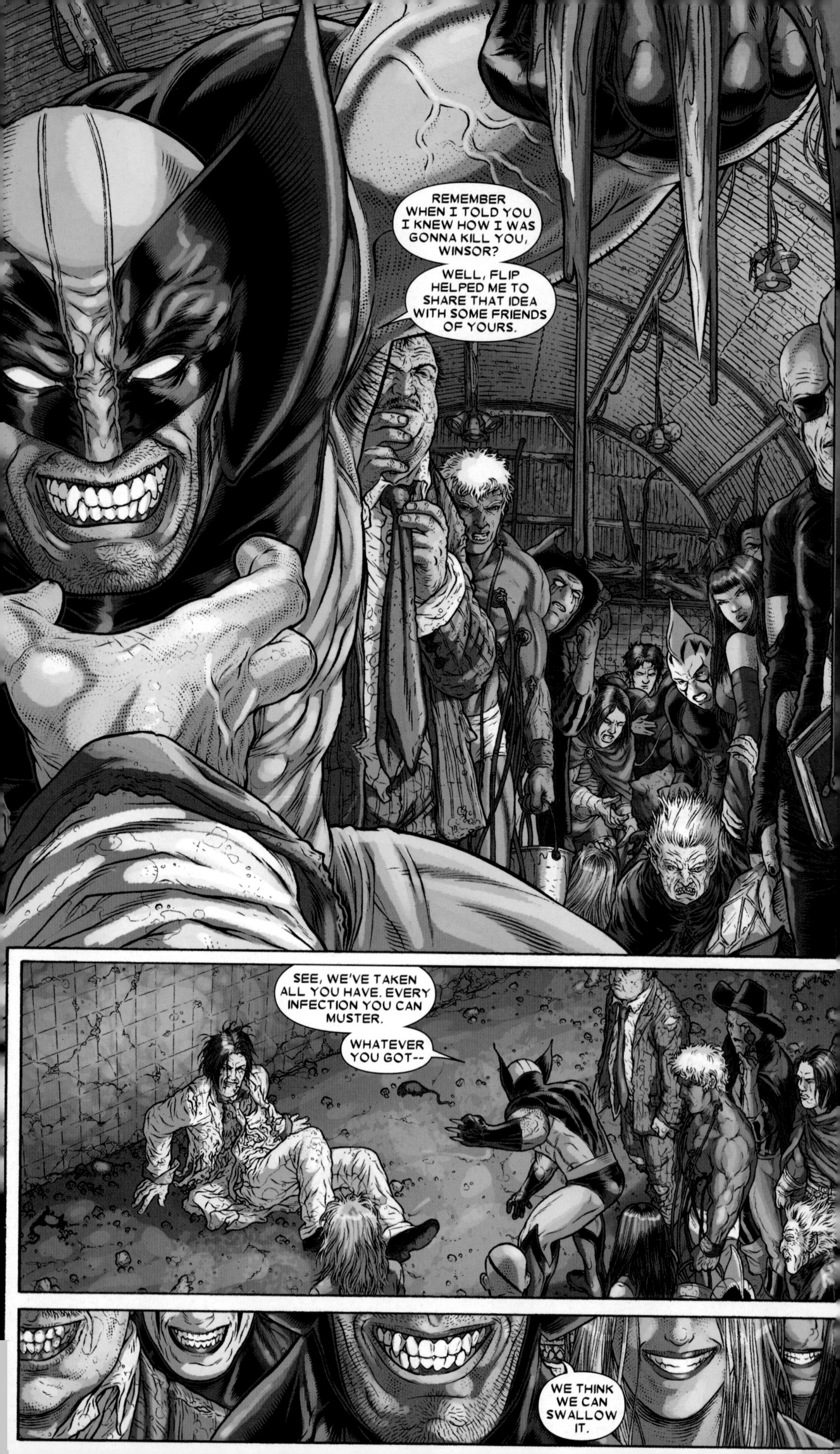
REMEMBER WHEN I TOLD YOU I KNEW HOW I WAS GONNA KILL YOU, WINSOR?
WELL, FLIP HELPED ME TO SHARE THAT IDEA WITH SOME FRIENDS OF YOURS.
SEE, WE'VE TAKEN ALL YOU HAVE. EVERY INFECTION YOU CAN MUSTER.
WHATEVER YOU GOT--
WE THINK WE CAN SWALLOW IT.

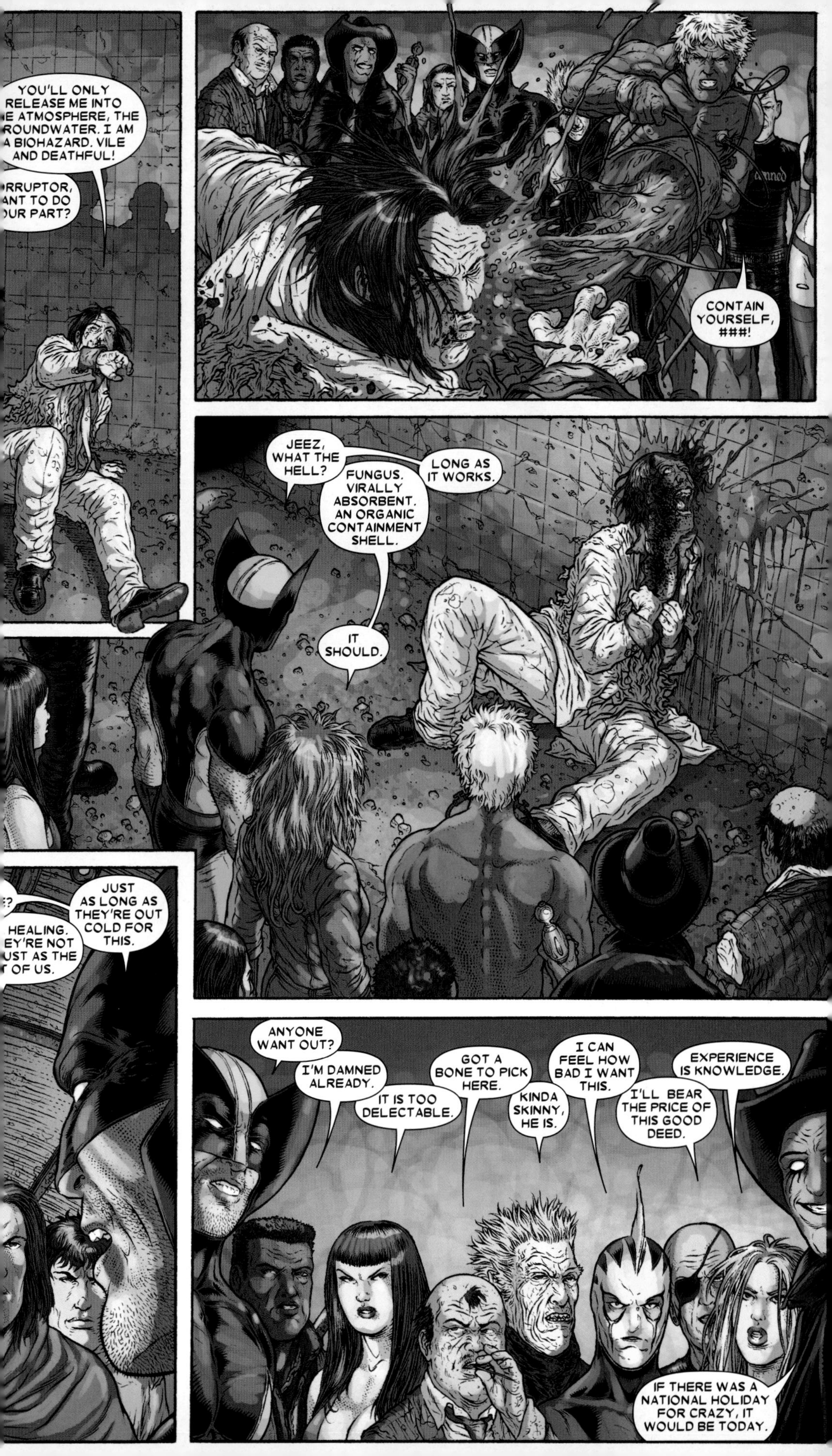
YOU'LL ONLY RELEASE ME INTO E ATMOSPHERE, THE ROUNDWATER. I AM A BIOHAZARD. VILE AND DEATHFUL!
RRUPTOR, ANT TO DO UR PART?
CONTAIN YOURSELF, ###!
JEEZ, WHAT THE HELL?
FUNGUS. VIRALLY ABSORBENT. AN ORGANIC CONTAINMENT SHELL.
LONG AS IT WORKS.
IT SHOULD.
E?
HEALING. EY'RE NOT UST AS THE T OF US.
JUST AS LONG AS THEY'RE OUT COLD FOR THIS.
ANYONE WANT OUT?
I'M DAMNED ALREADY.
IT IS TOO DELECTABLE.
GOT A BONE TO PICK HERE.
KINDA SKINNY, HE IS.
I CAN FEEL HOW BAD I WANT THIS.
I'LL BEAR THE PRICE OF THIS GOOD DEED.
EXPERIENCE IS KNOWLEDGE.
IF THERE WAS A NATIONAL HOLIDAY FOR CRAZY, IT WOULD BE TODAY.

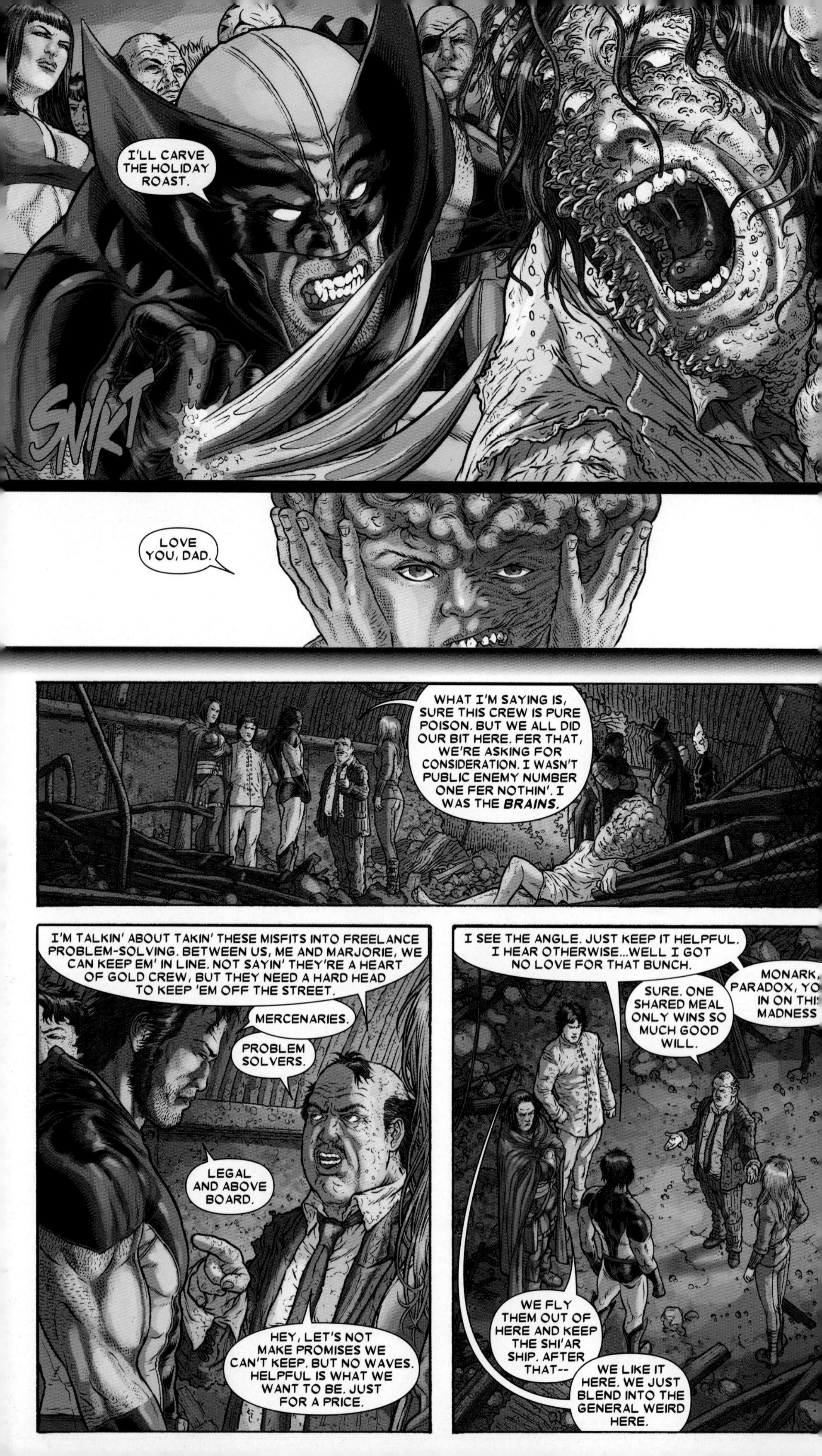
I'LL CARVE THE HOLIDAY ROAST.
SNIKT
LOVE YOU, DAD.
WHAT I'M SAYING IS, SURE THIS CREW IS PURE POISON. BUT WE ALL DID OUR BIT HERE. FER THAT, WE'RE ASKING FOR CONSIDERATION. I WASN'T PUBLIC ENEMY NUMBER ONE FER NOTHIN'. I WAS THE BRAINS.
I'M TALKIN' ABOUT TAKIN' THESE MISFITS INTO FREELANCE PROBLEM-SOLVING. BETWEEN US, ME AND MARJORIE, WE CAN KEEP EM' IN LINE. NOT SAYIN' THEY'RE A HEART OF GOLD CREW, BUT THEY NEED A HARD HEAD TO KEEP 'EM OFF THE STREET.
MERCENARIES.
PROBLEM SOLVERS.
LEGAL AND ABOVE BOARD.
HEY, LET'S NOT MAKE PROMISES WE CAN'T KEEP. BUT NO WAVES. HELPFUL IS WHAT WE WANT TO BE. JUST FOR A PRICE.
I SEE THE ANGLE. JUST KEEP IT HELPFUL. I HEAR OTHERWISE...WELL I GOT NO LOVE FOR THAT BUNCH.
SURE. ONE SHARED MEAL ONLY WINS SO MUCH GOOD WILL.
MONARK, PARADOX, YO IN ON THI MADNESS
WE FLY THEM OUT OF HERE AND KEEP THE SHI'AR SHIP. AFTER THAT--
WE LIKE IT HERE. WE JUST BLEND INTO THE GENERAL WEIRD HERE.

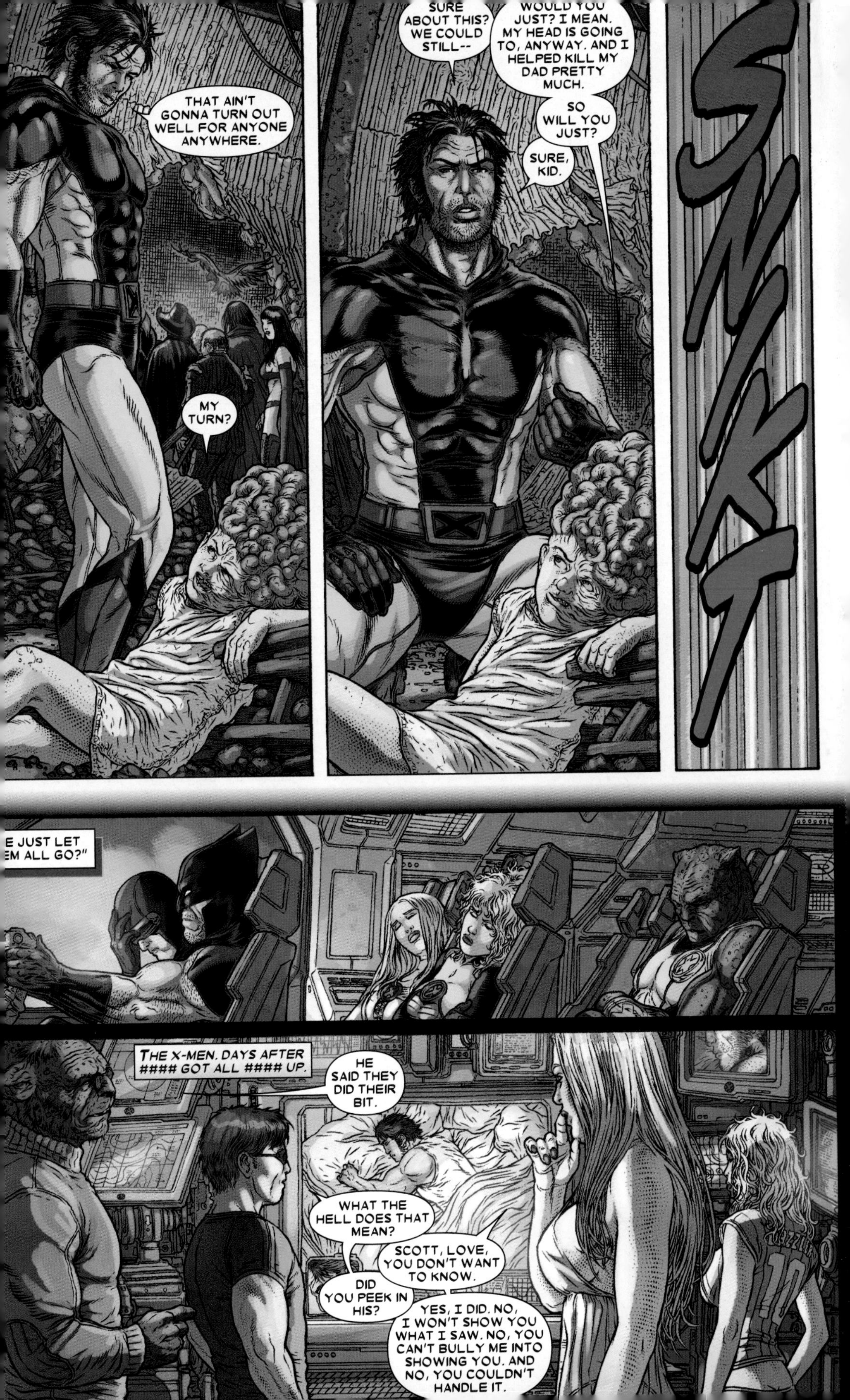
THAT AIN'T GONNA TURN OUT WELL FOR ANYONE ANYWHERE.
MY TURN?
SURE ABOUT THIS? WE COULD STILL--
WOULD YOU JUST? I MEAN. MY HEAD IS GOING TO, ANYWAY. AND I HELPED KILL MY DAD PRETTY MUCH.
SO WILL YOU JUST?
SURE, KID.
SNIKT
E JUST LET EM ALL GO?"
THE X-MEN. DAYS AFTER #### GOT ALL #### UP.
HE SAID THEY DID THEIR BIT.
WHAT THE HELL DOES THAT MEAN?
SCOTT, LOVE, YOU DON'T WANT TO KNOW.
DID YOU PEEK IN HIS?
YES, I DID. NO, I WON'T SHOW YOU WHAT I SAW. NO, YOU CAN'T BULLY ME INTO SHOWING YOU. AND NO, YOU COULDN'T HANDLE IT.

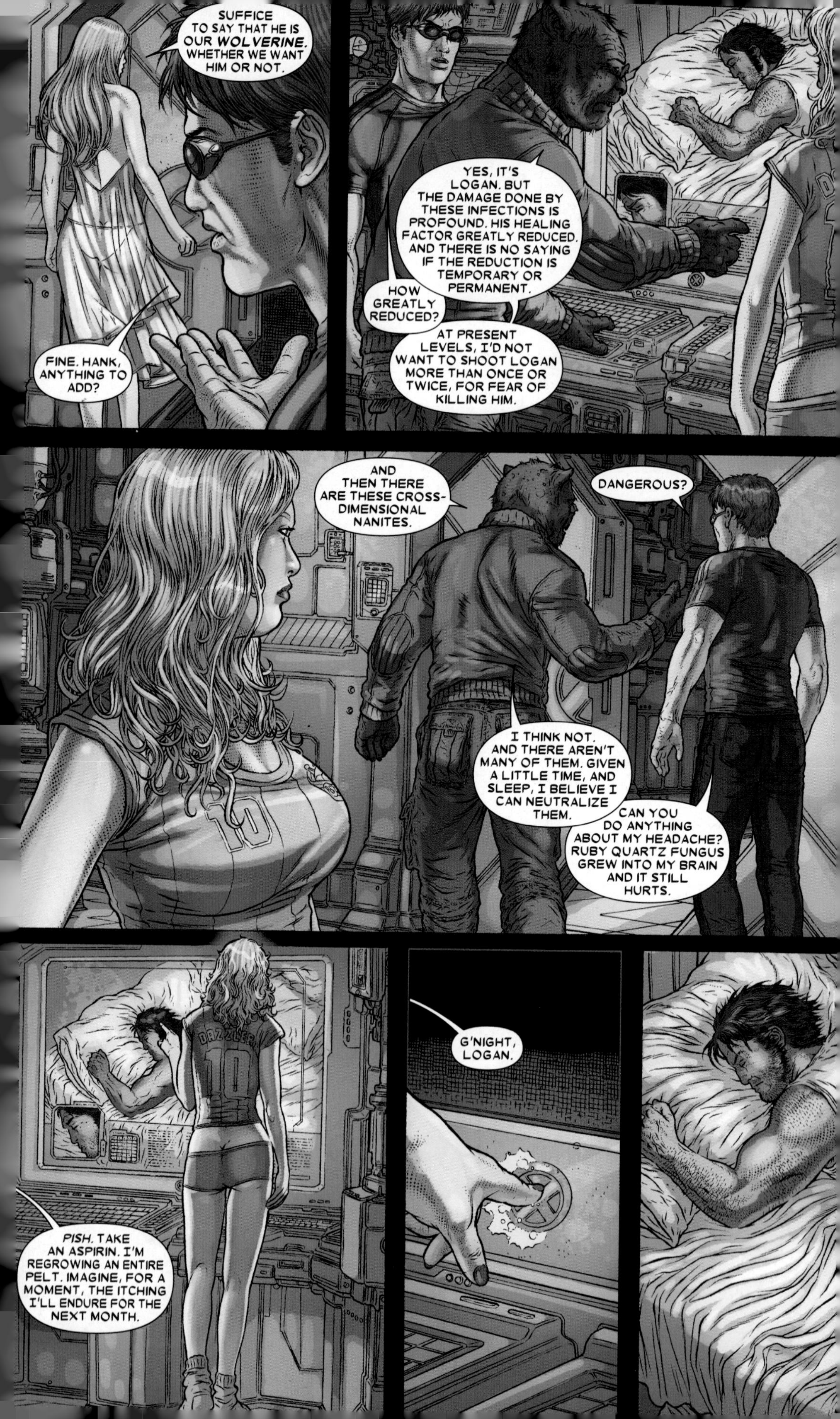
SUFFICE TO SAY THAT HE IS OUR *WOLVERINE.* WHETHER WE WANT HIM OR NOT.
FINE. HANK, ANYTHING TO ADD?
YES, IT'S LOGAN. BUT THE DAMAGE DONE BY THESE INFECTIONS IS PROFOUND. HIS HEALING FACTOR GREATLY REDUCED. AND THERE IS NO SAYING IF THE REDUCTION IS TEMPORARY OR PERMANENT.
HOW GREATLY REDUCED?
AT PRESENT LEVELS, I'D NOT WANT TO SHOOT LOGAN MORE THAN ONCE OR TWICE, FOR FEAR OF KILLING HIM.
AND THEN THERE ARE THESE CROSS-DIMENSIONAL NANITES.
DANGEROUS?
I THINK NOT. AND THERE AREN'T MANY OF THEM. GIVEN A LITTLE TIME, AND SLEEP, I BELIEVE I CAN NEUTRALIZE THEM.
CAN YOU DO ANYTHING ABOUT MY HEADACHE? RUBY QUARTZ FUNGUS GREW INTO MY BRAIN AND IT STILL HURTS.
PISH. TAKE AN ASPIRIN. I'M REGROWING AN ENTIRE PELT. IMAGINE, FOR A MOMENT, THE ITCHING I'LL ENDURE FOR THE NEXT MONTH.
G'NIGHT, LOGAN.

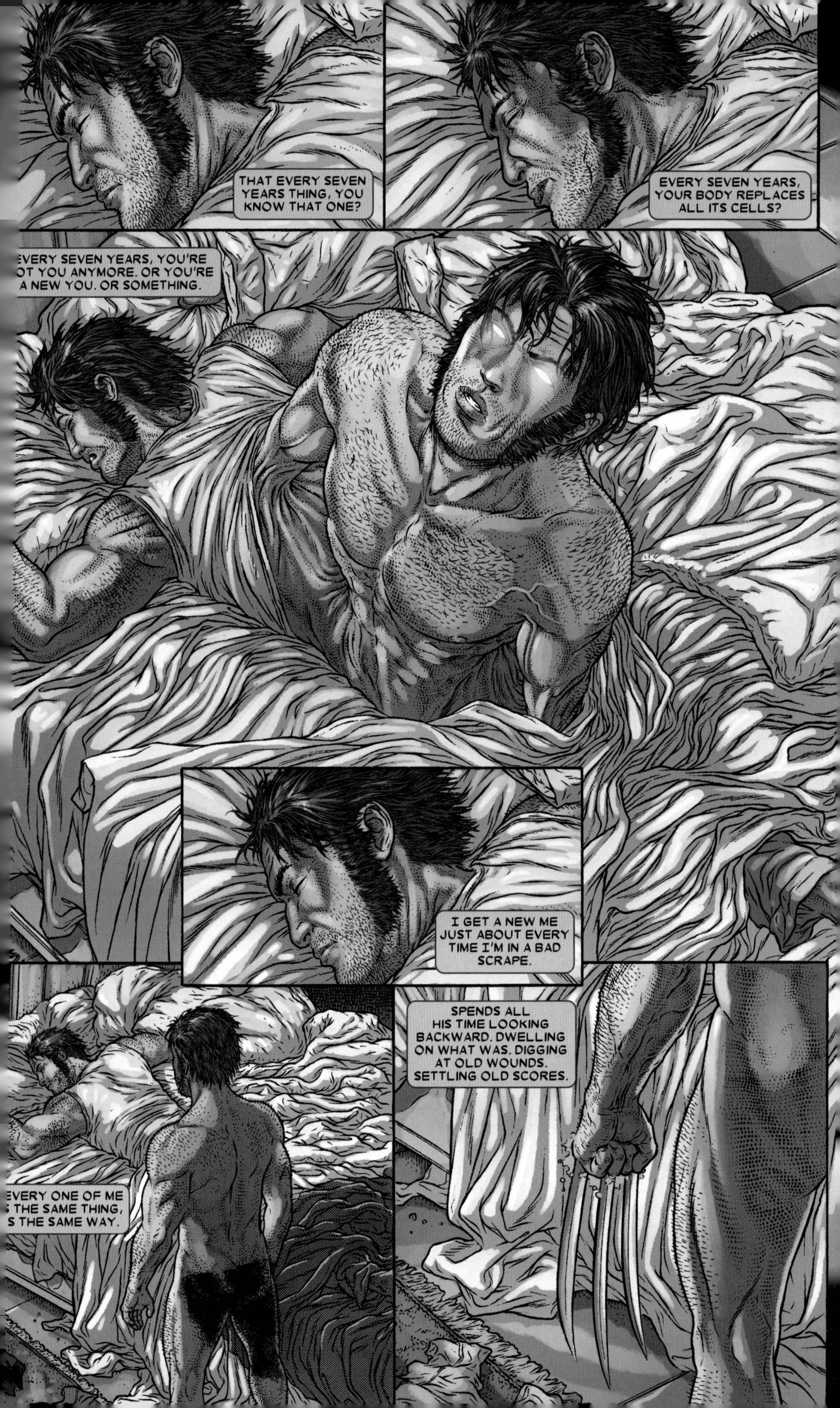
THAT EVERY SEVEN YEARS THING, YOU KNOW THAT ONE?
EVERY SEVEN YEARS, YOUR BODY REPLACES ALL ITS CELLS?
EVERY SEVEN YEARS, YOU'RE OT YOU ANYMORE. OR YOU'RE A NEW YOU. OR SOMETHING.
I GET A NEW ME JUST ABOUT EVERY TIME I'M IN A BAD SCRAPE.
EVERY ONE OF ME S THE SAME THING, S THE SAME WAY.
SPENDS ALL HIS TIME LOOKING BACKWARD. DWELLING ON WHAT WAS. DIGGING AT OLD WOUNDS. SETTLING OLD SCORES.

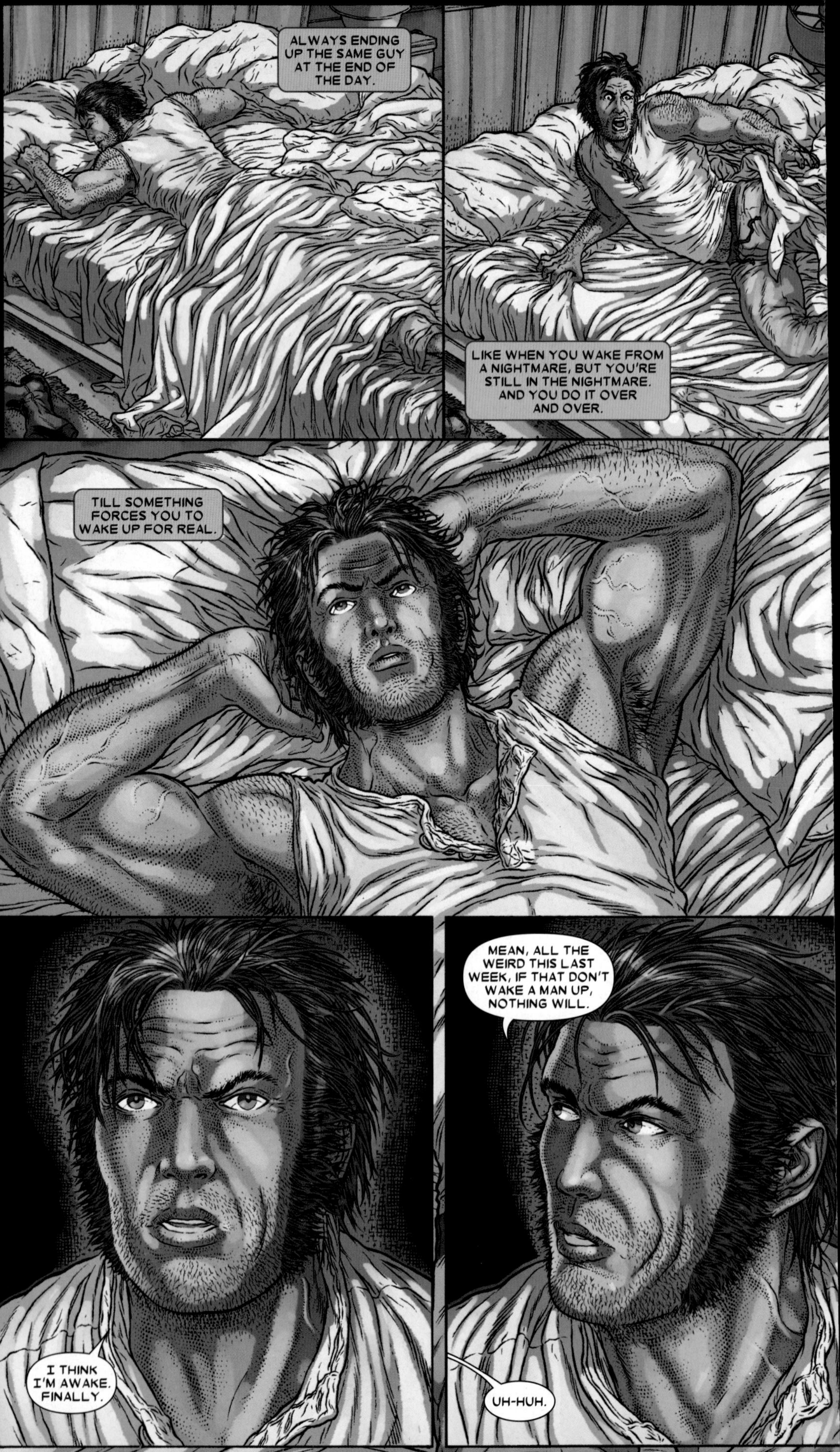
ALWAYS ENDING UP THE SAME GUY AT THE END OF THE DAY.
LIKE WHEN YOU WAKE FROM A NIGHTMARE, BUT YOU'RE STILL IN THE NIGHTMARE. AND YOU DO IT OVER AND OVER.
TILL SOMETHING FORCES YOU TO WAKE UP FOR REAL.
I THINK I'M AWAKE. FINALLY.
MEAN, ALL THE WEIRD THIS LAST WEEK, IF THAT DON'T WAKE A MAN UP, NOTHING WILL.
UH-HUH.

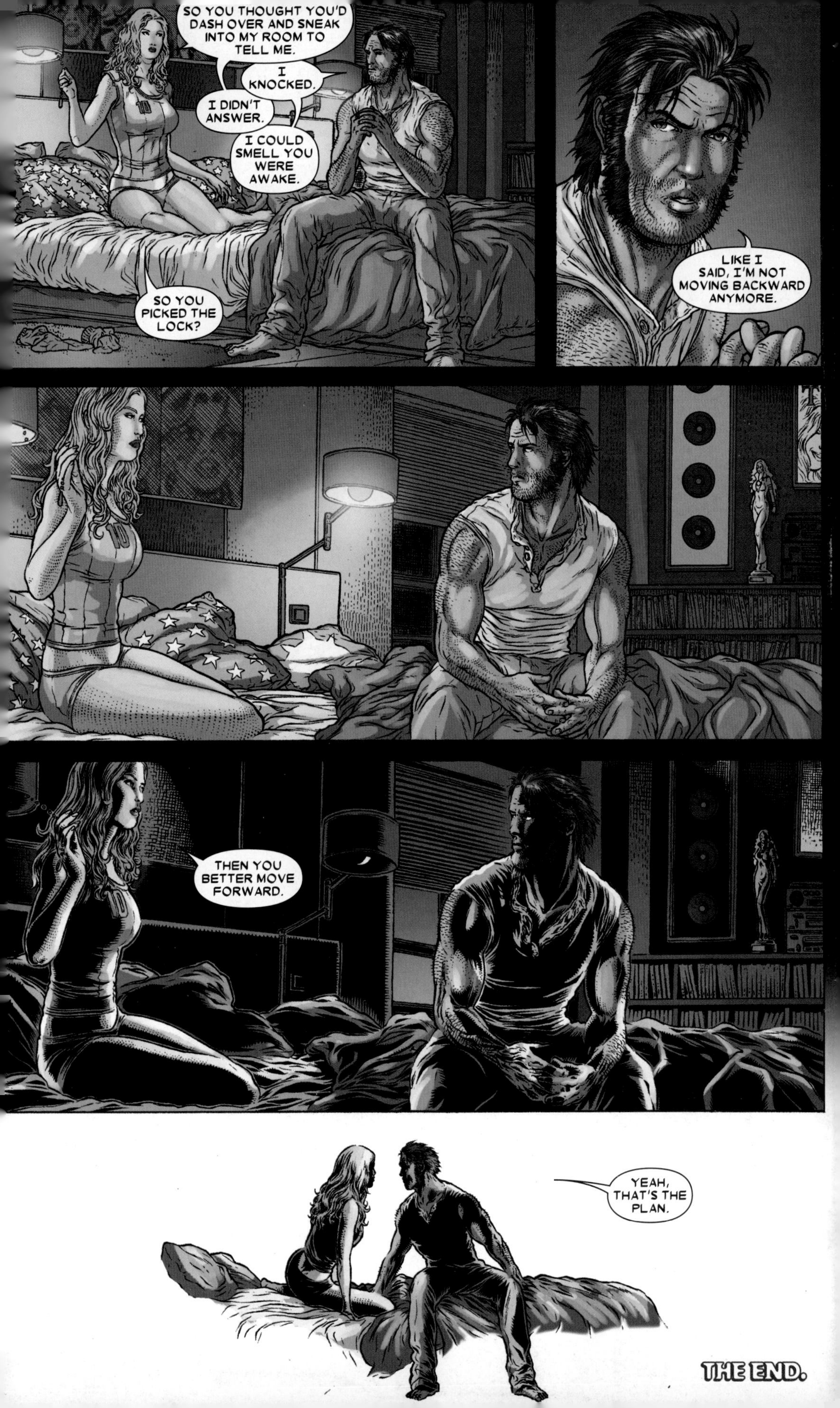
SO YOU THOUGHT YOU'D DASH OVER AND SNEAK INTO MY ROOM TO TELL ME.
I KNOCKED.
I DIDN'T ANSWER.
I COULD SMELL YOU WERE AWAKE.
SO YOU PICKED THE LOCK?
LIKE I SAID, I'M NOT MOVING BACKWARD ANYMORE.
THEN YOU BETTER MOVE FORWARD.
YEAH, THAT'S THE PLAN.
THE END.

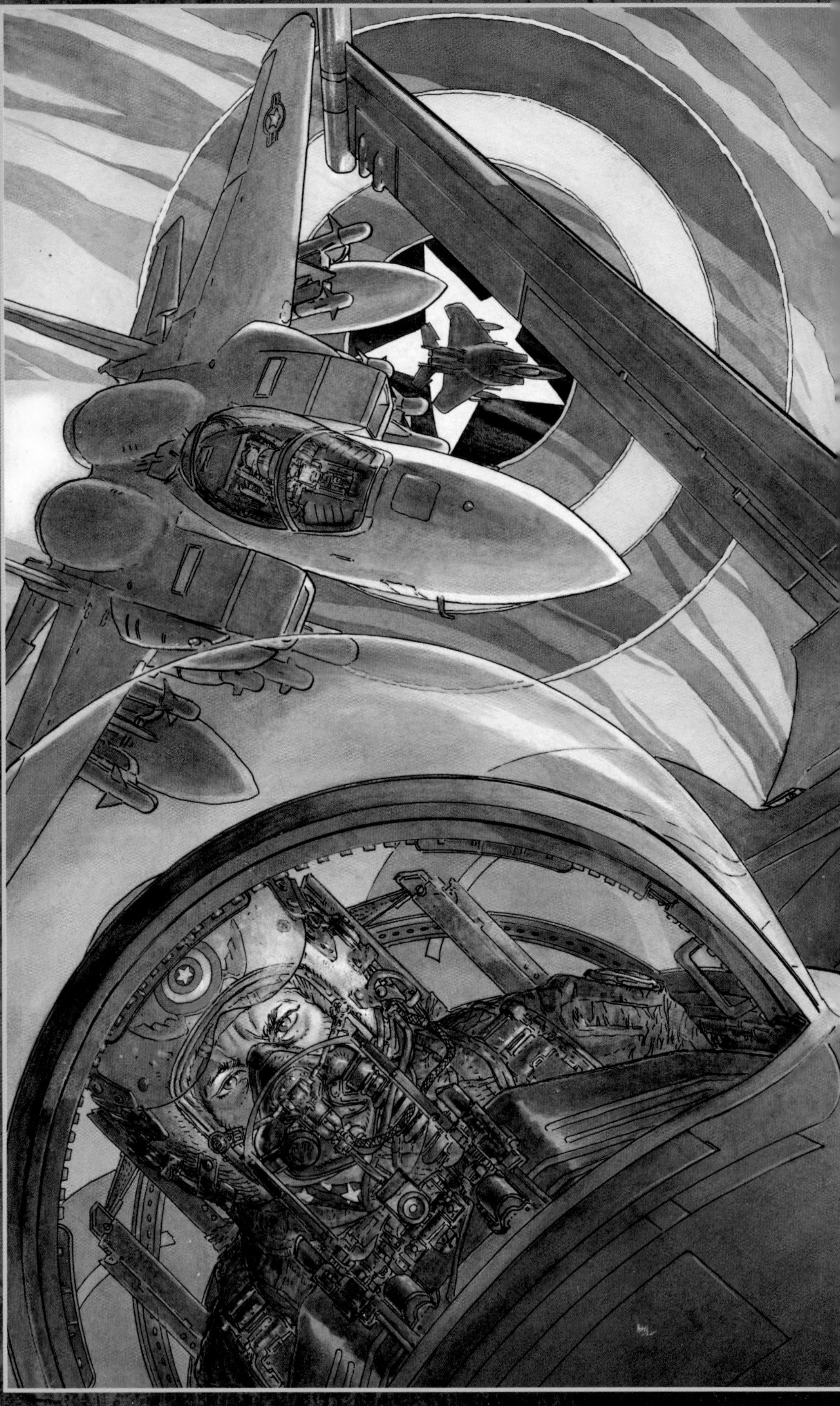

#7 I AM CAPTAIN AMERICA VARIANT BY **MICHAEL Wm. KALUTA**